Wifestyles

ALSO BY DAWN SANGREY

The Crime Victim's Book (with Morton Bard)

Wifestyles

Women Talk About Marriage

Dawn Sangrey

DELACORTE PRESS/NEW YORK

Published by
Delacorte Press
1 Dag Hammarskjold Plaza
New York, N.Y. 10017

Manufactured in the United States of America

First printing

Library of Congress Cataloging in Publication Data
Main entry under title:
Wifestyles, women talk about marriage.
Includes bibliographical references and index.
1. Marriage—United States. 2. Married women—
United States—Attitudes. I. Sangrey, Dawn.
HQ536.W53   1983   306.8'1'0973   83-1812
ISBN 0-440-09721-5

For Paul McKenna Fargis

Not a valentine.
A muscle.

A Disclaimer

Wifestyles is not a how-to book. It will not tell you how to survive being a wife, how to fix what you don't like about your marriage, or whether or not you should get married. I do not know the answers to these questions. Perhaps no one does, but if anyone does, it is surely you and not me.

Wifestyles is a collection of stories. Over a hundred women talk here about what they do in their marriages and what their marriages do to them. You may, indeed, learn something from listening to them. I certainly did. But I don't mean to be telling you what to do about it. I don't think one person can do that for another. All we can do is tell each other our stories.

CONTENTS

The universe is made of stories,
not of atoms.

—*Muriel Rukeyser*

Wifestyles

Introduction

LISTENING

I may as well begin by confessing that I am in favor of marriage. I know that there are other ways to live—I have lived some of them—and I certainly have days when I wish I could be free of this husband and that dirty kitchen floor and my fat belly with the baby in it. There are things about my marriage that I would change if I could. But I am happier living with my husband than I could be living without him. And in spite of all the old quarrels and primal wounds that marriage and motherhood reopen, I *like* being married.

I got married the first time when I was twenty-two and just out of graduate school. That summer I moved out of my parents' house and into a little apartment in the suburbs with my bridegroom. We decided to pay off our college loans before we started our family. My gynecologist prescribed the

Pill; he told me that it was just like the natural hormone in my own body, and I believed him. It was 1964.

I took my husband's name and went with him to live where he was working. I got a full-time job, but I also kept house as my mother had taught me. I ironed shirts. I baked Christmas cookies. I tried very hard, in the end desperately, to please my husband.

We separated after seven years. He put his clothes and his books in the car one day and drove away. There were no children, no ties. Quite suddenly the future that I had counted on all of my life was gone.

I was twenty-nine years old. I had never lived alone, and I was numb with terror. For a few months I did nothing— went to work, came home, told almost no one. Then, later in the spring, the terror lifted. I pulled off my wedding ring and threw it in the ocean. I took a lover. I quit my job.

For the next six years I lived by myself on Manhattan's West Side. I changed jobs several times on my way to becoming a writer. For the first time in my life I had close friends who were women, and I came to like most women better than most men. I dated sporadically, had a serious boyfriend from time to time, and eventually found some men who became good friends. A few years ago I took all of my courage in both hands and married one of them.

This second marriage is very different from the first. I am older and wiser, for one thing. Times have changed. My husband washes his own shirts. Nobody irons them. But so much has stayed the same. I still want my kitchen floor to be as clean as my mother's, and when it gets bad enough I still get down on my hands and knees and scrub it.

Listening

This book began in the tension between the way things have changed and the way they have stayed the same. A generation ago, when I was growing up in the 1950s, 70 percent of American households were made up of a breadwinner father, a housewife mother, and one or more dependent children. Ozzie and Harriet, Dagwood and Blondie. A generation ago the most reliable contraceptive available was the diaphragm. A married woman who had a job a generation ago was an oddity, often somewhat pitied. Only twenty-five years ago you could grow up in most middle-class American neighborhoods and never know a family that had been broken by divorce.

All of this has changed. In 1982 only 15 percent of the households in the United States fit the old Papa Bear-Mama Bear-Baby Bear mold.[1] The Pill and the IUD have revolutionized birth control. Divorce is rampant. The average woman who gets married today is likely to have more marriages than children, if birth and divorce trends continue in their current directions.

The last generation has also seen the rise of the social movement called women's liberation. Twenty-five years ago Betty Friedan was a Long Island housewife with three little kids and a problem that had no name. The standard apparatus for holding up a woman's stockings was a constricting device with four lumpy garters dangling down called a girdle. Jokes about how women can't make up their minds or park a car were standard comedy fare. No woman had yet begun a sentence with the words "I'm not a woman's libber, but. . . ." Today the issues of the women's movement are part of everyone's awareness. Grown daughters who visit their parents over the holidays are finding their fathers washing the dishes. The supermarket is full of husbands doing the weekly shopping. If a man calls me *girl* and I raise my eyebrows and look sour, he knows what I'm complaining about.

During the sixties when I was married and "safe," I was mildly sympathetic to the television version of the early women's movement. I became a feminist soon after my husband left. Trying to find a place to live in New York City when you're single and female and temporarily unemployed is enough to raise anybody's consciousness. Not to mention the rituals that surround contemporary dating among urban adults. My feminist anger supported me when I was alone. It gave me a way to deal with singles' bars and dark city streets and bosses who wouldn't give me the money I was worth. Being a feminist was less helpful once I was married again, but there's no turning back.

Somewhere in the early *Wifestyles* notes I wrote that I started working on this book because I wanted to talk myself into staying married the second time. I can't remember feeling that way now. We have a child now. We have (don't laugh) a cleaning woman now. But I was certainly going through some kind of a crisis. The euphoria of the honeymoon year was fading, and all of the problems I had never solved the first time around were emerging again. I was mad about a lot of things, and I was frightened. My mother had brought me up to live in a world that no longer existed. I had been okay as a single woman in this new world—mother hadn't raised me to be single anyway—but now that I was married again I didn't know what the rules were.

I wanted to find out how other women were making

their marriages work. I wanted to know what had changed and what had stayed the same. I wanted to know what the new rules were.

Because I am a writer, I have a professional incentive to learn. If the things I need to know are interesting enough, I can write a book about them. So I wrote a proposal, sold the idea to the Delacorte Press, designed a study, and spent a year traveling around the country talking to married women.

Throughout this book I will talk about the interviews as if I did them all, but there were actually three women asking the questions: myself and two others. I did seventy-six interviews in nine different states; Judith Thomas did thirty interviews in three states; and Harriet Arnone did eighteen interviews in three states. Each of the other interviewers gave me detailed descriptions of the people and places they visited, and, of course, I was able to listen to all of their interviews on tape. Judith and Hattie did their jobs so well that often I ended up feeling as if I had done a particular interview when, in fact, one of them had been there instead.

The United States Bureau of the Census divides the country into nine geographical divisions, which are roughly equal in population. Since I wanted to get as broad a spectrum of women as possible, I decided to visit several different places in each of these nine parts of the country. As I began to develop the itinerary for the study, I got in touch with someone I knew in each geographical division—a friend or relation who was willing to help me locate and approach the women I would interview. In research parlance such an intermediary person is called a gatekeeper.

I asked the gatekeeper to come up with a list of wives

—as many different kinds of women as possible—and to see if they were interested in taking part in the study. About two weeks before my trip to their area, I phoned each woman who had said yes to the gatekeeper. I told her what the interview would be like and answered her questions. If she still wanted to do it, we made a date.

I went north, east, south, and west. The women in the *Wifestyles* study live in fourteen different states. They come from small towns and from the suburbs and from the big city; the smallest community I visited has a population of less than one hundred and the largest a population of over 8 million. I talked to a coal miner's wife in the foothills of the Appalachian Mountains; a farmer's wife in the green cornfields of Iowa; a United States Congressman's wife in an elegant Washington, D.C., suburb; the wife of the local mortician in a tiny town in western Texas. I talked to young and old; rich, middle class, and poor; working wives and housewives; mothers and grandmothers and women without children; wives who love their husbands and wives who hate them.

There were 124 women altogether in the study.* A wide range of ages is represented. The average age of all the women in the study is forty years. Twenty-four percent of them were thirty or younger the day they were interviewed; 36 percent were thirty-one to forty; 25 percent were forty-one to fifty; and 15 percent were over fifty. The youngest wife was twenty; the oldest, seventy-three.

I talked to a woman who had been married for forty-four

---

*The Technical Appendix at the back of this book includes a demographic analysis of the sample and more information about sampling.

years and to another one who had been married three months. (The rule was she had to be legally married the day of the interview.) A little more than a quarter (27 percent) of the women had been married less than eight years. Thirty-nine percent had been married eight to twenty years, and the rest (34 percent) had been married more than twenty years. Most of the women (85 percent) were still married to their first husbands, but some women were contemplating divorce and some had been divorced and had married again.

The wives were in many different stages of motherhood. Almost a third (31 percent) had no children at home, either because they were childless or because their kids had grown and left home. Of those who had children at home, 26 percent had at least one preschooler; 28 percent had at least one child between the ages of six and eleven; 32 percent had at least one teenager (twelve to nineteen years); and 14 percent had children twenty years and older still at home.

Most of the *Wifestyles* women were employed—52 percent full time and 27 percent part time. Among the wives who work were a physician, a cleaning woman, a store manager, a radio and television producer, a printer, a baker, a bus driver, and several secretaries, teachers, nurses, and social workers.

The interviewing journeys were a personal odyssey. I saw parts of the country I had never seen before, and I learned to do a lot of things that are hard for me. I who hate telephones learned to call a stranger long-distance and persuade her that it was okay for us to meet and talk about her marriage. I drove unfamiliar cars down unfamiliar roads in the dark and the rain to the homes of these women I'd never met before. I learned to listen without passing judgment and without giving advice. The first time I talked to a woman whose husband beat her, I wept and hugged her and said, "It's going to be all right." Then I went home and read a handbook for counselors of battered wives; it said, "Above all, don't tell her it's going to be all right. It's *not* going to be all right." So I learned to keep my mouth shut. I talked to women who enjoy relationships that I could not tolerate, and I began to understand that everybody does not need the same things in marriage.

The year that I was on the road I was also the mother of an infant son. Christopher was eight months old when I started interviewing, and there was no way I was going to leave him at home. So I gave up my carry-on luggage and learned how to put the baby in the pack and then get the pack on my back without spilling him out. The gatekeeper in each region usually also played host to Christopher and me during our visit, so I didn't have to learn how to operate out of a motel by myself with a small child. When we did stay in motels, we always had somebody else with us to help out.

But there were challenges enough. I learned that there is always something on the menu the baby can eat—toast, mashed potatoes, applesauce, cottage cheese. I found that it was okay to dress him in the same pajamas he had worn the night before and that he wouldn't die from a bottle washed out in hot tap water. I learned how to leave him with strangers while I went to work. The babysitters were always carefully selected by trusted friends, but still, it was hard. One week in Idaho he cried all day long the first three days I left him. I kept saying to myself, "I have to do this. I came 2,500 miles to do this interview, and I have to do it." And, then, mercifully, he stopped crying. Today he is remarkably poised with strangers, and I am probably a more relaxed mother than I would be otherwise.

Everyone, everywhere, was kind to me. I can't think of a better antidote for late-twentieth-century cynicism than spending six hours with twenty-four pounds of squirming Christopher on an airplane whose every seat is filled and discovering that the person sitting next to me (1) loves babies, (2) thinks it's marvelous that I'm giving the child the experience of all this travel, and (3) would love to hold him while I eat my lunch. And when I got wherever I was going that day, there was a warm hug at the airport from the friend or relation who had offered to shelter and feed us. The women I interviewed welcomed me into their homes and their lives as if I were a neighbor. They gave me coffee and answered my questions and helped me find my way to the next interview. There were a few I didn't like and a few who held out on me, but most of the *Wifestyles* women were generous and open beyond my expectation. I could not have written this book without the kindness of all these people.

There were some bad times. I had three great failures of nerve, moments when I suddenly felt that I wouldn't be able to pull it off. The first was in Oakland, California, on my way to the first interview there. I had gotten lost, and I was late, and I was hurrying when I finally found the place. It was a little ramshackle bungalow pressed right up against the freeway. A set of rickety stairs led up to the front door. The screen on the door was torn, and the paint was peeling. At the top of the stairs, sleeping peacefully, was a large black and tan German shepherd. I didn't see him until I had dashed halfway up the stairs, and then I just stopped in my tracks. I could see the gray glinting in his muzzle. I backed down the stairs, went to the side door on the first floor, and listened. I could hear a television blaring. I banged on the door and shouted. No one came. I went back to the foot of the stairs and looked up at the dog. Still sleeping. I went to the first-floor window on the other side and banged on it. No one came. So I took a deep breath, walked carefully up the stairs, stepped over the sleeping dog, and banged on the front door until the woman I had come to interview opened it. Neither of us ever mentioned the dog, and he was still sleeping when I left two hours later.

The second great failure of nerve came on a foggy morning on a dirt road in the hill country of West Virginia. Christopher and I had come in late the night before, and nobody had much sleep. The friend who put us up drives a school bus. She got up at five the next morning. Her dogs barked and woke the baby, and he wouldn't go back to sleep so I had to get up too. She left me her car, an old Volkswagen Beetle, and a map to the babysitter and the first two interviews of the day. As the fog began to lift, the sun came out and sparkled on the frosty fields. It was perfectly quiet in the little valley.

Christopher and I set off a little before eight. A sharp edge of his car seat poked my right shoulder as I tried to watch the road and the map at the same time. It was pretty rough terrain, hilly and full of bumps, and I was still in second gear when I came to the bottom of a little hill, hit some gravel, and started to slide. I let the clutch out and the car clunked to a stop. We hadn't been going very fast and we were still on the road, but suddenly I was overcome by panic. I couldn't remember how to get the car started again. And I thought, "My God, what am I doing here? I don't know where I am. I don't know how to get home if I get lost. I won't know what to do if the car breaks down. What am I doing here in the middle of nowhere with my baby?" We sat there in the middle of that deserted intersection for what seemed like several minutes. Somewhere out of sight a persistent cow was mooing and mooing. Finally I took another look at the map, got my bearings, put the car in gear, and drove off.

The third great failure of nerve—the worst one—came in the second year when the interviewing was done, the data was almost ready for the computer, and there was nothing left to do but write the book. I sat down in front of the typewriter and nothing happened. I sat for a whole day with the meter running at the babysitter's and wrote nothing. Daydreamed. Boiled water for innumerable cups of tea; drank it down, scalding; boiled more water. Filed my nails. Chewed four packs of gum, one pack at a time. Waited. Called my mother. Stared at the encouraging note from my editor that I had taped up on the wall. Waited. Finally I said to myself, "I can't do this. I don't have a Ph.D. in social psychology or anything else. I haven't read every article and book that's ever been published about marriage. I am *not prepared*. I couldn't possibly know what I'm talking about, and they will know that I don't. People will laugh at me." I never did write anything that day, but the next day I was able to allow myself a little competence, a little authority, and so I was able to start.

No one else ever wondered whether or not I could do it. The women I interviewed accepted me as writer, researcher, story collector—obviously I could do it; I was there. They were willing to let me set the rules. I asked them to meet with me when their husbands and children were not around. I had decided not to talk to husbands—what I wanted to know was how *women* were getting along. And I thought that most of the women would be more comfortable and would speak more frankly if we were alone.

But I was not always successful in keeping the husbands away. One afternoon in Berkeley, California, a very shy woman had just begun to explain to me that her husband drank a lot and sometimes slapped her around, when suddenly a pickup roared into the driveway and he came stumbling into the kitchen. He was very sweet to me, quite charming and quite incoherent. After a while he climbed back into the truck and roared away. He probably never even noticed the tape recorder sitting on the kitchen table.

Another day in Idaho I visited with a rancher's wife in their little trailer home while her husband worked in full view in the field right across the yard. He had clearly been told to stay away, but as we got into the second hour of the interview he worked his way closer and closer to the trailer until finally he threw down his hoe, circled the trailer once, and then came stomping in to demand his lunch.

There were husbands who banged on things in the cellar and husbands who came home unexpectedly from work and husbands who phoned several times during the interview. Once in New Hampshire an entire family sat in—first the teenage daughter, then the younger son, and finally the woman's husband joined us around the dining-room table. But usually the woman and I were alone.

Each of the interviews took about two hours.* I started by asking how it all began: the first time she met her husband, the first date, the decision to get married, the wedding. Then we talked about the first year of the marriage and about highlights and turning points through the years. We talked about the children, if there were children. We talked about her job, if she had one. I asked each woman how she spent her time and what a typical day in her life was like. We talked about housework and money and sex and fighting. I tried to leave room in the interview so that the women could talk about whatever was on their minds. And they did. When I was finished I had over three hundred hours of tape—three hundred hours of stories about marriage.

Then I came home and sat down and listened to them all again. There is enough stuff in those tapes for ten books. I had to decide what was important to this book and to transcribe the stories I needed so that the women could speak for themselves here. I collected two things in the interviews: the stories and data for the computer. In addition to descriptive statistics (age, length of marriage, number of children, education, employment history, etc.), each woman's answers to over seventy specific interview questions were coded and put into the computer for comparison with the others. One result of my journey is the analysis of some of that data. But I am not a scientist, and I have chosen to emphasize the stories in the chapters that follow because I believe the stories are the most important part of what I learned. The statistics are useful, but the power is in the stories.

---

*There is a complete list of the interview questions in the Technical Appendix.

Wifestyles

I promised the *Wifestyles* women that I would keep private whatever they told me, and I have made every effort to keep that promise. All sorts of identifying details have been changed—the women have new names and new faces; their homes have been painted a different color and set on a different street. But the things that matter have not been changed. Women with small children in reality have small children in the book, with a minor change in number or sex or age. Interviews in rural locations have been kept in rural locations. And none of the words have been changed. Wherever a woman is quoted directly, her words are given as she said them. In these ways I have tried to be faithful to the women who participated in the study.

One of the people who helped me with the computer analysis talks about giving data "the traumatic eyeball test." You look at the numbers to see if anything really jumps out and clobbers you over the head. There were a lot of surprises in the *Wifestyles* study. One was the answers to the satisfaction question. About a third of the way through each interview, after we had talked about the history and present state of the marriage, I asked the wife to evaluate her marriage: "How satisfied are you today with your marriage? Rate it on a scale from 1 to 10, where 10 is high." I didn't expect an even distribution of scores, but the numbers still seem pretty amazing to me.[2] Forty-one percent of the women gave their marriages one of the two highest ratings for satisfaction, either a 9 or a 10. Another 32 percent gave a rating of 8. Only 27 percent gave ratings below 8. Most had something to complain about, of course, but when they were pressed to evaluate the marriage as a whole, more than two thirds of the *Wifestyles* women said it's pretty good. For the most part they are women who have chosen to stay married, and they are satisfied with what they have.

Another big surprise was an attitude: a deep-flowing loyalty to their husbands among these women. I suppose that every wife has days when she doesn't like her husband very much, but when the tape recorder is running, she wants to make him look good. Asked if she would marry him again, 92 percent said yes. Ninety-nine percent said that they liked their husband, and 98 percent said that they loved him. Seventy-three percent said they were satisfied with their sex life. I expected more anger and more griping. But almost everyone, even women who said they were unhappy and women who were abused, seemed reluctant to say bad things about their husbands.

The third surprise was the intense anger that some of the women I interviewed expressed about the women's movement. (Perhaps that surprise is just evidence of my East Coast, urban-liberal provincialism. I knew there were women who opposed feminism, but I don't think I'd ever talked to one before.) The question was one of the last in the interview: "Some people say that the women's movement has had a good effect on marriage and some people say it's had a bad effect. What do you think?" A third of the *Wifestyles* women said it had a good effect; 22 percent said it was bad; 21 percent said both good and bad; and 24 percent either didn't know or thought there was no effect at all. The numbers are hard enough to take. But the real trauma was to sit across the kitchen table from women I liked and respected and hear things like this:

I think so many of the women have gotten so full of their own importance they have forgotten to put family first. And to me family is very important.

I can't get into the women's movement and people try to lay a guilt trip on me, but I can't. Their solutions are sometimes . . . It's the guy's fault. But it's not the guy's fault. It's a cultural situation, things that are beyond the control of some of the women. Or it's their absolutely conscious choice to be where they are. But somehow it gets to be the guy's fault.

I think that the pressures on women are much greater. There have been so many books and programs about what women are entitled to and what they've been missing all of these years that it makes normally happily married women start to doubt and question whether they really have been happy, you know, and perhaps they should have been expecting more out of life than they got. I think it's made them more restless.

I think when women become too independent, then that will start breaking up marriages. I think she should be dependent on her husband.

Many of the women I talked to had positive feelings about the women's movement, which of course did not surprise me. But among these advocates, few had feelings as intense as those who were opposed.

Everything else I learned fits against the background of

these three central touchstones: satisfaction, loyalty, and feel-ings about the women's movement. When a woman who hates to make love and avoids touching her husband because she is afraid that one thing will lead to another tells me that her marriage rates a 10, the top score on the satisfaction scale, I understand that her sex life is not important to her but her marriage is. When a woman who works full time and whose husband is unemployed tells me that *he* supports the family, I understand that she is expressing her loyalty to him; she means he would if he could; she means she loves him anyway. When a woman who condemns the women's movement and says she has always just wanted to be a housewife then tells me, with enormous pride in her voice, that her only daughter is the first woman to graduate from the local university exten-sion as a diesel mechanic, I understand that her problem with feminism is not its substance but its image. A lot of the things I heard made better sense when I remembered to pay attention to these three touchstones, and we will come back, again and again, to them.

This book is about a journey made by a woman who needed to answer some questions about marriage. It is about the answers she found; it is about the process of finding the answers, and it is also, inevitably, about the woman who went looking. I considered leaving myself out of it, but that seems less honest to me and also less true. I also had the temptation early on to do things like make up some catchy-sounding categories to put the women I interviewed in, but I decided they wouldn't fit. The book is a lot less tidy and perhaps seems less objective because of these decisions. That's all right with me because I think if there are any answers to questions such as how has marriage changed and what good is it anyway? they are found in the heart as well as in the head. Think of *Wifestyles* as soundings, impressions, not science. Listen to the stories. The power is in the stories.

One

GETTING MARRIED

I take thee to my wedded Husband, to have and to hold from this day forward, for better for worse, for richer for poorer, in sickness and in health, to love and to cherish, till death us do part, according to God's holy ordinance; and thereto I give thee my troth.

—The Book of Common Prayer

. . . why do people marry? Why is it that people continue to behave as if true happiness, that forever-after-and-lasting kind of happiness, will be found within the context of this demanding and engulfing commitment?

—*Maggie Scarf,* Unfinished Business

About my first wedding I remember, understandably, only bits and pieces. It was July and very hot—100 degrees or better—and I was strangling in white taffeta—up to my throat, down to my wrists, down to the floor. There is a home movie that opens with me putting that wedding gown in the car for the half hour journey to the church. I ease the dress in, run around the car one way to close a door, run all the way around it the other way to close another door. When we first saw the movies we all laughed at Dawn running around in circles on her wedding day.

A photograph of the bride and groom in their traveling clothes: There we sit in the getaway car—his big old white Chrysler—smiling and sweating and indecently ready to get out of there. My face says, "There. It's all over. I made it."

The first marriage "ended in divorce," as the newspapers say. I hadn't realized that people like me could get divorced. Once separated, the two of us lost touch at once, even before the papers were final. I remember vividly the night that a mutual friend told me my first husband was married again. It was an astonishing sensation—I felt as if she had struck me physically. After that I stopped waiting for him to come back.

And so, eventually, I met my present husband, on a blind date arranged by his best friend, who turned out to be married to a woman I had known when we were both in the same high school, in another state, years before. We took the coincidence to heart: a good omen. The first date was lunch at the Helicopter Club on the top of the Pan Am building. Filet of sole and white wine. The fish was cold when it finally arrived, but neither of us complained. I remember running down the escalator ahead of him after lunch, exuberant and hopeful, feeling his eyes on me.

We got married in April in a room full of spring flowers and people who loved us. They broke into spontaneous applause at the end of the ceremony. I have never been as happy in my life as I was that day. Giddy happy. High happy. The-world-is-my-oyster happy—for this moment, for this day, to finally have what I wanted more than anything: to be married again.

Weeks before the wedding, I remember trying on rings in Fortunoff, by myself. I just went in to see which of the small, simple bands was exactly right, feeling easy and casual (just another prewedding chore). The smiling young man pulled out a tray—all those bright golden rings on blue velvet to show them off. I picked up one of them, slipped it on my own finger, and—zing!—felt an intense shiver of excitement and delight, like an involuntary start except that it was warm, not cold.

I drove out from Parkersburg, West Virginia, in my friend's aging Volkswagen Beetle to meet with Esther Jonas. It was November, a little before Thanksgiving. The fields were all stubble, browns and grays and golds. It's a rough and somber landscape. I passed a lot of abandoned buildings on the road, unfinished wood weathering to silver and buff. A huge sign painted on the side of a falling-down barn: Chew Mail Pouch Tobacco/Treat Yourself To The Best. The water in these hills is so hard it dries up your skin overnight.

The railroad tracks run straight through the middle of town where Esther lives. There is a truck stop, a gas station, a post office. Esther and her husband have both lived here since they were kids. He used to play ball with her big brothers. His mother lives just up the street in the white house there on the top of the hill, and after he was grown and driving trucks, he still used to stay at home when he was in town.

He'd be off on his truck route most of the time. But he

started hanging around the service station where Esther worked, bringing his truck to be serviced and just sitting around and talking to her. Then one day Esther was walking by his mom's house, and she put her head out the screen door and said why didn't Esther come in and have a cup of coffee. So Esther started stopping in there on her way home—first just for coffee, then for coffee and pie, then for a meal sometimes. Usually he wasn't around, but sometimes he was.

He never did ask her out, but he'd get home from his route and call her up to talk. He called her up one time at 12:30 A.M. and talked to her for two hours. And then he started coming over to the house, just to sit and visit or watch the TV.

Esther Jonas is a gentle, quiet lady with a soft drawl and a slow, easy way of moving. She doesn't confide much in strangers, but she couldn't resist telling this part of the story:

It's really funny the way he proposed. He came in from a trip. It was real cold although it was getting close to Mother's Day. That was the winter we had a real bad long winter here. And he had this Service Merchandise book, you know, it has jewelry and all this. And he was looking at it. We were sittin' in here on the couch, and he said, "Uh, what kind of ring would you like?"

And I said, "Well, what do you mean, what kind of ring would I like?"

And he said, "Mother's Day's coming up. I thought I'd get you a ring."

And I said, "Well, why would you buy me a ring for Mother's Day?"

Getting Married

And he said, "Well, I was more or less thinking about a . . . kind of . . . engagement ring."

The wedding was last year in the spring. Everybody in town was real pleased about it. Esther was widowed in 1976 by the black lung, and folks thought it was a shame for such a fine woman to be left by herself. She is in her mid-forties. Her new husband is fifty-two and has never been married before. He used to drink and hang out at the truck stop, but since he got married he just likes being at home with her. "Everybody just marvels at it," she said.

It was April when Jody Kovar and I talked—April in northern California, impossibly sunny and warm. You can see the Golden Gate Bridge from the second-story porch at Jody's house. The wildflowers everywhere were blooming riots of color—fuchsia and brilliant orange and a bright, spanking yellow that is nothing like the colors of the daffodils that bloom in the spring back East. I would have come for the view alone that day.

Jody lived with her husband for almost four years before either of them talked about getting married. They had rented this big old house in the Berkeley foothills, and they had a lot of different people sharing the space for a while. Everybody was still in school, and nobody was into exclusive relationships. But then something changed for Jody. "I thought that our relationship had gone as far as it could as a couple living together. And it even got down to kind of an either/or type thing. I mean, if we decided not to get married then I was ready to have our relationship end because I felt that it was important for me to find somebody who was interested in making more of a commitment. Not necessarily having kids right away but giving me what I felt that I needed at that time."

So then they talked about it a lot, she more than he. And finally they just decided to do it.

The day we decided to get married was on April Fool's Day, last April first. The hills and everything were so green around here. It was springtime. The year before and the year before that had been drought years. It was very, very dry. And this was the first year there had been so much rain. And I mean everything was lush —it was just beautiful. It was like springtime, and Easter was coming, and it just felt like a good time to get married. So we decided, that, you know, "Hey. Why not?"

So we announced it. We bought this big bottle of champagne—and nobody believed us. Because they thought it was April Fool. And they just thought, "Oh, you know, these guys are so crazy."

We said, "No. No. We're really getting married."

There were people who wouldn't believe it until they actually had the wedding and everything.

Two days later I had that appointment in Oakland at the little bungalow with the German shepherd on the porch. You could hear the cars on the freeway from the kitchen where

Sandy Lord and I sat at the Formica table. The wallpaper above the stove was peeling off in long strips, and the linoleum was worn through in front of the sink.

Sandy met her husband in Chicago. He rescued her and her two girl friends. That was how it all started. For some reason the motel manager thought that she and her girl friends were with the people in the room next to them who had been partying all night long the night before. Or maybe he just thought they were bad girls. (Sandy grinned and rolled her black eyes in comic mockery of her teenage embarrassment.) Anyway, this manager was throwing their stuff out of the room and yelling at them when her future husband and his buddy came along. And they just fixed it all up smooth as anything. They said, "Well, why don't y'all come over to where we're staying, and we'll find you a room over there." So they did.

And then his buddy left and Sandy moved in. "I had never been with a man before. He was the first man I had." She was sixteen and had just run away from home. She lied to him about her age. When he found out, he gave her some money and put her on the bus for home. But she was determined to have him, so she left some of her clothes at his place and came back a few weeks later. She found him with another woman, and this woman was wearing Sandy's new coat. So Sandy said she had to take off the coat and she had to leave. After that, he let her stay. "He was the type of man who always was taken care of. But when he took up with me, he got an apartment with furniture and everything. His family just couldn't get over it. He had a sister who came all the way from Texas just to lay eyes on me."

They lived together nine years common law. "We used to go to Reno and every time we went to Reno, we'd say, 'Okay, let's get married this time.' And then I said, 'Hey, it's about time. We got a kid, and we're about to have another one.' So then we got married."

Doris Sullivan has lived in New York City in the West Village almost all of her life. It was January and bitter cold the day she and I did our interview. The newspapers were blowing around in the streets outside. Doris gave me a good cup of coffee and the chair by the fireplace.

She and her husband lived together before they married. She is an ardent feminist, and he was violently antimarriage. For two years he said, "I won't marry you. I won't marry anybody. I won't marry you."

And for two years she smiled and said, "You'll marry me when you get ready."

He was in the navy on active duty then, and he would be in Washington or some base in Europe for weeks at a time. One day he came home from a trip and sat across from her at the dinner table, silent and glowering. Finally he burst out, "Okay. What kind of a wedding will you settle for?" Now he's sixty-eight and she's sixty-four. They've been married for more than thirty years.

I've got a million of them. Well, a hundred anyway. Almost every woman who talked to me had a story about the way it all began. Some could say what day of the week it was when she first met him—ten, twenty, forty years ago. They remember the weather, the dress they were wearing, the gleam in his eye. Asked about their first impression, more than half of the *Wifestyles* women remember feeling drawn to their future husband. Thirty percent were strongly attracted the first time they saw him. Or so they say. There's no way to calculate the effect of romantic hindsight, no way to know how many other boys with gleams in their eyes she has forgotten because they came to nothing.

The storytelling part of the interview started with this question: "Tell me about the day you met him." Occasionally a woman would look blank and say she couldn't remember, most often when she and he had grown up in the same town. Some talked for half an hour about their courting days, dancing at the teen canteen, joy-riding up and down Main Street —straight out of *American Graffiti*. But most of the women had one or two brief courtship stories, little vignettes they had treasured away: The First Time I Saw Him ("I thought he was the cutest thing I ever saw."), The First Thing I Said ("You're disgusting."), How I Caught Him ("I started going to the church choir.").

When I was growing up it was thought that the ideal girl-boy relationship began with a friendship and gradually blossomed into Something More. I remember my father advocating this approach, and I think I used to believe in it, but it doesn't seem to work that way. More than half of the *Wifestyles* women (62 percent) began dating their future husbands soon after they met them; 38 percent dated him exclusively from the start; 24 percent dated him and also dated others soon after they met him. Only 38 percent knew him as a friend before they became romantically involved. (Serious dating is partly a function of age, of course. A twenty-four-year-old woman is more likely to date one person exclusively than, say, a fourteen-year-old. Only about 30 percent of the *Wifestyles* women met their husband while they were of high-school age or younger; most were at least in their late teens when they met him and, presumably, more ready to get serious when he came along.)

I had an idea before I did the study that women older than me—those in my mother's generation, perhaps—were more sensible and less romantic than women of my generation and younger. Perhaps this is an illusion of every generation of daughters. In any case, I couldn't find much evidence to support it. The courtship stories of the *Wifestyles* women in their sixties and seventies were not very different from those of the women in their twenties and thirties. Some were romantic, some were not, but the difference seems to be a matter of personality rather than age. There are, in fact, no statistically significant differences by age groups in answers to the question about her first impression or to the question about their initial relationship.

And some of the most impulsive matches are made by people who are ordinarily quite sensible. Deborah Rosen is the picture of practical, down-to-earth reliability—the sort of woman you would ask to watch your kids in the supermarket if you just had to go to the bathroom. She is forty-eight, but she has one of those ageless faces. Except for the fact that her hair is all gone to salt and pepper, she could be thirty-five. She works as a child psychologist in private practice, and we met in her office, a big sunny room on the ground floor of a mid-Manhattan brownstone. She was dressed in a soft rose color, a matching skirt and sweater, and nice-looking, sensible pumps.

Deborah has always been steady. She made the honor roll and practiced her piano every afternoon when she was a girl. As a young college student, she knew what she wanted and what she didn't want.

> I had decided when I was an undergraduate student that I was not going to marry while I was a graduate student. For many many of my friends the value was to have your MRS. by the time you finished college. In the group that I was, the middle-class kind of community that I was raised in, this was a very very important value. And I would imagine that, oh, maybe 80 percent of my high-school classmates were married at least once by the time they graduated from college. And I had made a very conscious choice not to do so. So I had been dating a lot but with a very kind of unstructured notion that I wasn't going to get married.
>
> I knew I wanted to have some kind of a career, but that wasn't the reason. I didn't think that I was . . . ready to get married. As a teenager, I knew that every year I seemed to have an entirely different perspective on the world. I would say, "God, how could I have liked *that* last year. How could I have thought *that* was important?" And I noticed that the same thing went on with people, both girl friends and boyfriends. That you go through these stages of feeling very

intense about someone or something. And then suddenly you're almost as *un*intense. I had just been aware of those things.

And I wanted my college to be an exploratory period when I'd get a chance to meet with lots of people—and I like people—I mean, I had some really warm and really close relationships but not with the idea that I was going to lock myself into it forever. And I saw what happened to some kids who got involved with one individual, that they had to restructure all of their own personal decisions so they matched that other individual. And that was complicating.

And then when she was a senior, Deborah met her future husband on a blind date. "We kind of hit it off. He was a very serious, conscientious, systematic sort of person, and I had the sense that I understood what his thinking processes were. And he wasn't much of a bullshitter. He was pretty straight."

Seven weeks later they were married. He was finishing school and leaving town. It was 1955—before premarital sex or living together were accepted. He proposed and he pushed it, and finally she said yes. Their families and friends were astonished—everyone saw them as two of the most stable and serious people that they knew. And yet the match was right. "There was a lot of compatibility in our families. In fact, it was almost the kind of marriage that each one—that each family—would have chosen for their kids, and yet if the families had been engaged in it, it would have been no good. And if we had met four years earlier, it probably wouldn't have worked. It worked because we were ready at that moment."

After a small wedding and a three-day honeymoon, they put everything they owned in his brother's 1952 Buick and drove to Cornell, where he was to attend graduate school. "We didn't have a bed. We didn't have a table." And what was the first year like? "Oh, we could have lived on the other side of the moon, and it would have been beautiful. It was just a fantastic interpersonal year. We just loved being together." He gained twenty-five pounds the first six months they were married. And they've been happy ever since.

The second interview question was "Tell me about the day you decided to marry." I was looking for several kinds of stories—the day she decided he was The One, the day they turned to each other and said that they wanted to be together forever, or the day he dropped to his knees and pulled out a little box with a ring in it. There weren't a whole lot of formal proposals. In fact, when I was counting decisions to marry, I had a terrible time making up categories to put them in because every woman's experience is so unique. Finally I settled on three categories: a formal proposal, a mutual decision, and everything else.

If the man asked the woman to marry him and she saw his asking as the thing that decided it, that counted as a formal proposal, even if his words were less than formal. (One man proposed this way: "I think it's about time we get married.") Only 24 percent of the women in the *Wifestyles* study received a formal proposal even by this broad definition. It was more common among older couples than younger ones: 32 percent of the women over forty were asked by their husbands to marry them, while only 18 percent of those forty and under were.

If the couple decided together, neither asking the other formally but each coming to the understanding over time that they would be married, I counted it as a mutual decision. Mutual decisions are more common than formal proposals among *Wifestyles* women: 30 percent decided together with their husbands to get married. Most of these women are among the younger group; 38 percent of the women twenty to forty made a mutual decision, compared with only 18 percent of those over forty.

The biggest group is the "other" category, a group so varied that I couldn't find a way to categorize the decisions. Ten percent of the women were pregnant when they got married. Some of these received formal proposals or mentioned a mutual decision; others just said, "Well, I got pregnant and then we had to get married." One woman was pregnant by her first husband, whom she had just divorced, when she received a unique proposal. She said she knew her new boyfriend wanted to marry her when he offered to be her coach for natural childbirth!

There are women who resist. Jane Franklin finally divorced her husband after twenty years of neglect and physical abuse. She wasn't very receptive when one of the men she had been dating started to get serious.

> I just didn't really want to be bothered. I thought, well, I can make it and this is it. We can be friends but as far as anything else goes. . . . I just thought I

just didn't even want to be bothered again with somebody telling me what to do. But then he was such a
totally different person. And one day he just said,
"Why don't we get married? Why bother to have two
households?"

And I said, "Man, are you crazy? Here I am with
four teenage children and you want to marry me? You
gotta be nuts. You must be out of your tree." And this
is exactly what I told him.

And he said, "No. I'm not. I'm old enough to
know what I'm doing."

Still she put him off, and finally her woman friends in the
office bought her a beautiful new suit for a wedding outfit.
And then she married him.

There are men who want to ask the question without
taking the risk.

We went out quite frequently—I had it in the back
of my mind that he would probably ask me to marry
him, but I thought it might be in December at Christmastime. And then we went to a wedding in October.
And we were sitting—he's the type of person, I think
he was afraid. He's kind of the life of the party, center
of attention all the time. The type that you think
nothing bothers them, but really he's supersensitive
and keeps everything inside. So he was afraid to ask
me to marry him because he was afraid I might say no.
And he's like Mr. Joke, you know.

So we were sitting at the reception after, and he

said, "Pass the potatoes. Pass the roast beef. Do you want to get married?" One of those—in front of everybody—figuring that if I said no, he could say, "Oh, I was only kidding."

So I said, "Yeah."

So he took out one of those little calendars and said, "Well, when do you want to get married?"

And sometimes, *she* asks *him*.

It was more or less . . . you and I had better get married or I'm going to California, I said to him. He, I think, would have rather put me in dry ice for five years and then come back and got me. He didn't want me to leave. So he married me.

We eloped. One night he had a clean shirt and I had my hair done, so we got married. I knew he wouldn't go through with a big wedding. And I didn't think my father would pay for a big wedding and I didn't have any money, so one night—we had gotten our license—so one night at dinner he called and I said, "Why not tonight?" and he said, "Okay," and I came back to the table and said, "Anybody who wants to go to a wedding, get dressed." Everybody got up and got dressed. We went to the justice of the peace's house and got married.

The first time I got married, almost twenty years ago, women were expected to spend their adult lives as somebody's wife. "You know, you grow up and get married," said one forty-year-old woman I interviewed. "It never occurred to me that there was other ways of living."

"We didn't talk about it at all," said another woman of the same generation. "We just got married."

Nowadays we know all about other ways of living. Women are working outside the home in unprecedented numbers. More and more couples are living together without benefit of clergy. Alternatives to marriage jam the airwaves and leer from every drugstore magazine rack. And everyone knows that marriage is a risky business—the divorce rates are so high.

The difference between the two eras shows up in the answers to the expectations questions. ("When you were a teenager and you thought about your adult life, did you imagine this life?") In the *Wifestyles* group as a whole, some 20 percent said explicitly that they had not expected to marry, either because they didn't want to or because they just didn't think about marriage when they thought about their future life. Of the women who experienced this teenage disinterest in marriage, three quarters were younger wives. *But they all got married.* And so does most everyone else, sooner or later. It has been estimated that almost every woman alive in the United States today will be married, at least once, sometime in her lifetime.[1]

Among the women I interviewed there was a group in their late twenties and early thirties who had all lived with their husbands for some time before they got married. We talked about the difference between living together and being married, and I asked them why they had decided to marry. Their answers were no different from those of women in other generations: I want to be with him forever; I want to have children with him; I want to grow old with him. But for these women the decision to get married was a struggle.

Laura Chapman lives with her husband of two years in the French Quarter in New Orleans behind one of those lovely wrought-iron balconies. The apartment was hers before he moved in, and it looks both cosmopolitan and cozy—lots of books and mementoes around, old framed circus posters on the walls, plants grouped against the French doors. Laura is twenty-eight and pretty in a soft, almost pouting way—long fluffy brown hair, striking hazel eyes, a small full mouth. Self-assured and gracious, she is the picture of modern Southern sophistication. We sat on an overstuffed chintz-covered sofa. Ceiling fans circled lazily overhead.

When Laura was growing up, she said that she would never get married. "In high school I was really struck with the fact that I just couldn't imagine myself being out of college, out on my own. You know, I just couldn't imagine—'I'll die before then, probably.' Marriage meant not being independent to me, then. I really saw—now I look at my parents and I think they have a real good relationship—but when I was younger I thought they are so ingrown on each other. They are so interdependent. I thought that was really yucky. I thought it was real important to be on your own and to be real strong yourself."

After she finished college, Laura began working and moved into an apartment by herself. She enjoyed an active social life and had several lovers. "For a while when I was a teenager, I felt like, well, sex equals marriage. If I'm going to be able to have sex with this person, I'm going to have to get married to them. Once I decided it was okay to go to bed with somebody without being married to them, then marriage went out the window for quite a while."

By the time Laura was twenty-five her fear of dependency had lessened. She began to date the man she eventually married.

> Once I had spent a good time living in my own little apartment all by myself—realizing that I could do it and I wasn't going to crumple up and die because I was living by myself and there wasn't a man at my side— once I knew that it was okay to be in that situation, I could enter a relationship without feeling driven out of need. You know, it was more like—I'd like a relationship with this person. I have some things to share.
>
> Right before we got engaged, I got involved in a real short thing—a fella that I'd been friendly with. And looking back on it now, I wonder whether I didn't kind of get involved in that as—okay, this is going to be my last real fling. I didn't feel like that then. I think at that point I felt, I'm going to assert myself. And this is how you stay independent—you go and you have all these little affairs with everybody. And it was a disappointment. I think I felt like—oh, well this isn't any fun. What I really want to do is be with him [the man she married] and that's what's important to me. And I want to have other friends but, you know, what I really want is for me and him to be family.

Laura and her husband had lived together for almost a year before they got married. I asked her what the advantage of being married was, and she smiled. "I think one of the big motivations behind our actually getting married and having a wedding ceremony and all that was as a declaration. It's important to me in that respect. It's like—Look, you guys, this is a relationship we're in and we're going to do it." And then she laughed lightly and took it back. "It didn't feel too much different from living together. The only difference was, I guess I felt aware of other people. I guess when I got in a new situation, when this is a person that I'm just meeting, it wouldn't be cool for them to think that I'm living with someone. Now when they ask, 'Who is this man next to you?' I can say, 'Oh, well, this is my husband.' It's just more of a social convenience."

Toward the end of the interview, she told me again that she really was strong enough to make it alone. "I still think it's important to be strong—and if it happens that you're in a relationship with another person, that's part of what makes the relationship strong. We are dependent on each other, but I feel like I'm strong enough to make it on my own. And there might be a time when I'm by myself. Well, statistically there probably *will be* a time when I'm by myself. I think about that sometimes: Could I make a go of it by myself? I think I could. I think I'd be unhappy for a long time, but I know I could do it. And I think that's also what makes me stay. You know, one of the things that lets me be dependent on him."

So even this worldly woman is worried about what the neighbors will say. Or perhaps diminishing her marriage to a mere "social convenience" helps Laura tolerate the inevitable dependence of being a wife. She calls her marriage a "relation-ship," a cool and distant word to my ears. Her commitment to the marriage is "dependence." It's hard to talk about tradi-tional institutions in the vocabulary of the sixties. The fit is sometimes awkward, and the dilemma is real enough. How can new values be reconciled with the old?

Occasionally during an interview with a woman in her twenties or early thirties, I would run into some linguistic static. (I was always surprised—I think of myself as a feminist who is meticulous with words. *Girl* is my quickest trigger. I just can't stand it when somebody calls a grown woman a girl.) Several of the younger women were triggered by the word *wife*. One exchange went like this:

ME: What can you say you think an advantage of being a wife is?

SHE: Being a wife in terms of being the other half of a husband?

ME: I knew you wouldn't like the way I asked that question.

SHE: No, that won't do.

ME: Want to try "advantage of being married"?

SHE: That's fine. Advantages of being married—there are a lot, I think.

That same week—I was in San Francisco—another wife in her late twenties told me that the disadvantage of being married is "being called a wife. Sometimes being called Mrs.

People forget that I'm who I am, that I don't need to be labeled as a wife."

Negative feelings about being called Mrs. are not confined to metropolitan California. Carla Watkins is thirty and lives in Mason City, Iowa. She explained to me why she has kept her own name since she got married four years ago.

> I did it because I never could think of myself as Mrs. So-and-So. Because that's not who I was. I was Carla Watkins and I'd always be Carla Watkins. And no matter who I was going to be—Mrs. Smith or whatever—it just didn't sound right to me 'cause that wasn't me.
>
> And also I started thinking, too, in this day and age—sure you're going to try like heck to keep your marriage as long as you can. You know, it's work, that's for sure. But you have to be realistic too. You know, percentages aren't real good for you keeping one marriage all throughout your life. I thought—well, what if it did end up that I had to go through a divorce situation. I'd have somebody else's name, somebody else's financial background, somebody else's credit. I would be without anything at all if my marriage ended.

None of these women is saying she doesn't want to be married, but each of them is trying to balance the old and the new: to be involved in a permanent relationship and yet be strong and independent; to enjoy the commitment of marriage and yet retain her individuality; to make her marriage work and yet protect herself against the possibility that it will fail.

Traditional marriage does have its constraints. One of them is sexual fidelity, but here nobody's complaining. Indeed, several of the younger women in the study see their marriages as a haven from the demands of adult dating. Bobbi Webster, a pretty blond California woman in her early twenties who still looks like a teenager, put it this way: "I like the security of being married. I was talking to my girl friend yesterday—she's twenty-five—and she was saying that she's going through hell. A guy buys her a cup of coffee and expects to jump in the sack. I couldn't handle that." Asked how the first year of her marriage went, another young wife in Minneapolis said, "I just liked being married. I thought it was a big relief from being single and dating and all that." Laura Chapman talked about the disappointment of her last fling—"This isn't any fun." Another woman expressed physical distaste for her own earlier philandering. Wrinkling her nose in half-comic disgust, she said, "I like to make love, but, you know, this making love with all these different people who are just turkeys . . . it's just awful. Yek."

Diana Zimmer is an extreme example. Listening to the story of her teenage years was like hearing the recitation of a parent's worst nightmare. Diana was a teenager in trouble in the mid-sixties. She ran around with the local college boys and began to drink too much and then to use amphetamines and LSD. Eventually she became involved in a sex ring in which she was passed from one pledge to another in several of the fraternity houses. When she finally became frightened by what she was doing, she was able to break away from her old friends and move to another town where no one knew her. Soon thereafter she was married. "I was ready to get married—at nineteen, I think that was it. I was probably really ready to get married. Probably a lot because of what all I'd been through. My God, I'd just been devastated by everything, and I needed some port in the storm. I'd lived all I could handle —and I never did learn, and you know to this day it even scares me, if I were to divorce or widow or whatever. I don't know how to handle situations with men."

In one of my early interviews I talked with a woman who is about my age and comes from a background very similar to mine. She got married at twenty-two, just as I had, only her first marriage lasted, and she is now the mother of four teenage girls and a settled suburban housewife. But something is gnawing at her. She has never made love with anyone except her husband. She loves him and has a good time with him in bed and all that, but lately she has begun to feel that she has to have the experience of another man, another lover. I had learned by then not to give advice, but I wanted to tell her that I had found the sexual freedom of the divorcée to be a vastly overrated experience. Along with its many other attractions, marriage has the effect of taking one instantly and permanently off the meat rack.

Some women flee gratefully into marriage. Others are so ambivalent they have to be dragged to the altar. Susie Patterson managed to stay single until she was thirty-five. "I always remember, as a little kid and as a growing-up girl, I remember saying this to people: 'My God, when you get married, you've lost it. Then, whoever your friends are, are who your husband's friends are. Wherever you go depends on where his job is. I mean you just lose it.' And I don't want that to happen to me. I felt so able to move around and get places and not have this millstone dragging me back."

Susie has just turned forty. She grew up in the mid-fifties, when most young girls wanted to get married. I asked her where her ideas about marriage had come from. "I think I got them in this little farm town in Iowa I grew up in where all the girls got married the summer they graduated from high school. I was one of two girls in my class who went on to college. And my own mother gave me some of those ideas too, because she had gone to college when it was unheard of. And she always said, 'You've got plenty of time to do all that.' "

Susie still looks like an Iowa farmgirl, blond and pert, with a small, nicely rounded body and a lightly freckled pug nose. I loved doing this interview. I had had a rotten cold all during that long trip from Minneapolis to Mason City to Chicago, and I was very tired. The last few interviews had been difficult: a shy woman made more reticent by my tape recorder; a sad woman whose husband was having a long, messy love affair. Talking to Susie was like opening a window to let in the sun. She is a funny, savvy lady, and her story has a happy ending.

She left the farm to go to college and never went back. When school was over, she moved to the city, got work in public relations, and began a very successful career. She lived alone, had many friends of both sexes, enjoyed the local museums, the opera and the symphony. She made enough money to buy herself nice clothes and go on nice vacations. And then she was thirty-five, beginning to feel that what she had was not enough.

Susie knew that she was afraid of getting married. "What if I bet on somebody wrong?" But this man she had been dating was clear—he wanted to marry her. And finally she agreed. The wedding day: "Just stark terror, fear, and loathing."

The first year of her marriage it was really touch-and-go. "It was awful for me. Partly because I was terrified to get married, just fucking terrified. Because I thought: What will I do if I hate it? What will I do if this isn't the right thing for me?" Susie remembers a particular night when she began to understand what it was that so frightened her about being married. "We had gone to the movies or something, and we came in this apartment and shut the door and I walked into the kitchen and I turned around and he was there, and I thought: My God. He's still here. He's gonna *be* here. *He lives here.* This is it. My God. If I turn around and he won't go home . . . he won't have anywhere to go. Oh. That just drove me nuts. Nowhere to hide."

The happy part of the story is that they worked it out. Together and with some good professional counselors, Susie and her husband were both able to face their fears of marriage and to grow beyond them. As I was reluctantly packing up my briefcase after our interview was over, she and I were joking about how the story of her marriage is like an old-fashioned movie: bright, successful career woman finally finds Mr. Right and settles down to domestic bliss. Well, that wasn't exactly the way it happened.

The fear of getting married can come from many places. Women who have been divorced have a good reason to be afraid. Despite the ballyhoo about its potential for human growth, divorce is a hell of pain and disappointment. Most women (and men) who get divorced do marry again, which seems evidence to me that people have a lot more courage than we generally give them credit for.[2] Part of the problem is learning to believe in marriage again. That old romantic forever-and-ever stuff does tend to get knocked out of you.

One solution, of course, is to say you don't believe in it but you're going to get married anyway. That was Josie Serrano's strategy. Josie got married again last summer to a man who has also been divorced. They are both twenty-six. The story of their decision to marry has a kind of halting drama: one step forward and two steps back.

> That was a real off-and-on kind of thing for a long time because neither of us was real sure that we wanted to get married again. We decided to live together for a while and sort of see how things were. And things went along fine. And then we . . . we had joint charge accounts. I mean we were really, for all intents and purposes, you know, socially married. We were just not legally married. So we talked about it for a while.
>
> And I was getting a fair amount of pressure from my family—very conservative, sort of Bible Belt people—and we just decided that there were a lot of things that we could probably straighten out, not necessarily with the family because I was pretty rebellious at the time and didn't really want to give in to any of their wishes. But we just decided to get our insur-

ance straightened out. And it was really for a lot of these real practical reasons, we said, "Well, why don't we get married?"

I finally got my divorce, and we still went along, not real sure about this, you know, "Why get married again? It's been so comfortable living together. There's really no problem with this." But I don't know, I'm sort of a romantic at heart so I think probably that was the real issue: whether or not we were going to just do this and call it "second attempt" or whatever.

For a few months they teetered back and forth. He asked her to marry him; she said she didn't know. He would bring it up, and she would say no. Then she got interested, and he said he wasn't sure. Finally the week came when they were both sure at the same time.

The wedding was small and informal. Josie's description of it is telling. "We just balked at all the traditional things. The judge came and married us—that took about five minutes. And we had our little witnesses, and everybody stood around, and then we all came in here and we just started drinking champagne. It was really fun—not taken too seriously. I think it was taken in the vein that we meant for it to be—it was sort of a social thing. Neither of us had real preformed ideas that this was going to be the romance to end all romances—although that's always in the back of my mind."

What's in the back of your mind certainly counts. This sounds like longing to me, a wish for the marriage to be solid and sweet and loving, barely disguised in some talk about practical reasons and social occasions. But I can hear the fear too.

I once attended a wedding in which the bride was a picture of terror coming down the aisle. She was a young woman who had been supremely self-confident since she was a small child. Magna cum laude, winner of awards and trophies, second in her class at law school. The night before the wedding we had chatted at the rehearsal dinner. When I asked if she was nervous, she laughed and shrugged her shoulders. "The ceremony can't be more than ten minutes long," she said. The next time I saw her she was leaning on her father for dear life, her mouth twisted in a grimace of fear. I felt satisfied by the transformation, I remember. She had seemed frivolous to me the night before. Now I realize that she was just scared to death, so scared she didn't even know it.

When I first designed the *Wifestyles* interview, I planned to spend some time talking with each woman about her wedding day. It was the third question, after the day you met him and the day you decided to marry him: "Tell me about the day you got married." But it turned out that very few of the women were interested. I had expected people to drag out their wedding albums and get misty-eyed in front of the eight-by-ten glossies. Nobody did. The wedding is neither as memorable nor as fondly remembered as I thought it would be.

Oh, there were a few Cinderella stories—white satin and heirloom lace under an arch of swords, the dress blues of his officers' school classmates shining in the sun. And a few funny stories—an evening reception at home on Halloween and nobody remembered that all these little witches and goblins were going to show up looking for treats. The guests gave them champagne and wedding cake, and they kept coming back and ringing the doorbell again. Some sweet stories—a soldier home on short leave proposed on Friday; he had to go back Tuesday morning. Her three sisters worked on the wedding all weekend: One made the wedding dress, one baked the wedding cake, and the other did everything else. The couple was married on Monday evening in front of a hundred guests. There were sad stories too: brides who were pregnant and ashamed; a woman so exhausted on her wedding day that all she remembers is how much her stomach ached; a mother who was too busy to help her only daughter make a dress to get married in. But for the most part the *Wifestyles* women are like one bride I talked to who purchased an elaborate keepsake bridal book before the ceremony and never finished filling it afterward. As soon as it's over, most people lose interest.

It isn't that a wedding is unimportant. Getting married is a significant human occasion. What my sister, who got married recently, calls "the wedding doo-dah" is one of the few surviving ceremonial events in the ordinary person's life. Weddings are for showing off, for doing the loveliest, most romantic, most beautiful things one can muster: music, flowers, gowns, ritual words. Everything that says: This is important. This matters. In the most public way, in the most vivid display the couple present themselves: Here we are. Look at us. Watch us make this impossible promise to each other. See how we believe it. Remember how you believe it too.

When my sister was married, I got to take care of her wedding dress, a gorgeous traditional white confection. Getting it in and out of the tailor's for a final pressing was a three-person job, two to carry and one to open doors. We hung it in the upstairs porch over a floor carefully draped in bed sheets and covered up all the windows with towels so nobody would see. When the day finally came, my mother and I lifted the dress tenderly and dropped it over the waiting bride. Every time she moved, somebody had to hoist up the train and rearrange it. More sheets all over the floor of the car on the way to the church. After the reception I took the dress out of the back of our car and crammed it into a shelf in my closet where it lay with its lace black from the dance floor for several weeks before I finally took it to the cleaners. Once a wedding is over, it's over.

And *getting* married has almost nothing to do with *being* married. When I was growing up, I had a romantic fantasy about the sort of wedding I would have and a vague notion of a pleasant domestic life after that—husband, children, white house in the country. I didn't have much of an idea of what it would be like trying to live with another person. I never thought about that. Among the women in the *Wifestyles* study who said they had expected to marry, the same failure of imagination prevails. "I hoped to be married," one said. "The big hump was getting married. I didn't think beyond that."

"More than anything else, I wanted to get married," another said. "That was my goal in life. And once I got married, I thought, Hum. There's got to be something else."

The fourth interview question asks about the transition from bride to wife: "Tell me about the first year of your marriage." Many of the women were surprised by the first year —and some of the surprises were not so pleasant. Almost everyone acknowledged a period of adjustment at the beginning of the marriage. Some were dramatically unhappy. One woman recalled thinking, "Well, what am I doing in this? It just isn't at all what I planned it to be." Sixteen percent described a first year that was mostly unhappy. Another 30 percent had a mixed first year, with both good and bad times. Slightly more than half (54 percent) described a mostly happy year. This is another question that was answered differently according to age. Seventy-five percent of the older women, those over forty, said that the first year of their marriage was mostly happy, while only 38 percent of the forty-and-under group reported a mostly happy first year.*

Happy and unhappy alike had things to get used to. Many talked about specific areas of adjustment. Of these, the one most often mentioned—by 34 percent of the women— was her accommodation to the new husband's habits and expectations. He wanted her to cook breakfast; she liked to sleep in. She was ready to chat when they first got home from work; he needed some time alone to shift gears. He was used to mother ironing his permanent-press shirts; she hated ironing. I had expected to hear more about sex than I did in the answers to this question about the first year, especially from the women who were married before premarital sex was common. But only 12 percent talked about a sexual adjustment. Everyday quirks and differences in temperament were mentioned more often than whatever was going on in the nuptial bed.

Certain domestic details do need to be worked out whenever two people start living together: the times when meals

---

*See Table 1 in the Technical Appendix.

will be served and who will cook them, that sort of thing. In the traditional marriage many tasks are assigned by sex; much less has been certain among women who have married in the past twenty years. Several of the younger women talked at length about power struggles with their husband in the first year.

Sherri Caldwell and her husband are still struggling. Sherri lives on the crest of a dusty hill overlooking a country road in Nashville, Tennessee. It's a little red brick house. She and her husband are renting right now, but they hope to buy the house eventually, and they're working on it as if it were theirs already. Two weeks before I visited they had stripped and sanded all the floors and begun to refinish them. The front rooms were still closed off. She let me into the kitchen by the back door. It's a small, dark room. The ceiling light was on in the middle of the day. They're planning to put in a skylight when they remodel in here, she said.

At first glance this pleasant, open young woman might be taken for a high-school senior. She has dark hair, dark-brown eyes, and the compact athletic body of a good volleyball player. She was barefoot and wearing an Indian cotton print sundress. As I sat across from her at the kitchen table, there were times when she looked no more than seventeen. And then I would notice a line between her nose and mouth, the darker circles under her eyes, the roughness across the backs of her hands.

Sherri has just turned twenty. She and her husband were married a year ago last fall. They moved right into the little red brick house, had their first big fight the second day they were there, and have been trying hard to make the marriage work ever since. She now feels that neither of them was prepared for the realities of being married.

> And I thought, well, when we get married, we're really going to have . . . you know, I thought when you get married, you make love every night. And I thought it was taking showers together. But after we got married I said, "Knock before you come in the bathroom. Don't just come in on me."
>
> And I just wasn't used to sleeping with someone. He doesn't snore or anything, but he likes to sleep in the middle of the bed. And finally I told him, "We got to get something straight: You stay on your side of the bed, and I'll stay on mine."

I asked Sherri what she thought the main problem was between her and her husband. Was there one thing that kept coming up? She sat for a minute and thought about it. Then she frowned, deepening the crease between her eyebrows.

> In Engaged Encounter, they had a question: Who will be the boss in your family? Who is head of the family? You know, husband or wife? And he just put on his little notes "Husband." And I just didn't feel like husband should be the head of the house. You know, that's the old saying: Husband head of the house. Husband say what goes. This, that, and the other. And I just don't believe in that. I mean, it's not what my mother or . . . Daddy's the head of the house over to my house. But I'm not that type of person. I want to

be in there just as much as he is, and I want to get just as many yes or nos about the things we do or the things we buy—as much as he is. And he doesn't feel that way. We argue now about it, *still.*

She smiled suddenly, and the seventeen-year-old came back into her face. "I don't want marriage to be like this. I want to be a good wife and I want to do what he says, but then again I want to do what I want to do too." Torn between a traditional notion of what a good wife should be and her wish to stand up for herself, Sherri has been unable to resolve one of the fundamental issues of a young marriage: Who's in charge here?

Another woman who was also married at nineteen described a similar struggle in the early days of her marriage. Asked about the first year, she grimaced. "Horrendous. We were just talking about that at work. So and so was saying, if anything happened to her husband, she would never marry again. And I said, 'I certainly understand that. I'd never want to go through it again either.' Not because the marriage is unhappy, but I would never want to go through that first year. It was—to see who was boss, to see who could get away with what. Just stupid stuff. I mean, I can remember going home to my mother once. Lasted about two hours, I think, before he came and got me. Just really what I would consider real childish, immature ways of acting. My parents' marriage wasn't happy, and his parents were together and stuff but I would consider it a hopeless kind of thing, so neither of us had a model to follow."

Wanting to do better in her marriage than her parents

had done, another bride set high standards for herself. "I wanted to be the perfect wife. My idea then was—I was very immature—I guess I thought the perfect wife was somebody that would do everything to please her husband. Everything. Whether it be to always make his meals and have the house looking really good and if he wanted to do something, fine, go along with it, and don't argue. I just didn't want any arguments. . . . My mother and father never got along that well, and there was a lot of arguments, and I always said, when I get married, I'm not going to treat my husband the way my mother treated my father."

The way her mother treated her father will inevitably color the first year of a woman's own marriage. Her parents' relationship is the marriage she knows best. Whether she chooses to emulate it or to have a completely different marriage, its influence will still be felt. Later in the interview I asked each *Wifestyles* woman to compare her marriage with her mother's. Most (48 percent) felt that there were both similarities and differences; a little more than a third (37 percent) said that their marriages were very different from mother's, and the smallest number (15 percent) said that they were quite similar. One woman talked about how her mother's example seemed to overwhelm her own good judgment in the first days of her marriage. "I did notice, especially when we first got married, in certain situations that I reacted the same way as my mother would have. And it took me back. I said, 'This isn't the way I really feel.' It was just this behavior that I had seen all these years and been around. And I said, 'I'm acting just like my mother.' Maybe in the kitchen, my husband would be picking up the pot covers and looking in. And that's one thing my mother hates my father to do, and he does it all the time. She doesn't tell him. [She laughed.] So it was something like that. It wasn't anything serious—just one of these daily interaction things."

One of the surprises of the first year is how persistent the ways of one's mother can be. Another woman compared her own marriage to her mother's. "On the surface my marriage is entirely different. But I find myself doing things that my mother would do, things that really, ideally, I don't believe a person should do. In her I see: cooking, cleaning up, keeping the house, running the household, doing all this supporting my father and the boys. Not even getting them to clean up their rooms. And then I say, 'That's not how it should be. You know, you ought to have more of your own life.' [She laughed.] And then I turned around and look at myself, and I'm doing almost the same thing. Um, she doesn't quite have the freedom that I have. I'm not tied down to the kids because I don't have any. I don't think that I would treat a child the same way that I saw her treat my younger brothers, but then again I didn't think that I would treat a husband the same way."

Sometimes both wife and husband will find themselves influenced by the traditional roles in spite of their conscious commitment to a more egalitarian marriage. Pat Hinton and her husband are both in their early thirties, college educated, and working in the professions. She is a copywriter for a major advertising firm; he works in university administration. When they got married they decided to stay in the city instead of moving back to the suburbs where they grew up. It was to be a thoroughly modern urban marriage, but gradually Pat began to see that she really expected something else.

He's not traditional in the sense that he's not very good at figures and not very good at bills and taxes and fixing things around the house . . . and I'm not either. I couldn't care less about that sort of thing. I actually don't enjoy fixing cars, thank you very much, and I hope I never have to learn. And he doesn't either. [She laughed.] But he was suddenly thrust into a position of feeling like he should because he's a man . . . and so he's suddenly feeling like he should know how to do all these things, and he didn't, and it was hard for him.

It was real difficult. It was hard for me too. That was another thing about my father—he could do anything. He could get anywhere. And that was kind of an expectation that I had for marriage—that I would be taken care of to a certain extent. It was real funny because I had all of these very strong feelings about not being taken advantage of because I was female. You know, that we should have an equal share in the cooking and the cleaning and the housework and dee-dah, deedah, dah. And if I brought in as much money as he did, by God, I was going to have an equal say in how it was spent. All that. And yet at the same time, in the first year I realized also that I had expectations of him because he was male that never even occurred to me—those traditional things that I just expected of

him. I think I did expect that he would be like my
father is and that I would be able to be like my mother
is.

Sometimes it's the husband who has the modern ideas.
Louise Finn has been married for almost twenty years to a man
who knows very well that he doesn't need to take care of her.
It took her a little while to get used to the idea.

I think I had the idea as a teenager: You marry a man
and he works and you stay home and raise the children
and keep the house and so forth, and he takes care of
you. This was the idea of marriage that I grew up
with. But it's not like that. At least not in our marriage. I don't think my husband married me with the
idea that he was going to take care of me, because I
was twenty-five years old at the time and I guess he
thought I'd been taking care of myself all this time and
I really didn't need anybody to take care of me. But
in the back of my mind I still had this idea that I was
going to get married and I was going to be taken care
of. I may not have agreed then that I was thinking
that, but I think I probably was because it's been a real
adjustment in my thinking.

When we lived in Oklahoma, if I wanted to go
all the way across Kansas to visit my parents, he would
say, "Go ahead. That's fine. I'll stay here. I don't mind
your going." So I would get in the car and drive nine
hours with the kids and stay a week with my family
and visit. And I had friends whose husbands didn't

want them to drive twenty miles to the next town by themselves. And sometimes I thought, you know, well, I wonder if he cares what's going to happen to us on this long drive. But I'm convinced now that he figured I had enough sense to know what to do if something happened to the car. So I learned to accept that as not being unconcerned.

In a lot of ways I'm still very traditional and in a lot of other ways—because of circumstances and being forced to—I've been changed into a changing woman.

Another surprise: sometimes a woman who starts out full of feminist fervor will find that the traditional role really suits her better. Hannah Brown has been married seven years. Talking about the first year of her marriage, she said:

Most of the problems I really think originated with me. I was going through that period of was I feminist or not—you know what I'm saying? So I was having trouble feeling good about washing dishes. Is this fair? and everything. Now I finally—I have a little bit of trouble, but—I really don't want to work. I don't like to work. If I have a choice, I like being home. I love doting on him. I love fixing up his tray and taking it into the bedroom and handing him his food.

And for the longest time so many things you'd read would say that's—you know, you're being a slut. He's chauvinistic, and all that. But I finally have come around to—No. I think it depends on why people do that. I really enjoy it. I love doting on him, doing for him. And I think that in a way I should do it in that I should work in one way or another. And since I'm not working outside of the home, then I shouldn't sit on my rump all day and expect him to come home and do the dishes and clean the house and, you know. That's silly. That's not even fair.

I had problems finding where my niche and my role was because the idea of a role meant that it was wrong. And I think now that I've come to the realization that there is nothing with roles. Everyone does have a role. The thing is finding the role—maybe it's career wife-woman and not really so much wife but more career woman. But everyone chooses a role of some sort in life. And then the thing is to choose the role you're happy with.

It may be that people reconstruct the past to fit their expectations of it. At least most of us remember selectively. Many of the *Wifestyles* questions were answered in similar ways by the older and younger women in the study, with no significant differences according to age. But two of the questions we've considered in this chapter did show very different answers depending on the age group: the question about expectations and the question about happiness in the first year. Most of the women in the study who have married in the past twenty years, since the beginning of the sixties, say that they are not getting the life they expected; they also report that their first year of marriage was not a particularly happy one. Most of the women who married earlier, before the sixties, remember a happy first year of marriage and feel that the life they have is the one they expected.

Among many of the younger women there is a sense of surprise, perhaps of disappointment in themselves. Some are surprised to be married at all—they had other, more exotic dreams: travel, a glamorous career. Others are surprised by the wives they have become—they thought they could be so different from their mothers. Their marriages are still relatively new, and the difference between the dream and the reality is still painful.

The older women sometimes told a kind of story that I call Early Adversity Fondly Remembered. These are funny little anecdotes, often tenderly told, about the hardships of their early married years. How it was the depression and they were engaged for three years because nobody could afford to get married. How she found a mouse nest in the flour bin the day they moved into their first house. How they lived in a homemade sixteen-foot trailer on the farm and were never ahead by more than a month's wages. "All of our friends were in the same shape we were—nobody had any money. We couldn't go anywhere and do anything, so we played cards and drank Kool-Aid." It may be easier to laugh about not having enough money to buy anything but Kool-Aid some years later, when one's wallet is fatter.

Women who have married in the last twenty years are struggling to reconcile a rash of new values with the more traditional ideas about what a marriage should be. They also lack the comfort that can come from being married forty years. And nothing but time can bring them that. All of those old, sweet stories notwithstanding, it was hard enough to be a bride when times were steady and everybody's expectations were modest and clear. These days people actually make jokes at a first wedding about what the second one will be like. And I think we expect more out of life than we used to, especially we women. If getting married is harder than it used to be, it's no wonder.

Two

KEEPING HOUSE

Industrialization has had these lasting consequences: the separation of the man from the intimate daily routines of domestic life; the economic dependence of women and children on men; the isolation of housework and childcare from other work.

—*Ann Oakley,* Woman's Work:
The Housewife, Past and Present

Elizabeth Middleton's house is classic New England saltbox, white with green shutters, maple trees in the front. It is immaculate. In all of the windows, the panes of glass have that invisible quality that only lasts for a week or two after you wash them. The antique mahogany sideboard came from her mother's side of the family. It smells of beeswax. The house is full of beautiful things: rainbow afghans, doilies crocheted from string, needlepoint footrests.

Elizabeth has been married thirty-nine years to the local pediatrician, still practicing. They met, fell in love, courted during the depression in this small Vermont town. Married right after the war broke out. He enlisted, went overseas, survived, came home to start his practice up again. She wanted to help—type and keep the books—but he thought there was no place for a wife in her husband's office. Telling the story, years later, she said, "My job was to make things pleasant at home."

Here's the best description I've ever heard of the housewife's job: to make things pleasant at home.

Twenty years ago Betty Friedan wrote a book in which she said that being a housewife imprisons a woman in "a comfortable concentration camp" because neither the work of keeping house nor the role of the housewife is enough to sustain an adult human being.* She argued with stunning conviction that women need to have more important things to do. The modern feminist movement is often said to have begun with the publication of that book, *The Feminine Mystique.*

Nine years later, in the first issue of *Ms.* magazine, Jane O'Reilly described the "click!" that occurs when a woman realizes with "the shock of recognition" that "we are all

---

*Ms. Friedan has recently characterized this metaphor as "rather extreme" (in *The Second Stage,* New York: Summit Books, 1981), but she also notes that for her and the other women who founded the National Organization for Women, "equality and the personhood of women never meant destruction of the family, repudiation of marriage and motherhood, or implacable sexual war against men" (p. 47).

housewives, the natural people to turn to when there is something unpleasant, inconvenient, or inconclusive to be done."[1] She argued that the members of a household—male and female, children and adults—ought to share the work of the household.

And it was Norman Mailer, of course, who said that all this woman's liberation business really comes down to one question: Who's going to wash the dishes?

All right. Who *is* going to wash the dishes? In most of the households in America, most of the time, dirty dishes are loaded into dishwashers or stacked in pans of hot, soapy water by the woman of the house.

A typical housewife is still a person who goes through "her" house on automatic pilot—picking up, putting away, smoothing and straightening, wiping—all day, every day, as much of the day as she is home. Washing her hands, she rubs absentmindedly at the splotch of toothpaste left on the tap. When her shoe sticks on the kitchen floor, she stoops to wipe the sticky place away. She sniffs towels and garbage pails. Driving past the supermarket, she remembers that there is no milk in the house. She stops to get some. It is, as Jane O'Reilly said, *on her mind.*

Not all wives are like this, but most of them are.

Keeping house is still woman's work. It is what wives do for husbands. Somehow, somewhere, women who get married learn how to cook, how to clean, how to wash dishes. And they expect to do it. They still see it as their work. Many of them won't give it up. And most of them don't seem to mind. There are exceptions: children who do their own laundry, wives who never wash the windows, husbands who always wash the dishes. But then there always were. So while things are not exactly the way they used to be, they're not all that different either.

The traditional division of household labor by sex is well known: She does the cooking and the marketing, washes the dishes and the clothes, keeps the house neat and clean. He mows the lawn, takes out the garbage, and does small household repairs if he is "handy." (Traditionally certain other responsibilities are also divided by sex: She takes care of the children, and he earns the money to support the family. Child care and employment, both hers and his, will be considered in the next two chapters.)

We talked in the *Wifestyles* interview about keeping house, off and on, most of the time. Get the average husband talking about himself, and he'll tell you about his job; the average wife talks about her house, her chores, her kids, her flower garden. Routine household work is mentioned by almost every woman as part of her typical weekday:

"I get up and I make the bed."

"I put the coffee on and make the kids' lunches."

"Then we run out to the store, do any other errands that need to be done, try to come back and get the dinner started by five."

"We finish supper, and I do the dishes . . ." The housework is the backdrop against which the rest of her life moves. It is always a part of her, woven into the texture of her life—maybe only half a dozen strands, maybe all the warp and woof, but always *there,* never *not there* as it is, every day, for most men.

The interview included a specific question about who

does what around the house. It was typed on a 5 by 7 card. The part about housework looked like this:

WHO DOES IT?

1. I do all or almost all of it.
2. I do most of it.
3. We split it 50–50.
4. He does most of it.
5. He does all or almost all of it.

Cooking
Home maintenance and repairs
Washing dishes
Yardwork and gardening
Food shopping
Laundry
Picking up the house
Cleaning the house

And the question was: "How do you and your husband share the responsibilities of your household? Using the 1 to 5 scale at the top of this card, read through the list of tasks underneath the line and give each task a number that shows how you and he divide the work. Number 1 means you do it all, number 5 means he does it all, and there are some grades in between." I deliberately left out anyone else in the household who might do some of the chores. Children, for example, were excluded from the scale so that I could look at just the division of labor between the wife and the husband.

(When I first got the scores back from the computer on this question, I was talking about them with a friend, and she said, "I really think you ought to check those numbers again. I just can't believe that we've made so little progress. Is this all the difference the women's movement has made?" So I suggested she rate her own marriage to see how her scores compared with those in the study. She did, and her numbers matched the scores of the average *Wifestyles* woman almost exactly. You might want to try it too. Just take a pencil and jot down your own rating for each of the eight household tasks.)

Most of the women I talked with seemed to know that there is a new standard: He's supposed to help out now. Often there was nervous laughter if most of the numbers were 1 or 2 as she read down the list. Arriving at something he did do, she pounced on it with relief. "Yardwork and gardening? Oh, definitely 5; he does all that."

And there was more than a little generosity: "Cooking . . . 2. (I do most of it.) He'll come in and if I'm doing something and he's hungry, he'll make himself a sandwich, you know. But I cook all the meals, of course. He's not here most of the time."

"Food shopping . . . 5. He does it all. I make the list, and he always tries to get everything on it. I help him lug the bags into the kitchen, and then I put the stuff away."

"Food shopping . . . 4. (He does most of it.) I write an order down and he really—in the last two years, he's really learned. I try to tell him, 'It's on such and such a shelf,' you know."

Even so, the results are clear. The work traditionally considered the wife's responsibility (cooking, washing dishes, food shopping, laundry, picking up and cleaning the house) was dubbed "Herwork" for the computer. When Herwork scores for each woman in the study were added and averaged, the mean (average) score was 1.8, which means that she still does all or almost all of those tasks.

If you add the two housework responsibilities that are traditionally his (home maintenance and yardwork, gardening), she still does most of it, though not quite so much. The mean score for "Housework," all eight household tasks, was 2.2.[2] (You can find your own Housework score by adding up your scores for the eight household tasks and then dividing the sum by 8.)

It comes down to this: You know that crack between the stove top and the counter that's just big enough for a raw chicken liver to slip through? Some women wipe the stove down every night and then move it a little and wipe up the floor under the crack; some women wash that part of the floor every time they scrub the rest of it; and some women only give it a swipe when they move the stove to retrieve the chicken liver and see what the floor looks like. But no one expects her husband to wash that part of the kitchen floor. He doesn't even know it's there.

How do married women feel about being stuck with the housework, trapped in the housewife's role? Almost all of the women I talked to accept it. Their comments range from strong defense: "That's the way it ought to be" and "I wouldn't want him messing around in my kitchen" to resigned pragmatism: "It's the only arrangement that would work for us."

Susan Cox lives in a gray shingle-and-stone ranch on a

quiet residential street. Her three kids have finally grown up enough that she can have nice furniture, and last summer she bought a whole new living-room set. It still looks brand new. The house is picked up but lived in—piles of newspapers in the den, kids' stuff in the hall, a fraying pink towel in the downstairs bath.

Susan's computer profile for Housework (2.1) matches the average woman's almost exactly. I asked her how she feels about doing most of the housework. "I guess I'm more or less for the way it is. I guess I'm a product of my dad, especially where he thought that the man worked and the woman stayed home. I don't like to think I'm just totally like that but still, if my husband has worked all day and he's the one who is basically making the living, then I feel like by the time he gets home at night that his evenings should be as free as they can." Is there anything about the way the housework is divided that she would like to change? "I think everybody gets tired of doing all housework—you know, a majority of it. But I guess I wouldn't change it right now. We have talked about—that if I chose to go back to teaching, there would be no reason why I couldn't have full-time help, if I were needing to be away all day. And I guess you'd say I've chosen this way instead. I feel like I want to be here."

Irene Walker lives almost a thousand miles north of Susan, up the Atlantic coast in a northeastern rural area. The white house trailer where she and her husband live sits back on a narrow lot. Red and white petunias bloom out of an old tire lying on its side. The grass is straggly, and the porch floor needs mending; there is a piece of plywood over a hole in front of the door. The lawn and the carpentry are his work, she told me, shrugging. We sat at the kitchen table: brown Formica. Everything is scrubbed up in here, all the dishes put away, a fresh pot of coffee brewing. Irene's Housework score is 2.3, just about average. When she talks about "my housework," there is no sense of outrage. "Men don't understand about housework. They really don't. They don't—he'll do things that I ask him to do in cleaning the house. But he just doesn't see that they have to be done and do them."

Three thousand miles away, in a California suburb, Bobbi Webster, who is twenty-four, employed full time, and childless, does almost all of the housework (her score is 1.75). She has two jobs—one at work and another one at home—but she doesn't seem to mind. "When he is through with his day at work, he is through with his day at work. When I am through with my day at work, I come home and I still get the laundry, cook the dinner, put the dishes away, empty the dishwasher, fold the clothes, put them away. . . . He's always saying, 'Come on in here and watch TV with me.'

"I say, 'There's things I have to do. My day's not over at four thirty.'"

Bobbi is pretty and blond, a cheerleader grown a little too chubby. She talks about her work at home without a trace of anger in her voice. (I am astonished by her; I would be furious in her position.) The fact that she does almost all the housework in addition to her full-time job seems to be just a part of the way things are.

When I began the *Wifestyles* study, I expected that women like Bobbi who are young and employed outside the home would have the best chance of getting help from their husbands with the housework. It turns out that neither the wife's occupational status nor her age makes any significant difference in how much her husband does around the house.[3] Among the women who work full time, 42 percent are at the top of the Housework scale, where he helps a lot; 31 percent are in the middle, where he helps some; and 27 percent are at the bottom, where he doesn't do much at all.* That's some difference, but not very much. There's even less variation in the two age groups. The Housework scores of those forty and under are almost equally divided: 30 percent in the top third, 34 percent in the middle, and 36 percent at the bottom. The scores of the over-forty group are also pretty even: 32 percent, 42 percent, and 26 percent.† Whatever influences a husband to pitch in at home, it isn't just that his wife works or that they are members of the younger generation.

Some wives *are* angry about the amount of housework they do. Occasionally a woman expresses anger about the work itself. "I like a neat house. I really like a nice neat, clean house. The problem is: I don't want to do it. And so—I'm willing to do some of it. [Bursting out.] I *hate* that! You do it, you know, and twenty-four hours later you can't even tell you did it."

More often the anger comes from not getting enough help. Judy Simpson lives in a big brown shingled farmhouse. She is thirty-three and has three children, one in second grade, the other two still at home. Her housework score is 2; her husband helps some, but it's not enough for Judy. "He doesn't think enough about other people. Like, wouldn't it have been

---

*See Table 2 in the Technical Appendix.
†See Table 3 in the Technical Appendix.

nice if I came home and found the table set? Or wouldn't it be nice if he just picked up the vacuum cleaner and did it because he knew that I was tired? He does it if I ask him; he just won't think of it all on his own. He helps. He'll do anything that's asked. It's just that sometimes I'd like him to think of it all by himself."

For some of the *Wifestyles* women this is the sorest point: She always has to ask her husband for help. He never thinks to do it on his own. A Nashville, Tennessee, woman who is otherwise quite happily married has a Housework score of 2 and sometimes gets mad about doing most of the work at home.

> Sunday mornings. [She laughed.] Oh, I hate Sundays. When you get up—he usually gets to the kitchen first, it seems, on Sundays—and he's always reading the newspaper. And I start right in on breakfast just like every other morning, and once in a while I'll get really bugged and I'll just sit down and just sit there. And finally he'll say, "When is . . . uh, when is . . . ?" And he always says, "All you have to do is ask." But I don't want to ask. I want him to just do it. I think that's the difference between men and women. All I would have to say is "Could you help me with breakfast?" But then I would feel like I was putting him out by asking. But if I breathe heavy, then he knows he needs to come and help.

Another woman in a small Idaho town complained about her husband's selective vision. "Picking up the house? I do all that. He can't see anything. [She laughed.] That's terrible. He can sure make a mess. Walks over his shoes. I even left them for a long time hoping he would see the mess. I just left the mess. He never ever saw it. So finally I picked up. He doesn't see it. As long as he can walk through the house."

Some of the angriest women are overloaded: wives who do all or almost all of the housework and are also employed full time; the mothers of small children; women whose housekeeping standards are high. Sara Corey meets all three of these conditions. Her home is an old Victorian house, carefully restored—white walls, bleached wood, pastels everywhere inside. She works as a high-school history teacher; three-year-old Wendy stays with an older woman in town. Sara likes things nice. The pitcher on the coffee table is lead crystal, and the tall glasses match. The lemonade she serves me is homemade, impossibly tart and sweet.

Sara's husband does not help. He has a full-time job; he takes care of the cars; he plays with Wendy and sometimes puts her to bed. Sara does everything else: all the cooking, all the cleaning, all the laundry and shopping. It is a major grievance. Asked about the effect of her job on the marriage, she says it's not so much that she works but that she has all these other things to do too. "It goes back to the household work that I do most of, and I think I probably take that out on him . . . not meaning to, but the hostility gets pretty strong. Standing there washing dishes and thinking, 'Boy, I wish he would come and wash these dishes. I wish I could sit down by myself for just five minutes.' That hostility builds up because I tend to hold it inside of me. And then I kind of feel like I'm running around in circles sometimes."

Later, talking about how she organizes her days, the grievance broke through again. She leaned back against the flowered sofa and closed her eyes. "I sometimes wonder if this is all—this big rat race—if this is all that life is meant to be, that you're continually having places to be or deadlines to meet and you never have time just to sit down and put your feet up and read something you want to read, or time to just be yourself."

I asked Sara how she felt about doing all the housework. She said, "I feel it's unfair . . . since I work, I really feel that it's unfair that I do most of it." Then she told me why he doesn't help more. "He would do more but it's a matter of waiting on him to do it, and I'm not willing to wait. If I want something done, I want it done then, not two weeks later. So I do it myself."

Had she ever discussed the problem with her husband? "We have before. Usually if you talk, you get more help for a few days and then it's back to the same drag." What does she think a fair arrangement would be? "I would split it. Not necessarily fifty–fifty, but I just think when you get up in the morning, if someone puts the coffee on and someone else would make the bed, so it weighs out to where you don't feel like it's all your responsibility." (This is a revolutionary thought for her, and probably heretical as well. She imagines the sharing gingerly—"if someone . . . then someone else . . ." —as if it couldn't possibly happen in her house.)

Sara told me a story about how she once tried to change her husband's housekeeping habits. He doesn't hang up his clothes at night; he tosses them on a chair or on the floor, and then she comes by later and hangs them up. She didn't think it was right for her to pick up his clothes, so she announced that she wasn't going to do it any more. It was fine with him. He just let them stack up on the chair next to the bed. "When the clothes were just up so high, I couldn't stand it. I couldn't take it anymore, and I did it. It's not worth it. I sit and worry about it. That stack of clothes: something needs to be done. I don't know if it's nervous energy or what—that craving to clean it up. So eventually I cleaned it up." And, needless to say, she is doing it still. (I love this story. I have been as angry about who does the housework as Sara is. And I too would have hung up those clothes, probably sooner than she did.)

Few of the women I talked to (only about 11 percent) said that they quarreled with their husbands about housework. It is not a fight that seems to go anywhere or to satisfy very much. Several other women said what Sara did about complaining: Things change for a few days, and then the old ways creep back.

If two people are going to share the housework, then she and he have to work out who's going to do what. Under the traditional arrangement, the work is already assigned—mostly to her. But for wives like thirty-year-old Pat Hinton, married two years, part of finding out what it meant to be married—and married to this man—was working out who did what around the house. Pat and her husband had agreed before they were married that they would share the housework, and "we were having problems making small decisions like grocery lists [she laughed] you know, housework, and it was just a hassle. Who was going to be there when the plumber came?" After some negotiation they achieved their goal—her Housework score is 3.0—and also came to a better understanding of their differences.

> We have, uh . . . he values things a little bit differently than I do. He's not into some of the same things I'm into. It's not a value for him to have a real clean house. It's not a value for him to have a nice garden. And I really enjoy all those things. I'm more possessions oriented, I guess, than he is. And I like to have nice things around me. They give me pleasure. And I want to keep them nice. He just doesn't value those things. But we've come to a place where, you know, I push him less to do things and he initiates more as a result.

Once upon a time, women knew what a clean house was, but sharing the cleaning means sharing decisions about standards too. How clean is clean enough? What's fair? And who decides? If she is the only one who wants the kitchen floor scrubbed every night, can she ask him to scrub it? If he works all day and then comes home to rest, is it fair to ask him to cook dinner? Every night?

Dorothy Hunt, who is seventy-three, lives in rural Appalachia in a falling-down woodframe house with cracked plaster walls and no indoor bathroom. She has been married for more than thirty years and yet these questions trouble her too. Reading through the list of tasks, she said, "Washing dishes? I do almost all that. Once in a while he'll say, 'Well, I'll dry the dishes.' But if he's out late I don't feel too much like saying 'You come and dry the dishes.' I don't think it would hurt him even when he's been out all day. Maybe I've been busy in here all day too." In short, she isn't sure what's right; she feels two ways about it. But she's still washing the dishes.

It's just so hard to give them up. Bobbi Webster finally did grouse a little about that man who wants her to come and watch TV: "He knows as well as I do when the laundry basket is full. He knows where I keep the laundry detergent." (He also knows the laundry is *her* job.) Another woman told me that her husband didn't like to vacuum, but "he'll clean my bathroom." (There is only one in the house; presumably he uses it too.)

Even when a woman is sure that the housework must be shared, it still has a way of feeling like her work. Chris Haynes is a forty-year-old insurance executive who recently remarried after many years of living alone. Her housework score is 2.5, and she's satisfied now with the way she and her husband divide the work. But the first year of their marriage, it was sometimes rough going.

When we moved in together, his furniture included this enormous Chinese Oriental rug—a beautiful thing, dark-dark burgundy with a delicate border of beige and peach flowers. He bought it at an estate sale —some big fancy house over in Scarsdale. So we put it in our new living room, and I think half the fights we had that first year were about the damn rug.

It was almost impossible to keep clean—some maid had probably vacuumed it twice a day in its previous life—and I used to get really upset about the dirt on it. I remember he had these old work shoes with deep ridges on the soles, and he would come in from working in the muddy yard and leave tracks, neat little ridges of dirt, all along this dark-wine rug. And I would just go bananas. The whole thing got quite out of hand for a while until he finally got rid of those shoes.

It was really amazing to me—even at the time, when I thought about it—how quickly that rug had become *my* rug and how the dirt on it was *his* dirt.

Marcie Evans is an attractive redhead in her early thirties. She works in a savings bank where she has recently been promoted to vice-president. She and her husband have postponed their children so that they can both concentrate on their careers first. A funny thing happened to Marcie when she was first married, six years ago.

I had kind of envisioned that all of a sudden I was supposed to just "be married" and not to do anything else. Being married was staying at home and spending a great deal of time planning out one's meals and having the house nice and looking nice when your husband came home. . . . Which now, when I think about it, is funny because my mother worked. She didn't spend her time kind of twittering around the house. Yet I thought, this is what I'm supposed to do. . . .

I remember sitting on the floor in our apartment and getting the Wednesday-night paper that had all the grocery specials in it and figuring where I was going to go and what I was going to get at each place and trying to plan out my meals. I spent an entire morning doing that—four hours—and then in the afternoon I just sat in a chair and thought about that.

And I realized that I was probably going through some kind of a depression at that point. It took me about three months, but I finally decided that I didn't really *like* sitting at home and refinishing furniture occasionally or something like that. And it's terrific. I'm so glad I spent that time doing that because ever since then I've realized that I could never just be at home.

In spite of her commitment to a professional career, in spite of the example of her own mother, in spite of twenty years of modern feminism—still the reflex comes: Keeping house is woman's work.

And I, of course, am no different. Last year, when it seemed as if this book would never take shape, when I sat in front of the typewriter for hours and nothing happened—I dreamed of doing housework: scrubbing floors, usually. My kitchen floor is an old cracked linoleum horror that needs to be scrubbed every day and usually gets washed up a bit every week or so. I longed to be scrubbing that floor, longed for the simplicity of it, the beginning-middle-and-end of it, the hot suds and the scrub brush asking only that my arm push and pull it against the floor. I actually did scrub that floor almost every day during one of the worst weeks.

As I said, there are exceptions. My favorite story about

a husband who does housework is called Bob Needs Some Bounce. It was told to me by Bob's mother-in-law, Veronica Miller.

> My son-in-law does the laundry. My daughter works, and I was over there one day in the morning before he went to work—she had already gone—and there were two loads of wash on the line, already almost dry. I thought, now how did she get all that wash done before she went off to work? And then he came out and felt the sheets and smiled. "My wash is almost dry," he said. *My wash* . . . he thinks it's his wash. She folds it and puts it away, of course, but still. . . . [Veronica is waiting for me to say something, to let her know what I think. I am not telling her.] And he doesn't do any cooking. But he cleans. [Another pause.] I was with my daughter in the Shop-Rite one Saturday going down the soap aisle, and she said, "Oh, Bob needs some Bounce."
>
> "What?" I didn't understand her.
>
> She said it again. "Bounce—you know, those little sheets you put in the dryer."

She thinks it's his wash too, and that makes it unanimous.

The most dazzling exception I've ever met is Doris Sullivan, a woman who shares it fifty–fifty right down the line. She lives in New York City, is sixty-four years old, and has been married, "to this husband," for twenty-five years. He's retired now; he used to be in the navy. She works part time as a writer. There are no children.

Doris is a feminist, once radical, now somewhat mellowed. "I've been a feminist since before Betty Friedan wrote the book . . . and he had to live through that, you see. He had to live through all of that development and the radical part of it. And it wasn't easy for him, I think now. He's a better feminist than I am at this point." She is also clearly pleased with her marriage and her husband. ("The first time I saw him, I said, 'I want that.' ")

Doris's philosophy might be summed up in a piece of advice she gave me: "If you want him to wipe it up, put a roll of paper towels right there on the wall where he can find it. And then, if he still doesn't wipe it up, let it go and don't worry about it." Here's her story of how she got him to share the laundry:

> While I was working and when he was home on extended leave, I said to him one day, "You know, if you did the laundry during the week" (remember, he's not working) "then on Saturdays I wouldn't have to do the laundry and I could play with you."
>
> So he said, "What would the neighbors say?" What the hell! You know, really, feminists forget.
>
> So I said, "What do you care? They're not paying the rent."
>
> "Oh, I don't know," he said.
>
> So he went to sea and came back and he said, "I do my laundry at sea, why shouldn't I do it at home? And, quite right, it would be nice to have you not going down to the laundry room when we could do something else." So he got the laundry cart and put

it in front of the door so I would fall over it to prove
to me that he was going to do it . . . and he does the
laundry every other time now.

They also share the cooking; he cooks one night, she
cooks the next. "When I'm cooking, I start at six. When he's
cooking, he starts at two. It just takes him longer. He cooks
more tentatively." And who is washing the dishes in this
exceptional household? "The one who cooks cleans up afterward. We tried it the other way [one cooks, the other cleans
up], but it didn't work."

So they split the laundry and the cooking and the dishes.
A cleaning woman comes in once a week. Because he likes to
take walks to the shops nearby, he does all the marketing. She's
neater than he is; she picks up the house. Overall, they share
the housekeeping quite equally: Herwork and Housework
scores are both exactly 3.

Now remember, as Doris said, he's not working. Still,
this couple is unusual. Fewer than 6 percent of the women I
talked to had scores of 3 or higher for both Herwork and
Housework. To put it another way, more than 94 percent of
the women do more than half of the housekeeping. Cooking
is the least shared activity; only 11 percent of the couples in
the study split it fifty–fifty, and 87 percent of the women
report that they do all or most of the cooking. Other candi-
dates for Least Favorite Housework Chore to Be Shared:
laundry (only 17 percent share it fifty–fifty), food shopping
(18 percent), and home maintenance (16 percent). The most
commonly shared activity is yardwork; 43 percent of the
women report that they share it equally with their husbands.

Next most popular is picking up the house (29 percent) followed by washing dishes (24 percent) and cleaning the house (20 percent).

Most of the *Wifestyles* women dwell at the lower end of the scale, down where she does all or almost all of the chores. For all of Herwork (cook, wash dishes, do laundry, buy food, pick up and clean house), 37 percent report scores of 1.3 or less; more than a third do all or almost all of Herwork all of the time. And the *average* Herwork score, to repeat myself now that we're looking at all these numbers, is 1.8.

Not only do most of the women still do most of it, a good number of them want to keep it that way. I asked this question: "If you could change something about the way you and your husband divide the household responsibilities, what would you change?" A resounding 49 percent of the women said "Nothing."* Another 43 percent say they would like some help from him, usually with one specific job (the one she hates the most): "I wish he'd do the dishes"; "I want him to take out the garbage"; "I wish he'd throw in a load of wash once in a while." *Fewer than 10 percent* say they want to split the household work fifty–fifty.[4]

We talk about the way things are and the way things ought to be. Some of us feel it's best to leave well enough alone. Verna Pisani is one. She is about Doris's age, equally outspoken, and wise in her own way. Verna lives about fifty miles north of New York City on the edge of the commuter belt, where the horse farms of the very rich and the modest homes of the working class are side by side. You can't see her

---

*See Table 4 in the Technical Appendix.

place from the road, but you can hear her rooster or the hens fussing. She and her husband bought the house about ten years ago, after the last of the kids was gone: a little two-bedroom cottage with a dormitory in the attic for visiting grandchildren.

He works in an auto repair shop—mostly expensive foreign cars. Verna does washes and sets at the beauty shop in the next town north. He gardens. She keeps chickens. After supper, he's out in the yard alone, puttering. Occasionally he will yell at her to get him something. She sighs, gets up, and gets it.

Verna kisses to greet and to say good-bye. Her face is unbelievably soft, delicately lined. She is friends with everyone. On Tuesdays, when she bakes bread, she stops on her way to work to leave a warm loaf with one or another of the neighbors close by. Often she is invited in for coffee. ("I usually accept. I can never stay very long, so I know it's not an imposition.") She told me she was puzzled by one of her neighborhood friends.

This one girl, only married a few years. She complains to me because her husband doesn't help with the dishes or the baby. I don't understand it. You know, her husband is a fine man, a good man. He works very hard, travels so far on the train every day. I told her, "Maybe you expect a lot." [Verna smiled, remembering how her advice was received.] She doesn't complain to me any more. . . . But maybe she does not really want him to help her. The house is the woman's place. Look. [She gestured toward the pots cooking on the stove] I decide what we eat for dinner every night of the year. I pick the color for the carpet. I keep the house the way I want it. He comes home, angry at some customer. I give him a little whiskey, listen to him complain for a while. We have some supper; he goes out to the garden; the peace is back in his eyes. Maybe she doesn't want to give this up so fast.

The peace is in Verna's eyes too. She feels so settled, so sure of what she should be doing.

Another woman in another wealthy suburb has that same settled quality although she lives in a world as different from Verna's as I can imagine. Katharine Lashley is the wife of a United States congressman. She has spent her married life supporting her husband: keeping house, entertaining, raising the children, working on his political campaigns, picking out his shirts, taking them to the laundry, taking them back when they aren't right. She hasn't had a paying job since their first child was born twenty-two years ago, but she is on the go from morning to night; in addition to the housework and the children, there are committees, appearances, a crowded social calendar.

She is small, not over five feet one or two, and has a slender, disciplined body, the sort of body that comes from doing situps every day. Her voice is full, deep, beautifully modulated. She is very much the lady, very much in charge. Reading down the list of household tasks, that rich voice sounded more and more amused. "Home maintenance and repairs—oh, well, sometimes 1, sometimes 3, sometimes 4. It all depends." (I laugh and protest: The computer can only read one number.) She continued, "Tell me this—how do you answer when the fuses blow or the hot-water heater breaks down or the well pump goes, and he is in Washington for five days, and I'm here at the farm by myself with three children? I can't wait for him to come home. So I do it all. I'm not going to climb up on the roof . . . *but I have.* You know. I'm here. And he's not."

This is more than the traditional division of labor: He works and I stay home. It is also division of power. Katharine manages her family's affairs with enormous competence and energy. She is proud of her contribution, and she is not interested in sharing the load with anybody. Here is her story about what happened once when her husband tried to help.

I've always handled the money. I think he just dumped it in my lap. He doesn't want to be bothered. He doesn't like those details. And, after a while, I don't want him in my checkbook because he forgets to put this or that. I've just always handled the money. I was away this summer for just about a month and a half, and I was making arrangements to have all the mail forwarded. And he said, "Oh, no, don't do that. I'll take care of it."

And I said, "What about the bills?"

He said, "I'll take care of them." And he got things all fouled up and ended up taking his checkbook in and having his secretary try to rearrange things. And thereafter he said, "I didn't know you were so valuable." I think he has learned his lesson. It only took me a month to get my things in order again after he bolloxed them up.

He may earn the money, but it's "my checkbook."

The wife of another powerful man was equally frank about the control she enjoys in her traditional role. Carole Baxter's husband also works in Washington. His picture was on the front page of *The New York Times* the week that I interviewed her. Like Katharine, Carole spends most of her time managing the household and helping with her husband's career. She had just gotten out of the shower when I arrived for our appointment. We chatted for a minute, and then she excused herself to finish blow-drying her hair. The living room is elegant, understated, blue and buff with touches of terra cotta. We agreed to do the interview in an hour since that was all the time she had.

He works long days, tries to be home for dinner with her and the children most evenings, always has to go out again after dinner for a meeting. I asked how she felt about doing all of the housework. She said, "There's no other way it would work for us." Carole likes being a full-time homemaker. She doesn't feel the least bit dependent or second-rate. "I think it would be tougher on him not to be married than it would me. I think he depends on having home to come home to. I know that I would always have home to come home to because I really make the home. But he needs this, and he can't . . . he doesn't make it himself."

For women like Verna and Katharine and Carole, keeping house is as satisfying as any paid employment. What they do at home is crucial, and they know it. They hold things together and make them work. Their husbands are somewhere else, doing something else. The men may be good at what they do, but they're not much help at home. The wife is usually too tactful to say so, even to me, but when he's around he's likely to be underfoot. And the simplest tasks can throw him.

A woman I interviewed went away on a long business trip without her husband. He phoned her one evening just as she was about to crawl into her hotel bed. "He had just put his shirts in the dryer, and he didn't know what to do next. 'Can I go to bed now?' he asked. And I said, 'Absolutely not. You have to wait until they're dry and take them out right away and hang them up carefully. Otherwise they'll just be all wrinkled in the morning.' She sounds like a mother talking to a slightly backward child.

At Christmastime Bobbi Webster does all of the planning, present buying, extra cleaning, marketing, cooking, and cleaning up for their family celebration. She told me, "It wouldn't get done if I didn't do it. He'd send out to McDonald's." And she laughed.

Another woman told me that her husband drove her crazy because he never finished anything: If he did the dishes, she had to come after him and wipe off the stove; if he changed the baby, she had to fix the pins; if he washed the floor, she had to go over it to get the places he missed. "Sometimes I feel like I'm a macho-mama," she said. That's it exactly. A macho-mama.

In a shopping mall outside of Boise, Idaho, I saw an apron, one of those bib kind that they sometimes sell for men to wear when they barbecue. Only this one was for a woman. It said on the front, in big red letters: Mary Martyr.

The kicker is this: When we women keep our houses all by ourselves, it is easier for us to see our husbands as silly overgrown children, to discourage their participation in domestic affairs, and to diminish their contribution to the family.[5] Whether this impulse comes from defensiveness (because we know that housework is really not such a big deal as we pretend) or from an accurate perception of the true worth of the work that has traditionally been ours, the end result is a profound separation of wife and husband. Girl's job and boy's job—woman's place and man's world—has the effect of keeping us apart, not only in our roles but in our understanding and sympathy for one another.

I myself believe that there is no such thing as separate but equal, not in school and not at home either. When wives and husbands go their separate ways, I am afraid that the chance they will be able to understand each other or even to think well of each other is significantly diminished. I am also aware that many—perhaps most—of the women I interviewed would not agree. Among the *Wifestyles* women there is no significant relationship between a woman's satisfaction with her marriage and her Housework score.* Thirty-one percent of the women whose husbands help a lot gave their marriages the highest (9–10) satisfaction score; 48 percent gave a middle satisfaction score, and 21 percent of those who were getting lots of help gave the lowest (1–7) satisfaction score. It just doesn't make that much difference to most of the women I

---

*See Table 5 in the Technical Appendix.

talked to. An Illinois woman who has been married more than twenty-five years summed up the majority opinion: "I would like him to be more willing to help around the house. But he's not going to, and I'm not going to worry about it. After all these years, there's no use fretting about it."

And yet women are asking questions that they have not asked before—and in the most unlikely places. Take the city I was born in, for example: Lancaster, Pennsylvania. In 1980, while I was still interviewing for the *Wifestyles* study, I was invited to speak at the Sixty-Third Annual Convention of the Society of Farm Women of Lancaster County. Earlier in the year a new chapter of the society had been formed in nearby East Petersburg, and the president inducted the new members with these words, which explain the society's purpose: "You are to perpetuate that which was good in the homes of our grandmothers and preserve their spirit of patriotism and sacrifice. Farm Women Societies strive to foster the love of farm and rural life today." The society song is an old gospel hymn, "Brighten the Corner Where You Are."

Do not wait until some deed of greatness you may do.
Do not wait to shed your light afar.
To the many duties near you now be true,
Brighten the corner where you are.

Lancaster is hardly a hotbed of radical feminism, and my mother was in the audience that day, so I was doing my level best to be inoffensive. My speech was about keeping house, among other things. In it I said that woman's work is very important work. Feeding people is important. Picking up the house, washing and ironing clothes, all those things we do to keep our households going are important. I said this work is too important for women alone to do it all; men ought to share the work.

The four hundred farm women present received me with gracious warmth. The strongest applause came after my speech, however, during the question-and-answer time when several of the women stood to give brief testimonials:

> I work part time. He takes care of the children. And if he scrubs the floor and it's not right, it's okay because we have love and gratitude for each other, and our faith is what makes our marriage.

> We've been married fifty-one years, and I have the best.

> Two weeks ago I broke my foot, and my husband and son have taken over the house—the cleaning and also the cooking. I'm very proud of them.

Somehow what I had said seemed to be an attack on their good men, and they were quick to set me right.

The bravest woman in the entire crowd was one of the last to speak. She and I managed to talk to each other there in the Farm and Home Center on Arcadia Road before four hundred witnesses about the things that matter most to each of us. It went like this:

SHE: I have a question and a comment. The question is: How do you teach your, ah . . . ladies to respect their husbands when you encourage them to take the women's side of the house? And my comment would be that I've been . . . I have a happy marriage and my husband shares in my things and I appreciate that. But I still think I have a place where I'm going to respect him as a leader in the home. And how do you encourage that kind of respect when we expect them to come in and share the role of the housewife?

ME: I'm very tempted to ask you a question in return: What is it about your husband's doing that kind of work that leads you not to respect him?

SHE: I think that there is a lot of respect when the household work is shared. But I think that there is a lot of respect that a man needs that is maybe something very important that we need to think about when we expect so much of our work to become their work.

ME: Absolutely. It's a dilemma for both men and women. But I think . . . I think you've got to face this: If you don't respect him when he washes the dishes, how do you feel about yourself when you wash the dishes?

One new question leads to another: How can my husband keep his respect if he's going to wash the dishes? How do I feel about washing the dishes myself? Where does respect come from anyway?

Some of the women I talked to are pleased to be keeping house. The housewife role feels good to them—it nourishes and satisfies. Others are not so sure. Marcie Evans, the bank vice-president who turned herself into a housewife when she got married, went through the motions for three months like a sleepwalker before she woke up and realized it wasn't for her. She describes the housewife's job as "twittering around the house." Fortunately, Marcie had a choice, and she is no longer only a housewife.

Many women are not so lucky. Jean Kreegar lives in rural Texas. She has been married seventeen years, has one school-age child, and has not worked for pay since her child was born. Jean is unhappy about being a housewife, but she doesn't feel able to do anything about it.

> I wish that I could contribute more to the livelihood of our marriage. My mother worked beside my father in the fields, in the barns, and I sometimes feel parasitic because I am not contributing in some way to the livelihood, the financial, or at least the physical suste-nance of the house. This [housework] is make-do. I don't enjoy being a homemaker. If I thought that cleaning house was the ultimate end, I could not abide that. I know it's not. And yet I'm not ready to go out and knock on doors to find a job because I don't have any skills, any qualifications.

Jean does almost all of the housework by herself, but she doesn't like the work or find it very satisfying. Her family eats out a lot. "I no longer find cooking fun or interesting." I asked her to describe a typical weekday in her life. "After breakfast I sit down, read the paper, watch a little TV, piddle around, clean up the house, maybe take a nap before my daughter gets home from school. . . ." She paused, looked at me for a moment, then looked away. "This is awful," she said. "It's such a wasted life."

Many women have more than housework to do, of course. We have children to raise and/or jobs to go to and/or commitments in the church and in the community. It has become terribly easy for those who have more than enough to do to feel superior to those who do not. I talked to another housewife who has a part-time job and three kids, the oldest about the same age as Jean's. Cathy Saks does most of the housework too. She is satisfied with her life, but she knows of women who are not. "A lot of times they're bored; they're bored with themselves and they're bored with housework and all that. But they're not giving it their all. I think you can easily become lazy as a housewife because you don't have to punch a card. You have to motivate yourself and that's what the hard part is, you know. I mean you could very easily get up in the morning and sit and drink coffee all day long, which some people do, and in their mind, they're saying 'I'd love to do this; I'd love to do that.' But they don't motivate themselves." Perhaps a housewife is just a nobody after all. Perhaps woman's work is worthless.

Jody Kovar lives outside of San Francisco. Jody is twenty-six and has been married for a little over a year to a man with whom she lived for several years before that. Both are employed full time, she as a nurse and he as a lawyer. His work schedule is more demanding than hers right now, but they still share most of the housekeeping tasks.

Jody loves to feed people. She is a magnificent and tender cook who grinds her own coffee beans, dries her own herbs, bakes her own bread. The kitchen is clearly the most important room in the house: a jumble of unmatched pottery mixing bowls, fruit slices drying in a sunny window, tall crocks of beans and rice along one wall. But she isn't at all sure about the value of this work, in spite of its importance to her. She worries about what will happen to her husband's respect for her when she has children and stays at home.

> I would never want him to be above me and feel that he's taking care of me or whatever. . . . A woman who is taking care of a little baby is just working her ass off all the time at home. But then, I think people in their minds think "You're just hanging out, drinking coffee and watching the soaps. And just what do you *do* all day?" I would never want to have a fight about it with him and have it get real ugly about, you know, he would say "Well, I'm . . . there you are at home all the time and I'm just out there just working and working and bringing home the paycheck." You know. I don't want to hear that. I don't need to hear that from somebody. So I hope I don't.

I hope she doesn't too. But I wouldn't count on it. I'm afraid most husbands think that keeping house is not quite grownup work. And I guess they'll continue to feel that way until they are keeping house too.

For myself, I know that what women (and men) do at home—cooking, decorating, washing clothes, cleaning, even mowing and weeding—is among the most important work there is. Because it nourishes the ones we love. Because the way we do this work affects the color and texture of our daily lives. And because it has to be done. Cooking dinner every night whether you feel like it or not is like being nice to your old boring Aunt Susie—you do it because it helps to keep the family together.

Housework is also not enough work for an adult. And there is no contradiction in that. No matter how important cooking dinner is, it's still a relatively routine and thankless task. (Most of the time my family eats a meal in less time than it took me to prepare it.) And there's no reason why a person should limit herself or himself to household work. There are only so many meals to cook and so many dishes to wash; if we share the work, we should all have time to do other things as well.

Three

RAISING CHILDREN

The wife takes the child.
The wife takes the child.
Heigh-ho-the-derry-o
The wife takes the child.

—The Farmer in the Dell

I suppose there isn't anything else that changes a woman's life as much as the birth of her first child. One day you can go places by yourself, think about yourself, put yourself first from time to time or all the time. The next day the child is in your life—and nothing will ever be the same. For days or years or the rest of your life, depending on who you are and what else you have to do, that child *is* your life.

My son, Christopher, was born on a perfect summer day three years ago. I was thirty-seven years old, and I had wanted a baby all my life. Having Christopher changes everything. Only superlatives come to mind: I have never grown as much, understood as much, felt as much, laughed, loved, trembled as much in my life as I have since this child came. He was—and is—a miracle to me.

Part of the miracle is that there's no turning back. Soon after Christopher was born, I was introduced at a party to a woman who is the mother of three teenagers. When I told her I was a new mother, she smiled dryly and said, "Welcome to the club. You'll never sleep through the night again."

A few weeks later I left my newborn son for the very first time with a carefully selected babysitter so that I could go shopping for myself. None of my old clothes fit, and I couldn't face my maternity jeans one more day. The local discount department store had racks of skirts and pants in my new, larger size—everything from blue denim jeans to front-pleated skirts with designer labels. Here's what I bought that day: one yellow print shirt, infant's medium; one red-and-white striped stretch suit, size 8–14 pounds; one carriage pad; two crib sheets: one yellow, one blue. It wasn't that I felt guilty about leaving the baby. I know that I'm entitled to some time for myself. But I just couldn't get him out of my mind. I hadn't realized how much a child can possess a woman, taking up all of her energy, all of her attention, all of her shopping time.

Women with children in tow talk to other women with children in tow—even women they've never seen before—on the street, in the store, at the playground. Some of it is loneliness, but even more, it's the bond that being a mother makes, the instant recognition of motherhood: shared pleasure, shared pain. Sometimes it's just a smile across the supermarket aisle, each with a baby in the pushcart seat. The meeting of eyes that says: I know what you've been going through.

I once had a man tell me that he thought pregnancy was the ultimate empathy experience: You are simultaneously yourself and someone else. It was a clever-enough notion for an outsider to have, but I instantly thought, No, the thing that happens between *mothers* is the ultimate empathy. Or maybe it's the thing that happens between mother and daughter. I remember listening to my mother talk to newborn Christopher; she was using the same words, the same intonations, the same little croonings that I used when I talked to him.

I got together a small book of photographs to take on my interviews so that I could show my family pictures when others showed me theirs. Since the interview was about marriage, I expected to see wedding albums. But of all the interviews I did, only two women showed me pictures of their wedding day. Dozens of women showed me baby pictures. Her children and her grandchildren decorate the mantel, the piano, the wall above the desk; Sonny in his band uniform; Susie in her cap and gown; the first grandbaby on the front lawn.

It may be that having children is what marriage is for. That's certainly what they told us. All of those baby dolls that drink and wet aren't tucked under the Christmas tree for nothing. Married women expect to have children—not every wife, but most every wife, even now.[1] It's still a part of the Dream of the Married Lady. I asked the women I interviewed about their expectations ("When you were a teenager and you thought about your adult life, did you imagine this life?"). Not everyone imagined herself married, as we have seen, but those who mentioned marriage almost always mentioned children too:

"Getting married and having kids—that was what everybody did."

"I didn't have any great ambitions—thought I'd be married, have kids, and stay at home."

"I guess I had the traditional American dream: finish school, work for a year or two, get married, stay home, have four or five children, and dote on my husband."

Even women who are very liberated indeed say "marriage and children" in a single breath, as if one inevitably follows the other. Anne Morgan is twenty-seven and has been married for five years. She and her husband lived together for more than a year before they decided to marry. She kept her own name—and her own checking account—just as they were before she got married. Her job, working with computer software in a university research lab, is "definitely a career"; she recently left another position because she felt she wasn't being paid enough. Last year Anne took four months off when her first child, Daniel, was born and then went cheerfully back to work full time.

I asked her why she had decided to get married. "It's a psychological security. I know that marriage is no more permanent than a live-in relationship or any other kind of relationship because you can get divorced—rather easily these days. I suppose there was a certain amount of commitment, and the implication, along with that commitment, that there might be children eventually. You were willing to be serious enough to think that far." Anne came into her adolescence in a time and place where birth control was as accessible as aspirin and as easy to take. She expects to hold down a paying job for the next forty years. Even so, for her the equation holds: a wife is a mother.

Nowhere is the assumption more clear than in the pain of women who expected to have children and do not have them. I talked with several wives who knew that they would never have a baby of their own. Rhoda Claybertson was one of them. She is a square-jawed woman with dark, blunt-cut hair who works as a short-order cook in a little town not far from Parkersburg, West Virginia. It was difficult for Rhoda to talk to me about her infertility; there were long, painful pauses in the story. The baby who would never be born had transformed her and her relationship with her husband.

All I ever wanted when I was a teenager and into my twenties was to get married and settle down and have a bunch of children. And that was always in my mind. I think that's what made me turn and do all the things I've done. . . .

We had a lot of rocky ground to travel when . . . I went to find out why I wasn't conceiving and they sent me to a specialist. There wasn't nothin' they could do but remove everything, and that was quite hard to adjust to. It was rough. We had a lot of problems 'cause I was hard to get along with. I just didn't care what I said to him to hurt his feelings. I just didn't care. You don't realize, I guess, until you sit back and look at yourself.

We had one other disappointment. We were supposed to adopt a baby, and we went and got all new furniture and everything and then when it came down to it we didn't get the baby 'cause the girl decided to keep it. So that was a letdown, and I just couldn't handle it. . . . I withdrew and I wouldn't talk about it. I cried a lot. . . .

I guess I've changed . . . whenever I see a baby, I just shy away from it. But I'm gettin' over it again.

I sat at Rhoda's dining-room table and wept when I heard her story. It pulled a great, keening sorrow out of me, the memory of years of sadness when I thought there would be no baby for me. We were both a little embarrassed. I didn't even have a tissue, and she had to jump up and find me one. But I think she was glad to talk about it too. She hugged me hard when I left.

There are married women, especially younger married women, who do not feel the way Rhoda and I feel about babies: women who are not sure they want children; women who are sure they do not want them.[2] Some of the magazines I read tell me that there is a new ethic among young marrieds; they've all decided to remain gleefully "childfree." I did not encounter this attitude in my travels; perhaps I did not look for it. I did talk to some women who weren't sure and to a few who had decided against having any children. But nobody was waving any flags about it.

For some, there are mitigating circumstances. Doris Sullivan is in her sixties. She lives in New York with her second husband; he's retired now. They're the couple described in the previous chapter who share the housework fifty–fifty. Doris says that she is "childless by choice." Then she explains that her mother was divorced before Doris was born and that she was raised in the home of her mother's parents, an only child among several rather formal and forbidding adults. "I suspect that my mother probably found me to be a bloody nuisance, and I'm sure they [the grandparents] did, when I look back at it. And I think my feeling about not having kids comes from that. And then I never felt secure in my first marriage at all. I never expected it to last. So I was not about to be saddled with something I couldn't manage. . . . In this marriage, we were too old—but I suspect we would not have had children even if we had been married early on."

Several women talked about the link between their own childhood and their feelings about having children. Sally Horowitz lives in Cambridge, Massachusetts. She is twenty-seven and has been married for three years to a medical student who is now in his last year of training. Sally works as a counselor in an inner-city teen center. She told me that she wasn't sure she would have children because she still has so many of her own needs to meet. "I had a great deal of responsibility as an adolescent in my parents' home. I feel that I did not have much of a childhood or an adolescence. My needs and interests during my adolescence were grossly interfered with, and I have a lot of compensatory needs to meet. I want to meet those needs before I have children. And I recognize that if I were to have children before I meet some of those needs, I could feel very resentful and be most un-happy. And would threaten, of course, my marital relationship as well as my relationship with my children."

(Later she said, so softly it was almost inaudible, "But I love the kids I work with." So I asked her if she thought she would have her own in the end. She looked down and then looked back at me and nodded her head up and down—yes.)

Once upon a time a wife just *had babies*. Now pregnan-cies can be planned. (A woman awakens. In the translucent light of early morning, she curves against the warmth of her husband. They make love. Afterward, lying together, they talk again about a baby. It is partly an age-old conversation: Would the baby have your eyes? My mother's curly hair? And part of the conversation is new: Should we wait? What for? What will happen to our life when this baby comes?) Implied, if not expressed, is a revolution: She can say, "Let's not have any children at all." Or less staggering, but just as revolution-ary: "Let's not have any more children. Let's stop with the one or two or three we have now. Let's leave room in our lives —especially in my life—for something else."

Married women who have waited to have their first baby face a decision that was unheard of only a generation ago: If they want to get pregnant, they have to stop using their birth control. Deliberately. Stop taking the Pill. Put the diaphragm away. Go to the doctor's office and have the coil removed. It's understandably difficult for some people to face that much responsibility head-on. Pamela Riley is twenty-eight and has been married for eight years. "I had originally thought I did not want children, did not want to bring a child into such a world as ours, and so forth. Now I don't know. He wanted one. Now he doesn't. Now I sorta do, but not enough to press the point, and I'm getting older and if I'm going to, it's going to have to happen soon, but . . . Nobody has made a major decision about the children yet."

Sueann Evans feels pressed to make a decision too. She is twenty-nine and newly married for the second time. She has just become a partner in the law firm where she has worked for the past four years, and she is acutely aware of the complications that a child would bring to her life. "We talked off and on about whether or not we wanted to have kids. . . . I was never real strongly family oriented. I'm not sure I want to spend the rest of my life raising kids. It's not just to get 'em over the twos and the threes. It's a life-long proposition." Again, the revolutionary thought: Let's not. Let's keep our money and energy and time for ourselves, each other, our work, something else besides children.

In psychological theory there is a notion called cognitive dissonance. Roughly speaking, it's the idea that it is hard for most people to hold two contradictory thoughts or feelings in their heads at the same time. It's hard, for example, to know that you both love and hate a person at the same time, so when you're really angry at somebody you love, you just feel how much you hate him or her and your love feelings become invisible at that moment. In the same way mothers seem unable to imagine or remember what it was like to be nonmothers.

I asked each of the mothers I talked to what her life would be like if she didn't have her kids. The answers were striking because they were so much alike:

"I can't imagine not having them."

"I never really considered not having children."

"My word! I can't imagine life without children."

Most of us who have them can't envision our lives without them. Once it's done, it's done. A husband can be divorced if worse comes to worse—many of us can contemplate that possibility—but you can't leave the children. Marriage is reversible; motherhood is not.[3]

We're stuck with them, that's the wonderful and terrible thing about children. Although they will, eventually, sleep through the night and go off to kindergarten and leave home to establish homes of their own, they never stop being our children. We never stop being their mothers. It is, as Sueann said, "a lifelong proposition." And nobody really understands what that means until it's too late.

"Well, suppose you had it to do over again," I ask in the interview. "Would you have the children?" Almost every mother I talked to—more than 94 percent of them—said, "Yes."[4] *Ninety-four percent!* Mothers of infants, mothers of teenagers, mothers of adult children long gone from home; mothers who had their kids fifty years ago, before World War II, before the Pill, and mothers who had their babies last year and this year; a mother in Appalachia in a backwoods farm, and a mother in a penthouse apartment overlooking the San Francisco Bay. For all of these women, so different in so many ways, this is the same. In spite of everything, they say they would have those babies all over again.

Louise Finn is one who said she would do it again. She lives in an outlying parish of New Orleans. The house is cool and dim, shutters closed against the late-morning glare outside. We sit in the family room on an old plaid loveseat. The blue-and-brown threads on the armrest are almost worn through. There is dog hair on the rug. Lots of trophies along one wall: tennis, swimming, sailing. Some scouting awards. Piles of *Boy's Life* and *National Geographic*. Her sons are fifteen and eighteen now. They're both good students, and school takes up most of their time so they don't play sports as much as they used to.

Louise is tall with striking eyes—pale green against a tanned face. She plays a couple of fast sets of tennis most mornings before it gets too hot, and she has just come from the shower. When she smiles her eyes crinkle deeply at the corners, and I notice that she is older than she looks, so I ask. She will be forty-seven next May. We talk about her boys. She says she has always just taken them for granted: Of course she would have children; of course she would stay home and raise them. But last year in her Sunday School class, the minister was talking about the young people who come to him now and ask why they should have children. "After that, I thought about it. I thought: *How simple life would be* without the children. [She smiled again, and her eyes crinkled.] But I wouldn't give them up for anything. And I wouldn't trade the last eighteen years, the experience of having them day after day in my life, for anything either."

I have considered that we say things like that because we're stuck with them anyway.* But I don't think that's the reason. I think it's simpler, purer, more elemental than that. Raising children happens to be among the most satisfying work on this earth. And I think almost all mothers would do

---

*I have also considered the possibility that my obvious pleasure in my own child influenced the way the women responded, but since I only did 61 percent of the interviews, that can't account for all the positive responses.

it again because it's so worth doing, so very very worthwhile.

I asked about the pleasures of raising children: "What do you like best about being a parent?" Some of the mothers just drew a blank, and several of them said outright: "That's a hard question." One woman struggled for a moment and then shrugged. "Oh, I don't know. I just like being a parent. I like it all." Another tried, "Oh . . . *everything.*"

Anne Morgan talked about physical pleasure: "I think it's the physical closeness that I like the best. I'm still nursing him, and I like being close to him. He's just such a fun little person —oh, this is a hard question." She looked at me helplessly, as if to say: How can I put this into words? "I like to hold him."

Claire Simpson's daughter, Lisa, is just three months old. Her little round face is all curves—cheeks, chin, bald head— and enormous eyes, that slate-blue color that baby's eyes are first, before you know what color they will be. Lisa sits in her infant seat while her mother and I talk; she is teaching herself how to make a fist, working at it as hard as anyone has ever worked. She closes her hand, focuses on it fiercely, and then moves her head the other way as she loses interest. Lisa's mother talks about the physical pleasures of a baby too: "I love her skin. I love her little body, so perfect, so soft. I love the way she smells."

The contentment of infancy gives way to other, more complex pleasures as the children grow. Sherri Caldwell's three-year-old son, Brett, has begun to talk in sentences in the past six months. What does she like best? "The rewards. The smiles. His little kisses. His saying 'I love you, Mommy. Please tell me a story before I go to bed.' You know, I enjoy all that. Giving him a bath. Watching him grow." There are so many good things, and each mother had her own catalogue. The last thing that Sherri mentioned—"watching him grow"—was mentioned by more mothers in their list of Best Things than any other single experience.

Feelings of closeness and love, good times when having the kids is fun, the satisfaction of the bond between mother and child—these are the pleasures of raising children. Each mother has her own special memories: the scent of her newborn nursing, the sudden stab of joy as she watches her toddler's sunlit head tossed back in laughter, the surprise of realizing that her teenager truly understands her, the thrill of a grandchild who looks exactly like her father from the nose down. These precious experiences add up to: Yes, I would have the children again.

Many women have a strong sense of identification with their children, a feeling of possessiveness and pride that is a major source of pleasure. New mothers suffer separation anxiety long before their babies are old enough to reciprocate by wailing when Mommy leaves them. I remember going out somewhere without Christopher when he was just a few months old and feeling disoriented all the time I was away from him, as if I had misplaced my arm. For some women, this feeling of identity with the child is the best thing about being a parent. One mother put it this way: "You have someone who belongs to you, whom no one can take away." Another said, "I love the idea that they are mine." And Louise Finn used the same words: "What do I like best? That they're mine."

A mother's pride can focus on what she teaches the child. Sherri talked about wanting to say "Hey, look! I taught him that! You know, his good manners and stuff like that." For

Polly Duncan, whose daughter is just the same age as Brett, the best thing is "to suddenly discover how you've made an impression on her." Another mother whose children are three and seven put it in even stronger terms. She enjoys "having some control over molding someone's life."

And, of course, mothers feel proud of their children's accomplishments too. Jerri Reynolds, whose two children are almost grown, grinned when I asked about the best thing. Then she said, "I think it's the sense of accomplishment that my children have. I like to brag on the kids. I really like to brag on them. I guess all parents are like that." Another mother of teenagers said her best thing was "the nice things people say about my kids." Hearing the good things about your children can be *so* gratifying. Some mothers are shy about repeating praise, as if it were not good manners to be quite so pleased about your own, but many of the homes I visited included a display of some child's achievement: a fingerpainting framed above the desk, a good report card on the kitchen bulletin board, a felt banner that just said "Yea, Kevin!" Kevin had made his first soccer goal the week before, and his mother was proud of him. I thought the boy and the mother were lucky to have each other, and it was a great banner—blue and white with red ball fringe.

There is more to raising children than the pleasure of loving them or the pride we feel in their achievements, of course. There is also a lot of hard work, some of it downright unpleasant. And there are days when raising children is full of anger and pain. Once upon a time, mothers weren't supposed to talk about the bad times. (It was a specific instance of the more general rule that women were supposed to be pleasant all the time. Remember the advice of Thumper's mother: If you can't say anything nice, don't say anything at all?) Nowadays a certain jocular frankness is more fashionable. One mother confessed, "I like them when they're really small and when they get to be twelve or thirteen. The in-between years, you should rent 'em out." (She has three children; they are fourteen, eleven, and seven.) Not everyone is comfortable with the new fashion, however. Another woman I talked to said a similar thing—about a span of years in each of her children's lives when she just couldn't stand them—and then made me promise I wouldn't quote her. (I did promise. I didn't quote her.)

The question following Like Best About Parenting in the interview is logical enough: What do you like least about being a parent? Some mothers couldn't think of anything— a little less than 9 percent responded this way—but most find it reasonably easy to complain about the difficulties of raising children. Two complaints top the list: the overwhelming responsibility that parenting entails and the loss of freedom that a mother experiences. Sylvia Collins, whose two teenagers leave her "tired and frustrated, maybe, but never bored," looked so grim when I asked what she liked least about parenting that I didn't know what to expect. What she said *was* pretty grim: "Being a parent is total responsibility and work forever and ever. We should work ourselves out of a job, but in this day and age, if a child grows up and has trouble, he just comes home to mother and father."

Another mother of teenagers put it more simply; what does she like least? "The constant demands."

Parents of preschoolers experience a different kind of

stress: the overload that comes from being "on" all the time. Mary Wolinski has a full-time office job and an eighteen-month-old daughter. The thing she likes least about parenting: "Not getting enough sleep."

The memory of those sleepless nights is strong with many women. A sixty-year-old grandmother of five was reluctant to consider what she liked least about her parenting experience —mothers aren't supposed to complain—but I pressed her a little, and she said, "Probably at times, giving up your own. . . . If they were up at night that probably was what I liked least."

For Naomi Bixler, who is thirty-eight and the mother of two preschoolers, the problem is global: "Parenting takes most of our energy. The day-to-day drag just wears us down."

Judith Simpson lives in a wealthy New England suburb on a lake. It was perfect early July the morning I drove up to see her: clear bright sky, warm sun, dry air, the lake just lightly rippling from the breeze. *House Beautiful* setting. *Better Homes and Gardens.* The house is at the end of a cul-de-sac, set back from the road on an enormous lawn that slopes gently down to the lake in back. It's a very pretty, very green lawn, tended by professionals, dense and fragrant underfoot. In the front of the house is an enormous swing set: three swings, rings, a rope to climb, a slide, a playhouse—the sort of stuff indulgent grandparents buy.

Judith met me at the door. She is a little shorter than I am, deeply tanned but certainly not athletic, just enough over-weight to look lumpy in her bright blue shorts and top—a costume for sunbathing, perhaps, but not for jogging. White kidskin sandals. Gold hoop earrings. We walked through the house on our way to the back porch to sit—deep, richly colored carpeting, wall to wall; large, framed oil portraits of three children above the fireplace in the living room. A collection of crystal and porcelain animals on a shelf in the hall. Everything expensive and tasteful.

Judith is thirty-three. She graduated from college, worked in advertising in the city for a couple of years, met her husband, married him, worked one more year, got pregnant with Adam, quit her job, and has been home raising children for the past nine years. She remembers the first year of her marriage wistfully. "We weren't tied down to a house. We each had our own car. We had no children. We went to the opera all the time. We went to [the] symphony. We went to sports events. . . . It was a nice year. We went out to eat *all* the time—what is this once-a-month business? Every other night we were going out to eat. It was just the two of us."

Judith's life changed radically with the birth of her first child, and she was not happy about the changes. "I was very resentful actually. I was resentful at having to stay home. I didn't like it at all. I didn't like not being able to go to work, not seeing people, not talking to people. I was resentful. I loved this little kid, but . . . you have a lot of time on your hands."

In the next six years two more children were born; they are nine, five, and three now. Judith talked about how difficult it is for her to be the mother she wants to be when there aren't enough hands or laps to go around. "The third child is the straw that breaks the camel's back. I always wanted three children, but . . . when we just had the two, you know, they would say you have two parents, one for each child. You have two hands, one for each child. So that when you're going places and doing things, two is a good number, and the third, somehow, you know. . . . I can't go places and hold three hands. We can't each have one sitting on our lap."

She gets worn out by the sheer need for her presence. "I'm so tired of looking. All day long, it's 'Mommy, look! *Look* at this.' " And the best relief is just to get away for a little while. "Sometimes my head is so full of little voices that I just want to say 'Hold it! Stop the world.' I'll take time to go grocery shopping by myself so I can go alone while he keeps the kids. It may only be an hour, but it's time I don't have to be listening to all these little conversations."

I asked Judith if she would have the children again. "Of course," she said. All three? "Oh, yes." Nevertheless, there's a fantasy about leaving it all behind. When we talked about whether she ever thought of leaving her husband, she told me how she sometimes wishes she could leave her kids. "You fantasize—you know, wouldn't it be nice to be foot-loose and fancy-free. I always say to my husband, if we ever get divorced, he gets the kids, you know, because nobody wants a woman with three little children. And if I did get divorced, I would leave. He'd have the kids, and I'd go. I'd go where there is more action. This year it's fantasy. I wouldn't leave him. I wouldn't leave the kids. But every so often I think it would be nice to be all by myself and to go see places."

A friend of mine who is the mother of three grown sons, the youngest now taller than his six-foot father, has a piece of sculpture in her home that I covet. It is a bronze figure of a woman, about eighteen inches high, cast in the lost wax method. She stands on strong legs with big-muscled thighs, her huge belly pushing forward, hands on hips. Her head is thrust back and the mouth is open—laughing or screaming? The figure is powerfully female, powerfully maternal. And there are two little figures of creeping children, also bronze, that can be hooked onto the mother figure at different angles; you can hang one of the children off of her head, for example, and set the other crawling up her leg. Or one can be perched on her hip, and the other cradled against her breast.

The sculptor who created this marvelous image is Rita Sargen-Simon. She calls the figure Earth Mother. Rita hadn't originally planned to include the babies in the sculpture, but as the work developed the figure seemed to call out for babies to make the concept complete, so she added them. Earth Mother's babies are remarkably heavy; they clang against her as you put them into place. For me they are a perfect symbol: how they weigh us down, these children. How they burden us. A mother's fantasy of leaving, of being alone, of getting some time away is a natural response to the continual and demanding presence of children. In some societies and in extended families in which the kin are close enough to help, mother gets a break because other women, or even older children, take the babies away for a while. But for Judith, isolated in her gorgeous suburban home, there is little relief. She can't shake them off.

In another town another woman struggles with many of the same feelings. Minneapolis in May, the street littered with "spinners" off the maple trees, everything washed with a green tint—bushes and lawns, iris blooming. Karen Baxter lives with her husband and two little kids in one of the big Victorian houses that line the streets here around the park. Inside the house is clean and bare, sparsely furnished, white walls, lots of books and plants. A small enameled children's table, bright yellow, in the far corner of the living room. Toys in some big baskets beside it.

The children were gone for the morning, off with their father doing Saturday errands. Jeremy is three and a half; his sister, Elaine, is almost six. There is one picture on the bookshelf, a snapshot: two towheads in a rowboat, laughing. Their mother looks like a schoolgirl: long, straight brown hair, dark eyes behind gold-rimmed granny glasses, jeans and a T-shirt. She is thirty-one.

I was not in the door five minutes before we were talking about our children. Christopher was nine months old and had begun to mind my leaving him; he had been crying when I walked out of the sitter's house that morning, and I was upset enough that I wanted to talk about it before I got to work. Karen and I settled right into the why-didn't-they-tell-me sort of complaining that young mothers do. I said I had no idea how responsible I would feel for this little creature. Why didn't anybody tell me? Karen's theory is that women don't trust one another. "Women don't believe each other. I don't think women have credibility, and I don't think women give each other that credibility for the most part. And there's always . . . there's so much competition between women. I think when you're really raised that way, you know, you always have to be the most beautiful and you always have to be the most talented, that sort of thing. I think that women really feel like —'Oh, well, maybe she has that problem but I'll handle it differently.' " I had never thought of it that way before. I can certainly remember vowing before Christopher was born that

I would never do a lot of things—I would never scream at a child of mine the way that horrible woman was—that sort of thing. But I think the main reason nobody told me about the burdens of mothering is that it's one of those things that can't really be explained. You have to do it yourself to know what it's like.

And, too, it's essentially mysterious. Why *do* women invest three or five or twenty-five years of their lives wiping bottoms and noses, driving children to birthday parties, taking them to the dentist, washing their socks? You just get so attached to them. Karen agreed that the attachment is mysterious. "Part of it is that you just can't explain it," she said.

Like Judith, Karen is feeling overloaded. Unlike Judith, she is finally not content in her decision to live with the constraints. When I asked her what she liked best about parenting, she paused and then laughed. "Let's see . . . is there anything? [She laughed again.] No . . . um . . . [more laughter] I'll think of something . . . generally, I . . . it's hard to pinpoint anything. I like my kids generally. In some ways I like the freedom that staying home with them has allowed me this last year. I don't know if I would have just stayed home [from work] if I did not have the children. Even though I was tied down a fair amount, it still was nice to choose more what I wanted to do, and I did a lot more reading this year." Like least? was easy; she said it in three words: "Being tied down."

Each mother makes her peace with that however she can. Some get live-in help. Some take the kids to visit Grandma every Saturday. Some take them everywhere and never think about how much simpler life would be without them. In Karen the peace is fragile. I asked if she would get married again. She isn't sure. "I guess I would choose to be single, but mostly I would choose to be childless. It's real hard for me to decide—my dissatisfaction, my restlessness, whatever—how much of it's due to having children and how much of it's due to being married. If I was going to do it over again, I'd have them later in my life. I would not have had them so early. There are times when I really wish I had not had them."

"Right now, at this moment?" I asked.

Karen smiled a sad little smile and looked away. "Right now I probably wish I did not have them." It was hard for her to say it and hard for me to hear it. Neither of us wanted to talk any more about the kids after that. But they came up once more when we were talking about Karen's future. "I foresee he and I staying together forever, sort of thing, especially with the kids. I think—if it weren't for the kids—[A long pause.] What's kind of hard for me right now is that I have a twin sister who's off traveling in Europe and having a marvelous time with her lover, and there's part of me that's really jealous. She has *so much freedom.*"

For most mothers the alternatives are not so vivid, and most have made more peace with the confinements of motherhood than Karen has. Few will *say,* "I wish I didn't have the children. I wish I were free." It's okay to want a day or two off, however. I talked to a mother in New York City who said the thing she liked least about parenting is that "you can't get out of the role." She would like to be not-a-mother for a few hours every once in a while.

Three hundred miles north, in rural New Hampshire, Mara Jackson expressed the same wish. "There are times when I would like to take a long drive and just go by myself. That's something you cannot say to my husband. He doesn't think that a mother should have to say that. She should say, 'Let's all go together.' Or 'Let's you and I go.' But he doesn't think that a wife or a mother should have to say she wants to be away by herself." (I get angry when I hear that. I wonder if Mara's husband has ever spent twenty-four hours alone with their two school-age children. It's a troublemaking question, and I decided not to ask her.)

There are women who agree with Mara's husband, of course. There are still mothers who see the raising of children as a full-time lifetime occupation. I talked with a woman in Birmingham whose children occupy every corner of her life. Phyllis Stair met me at the motel where I was staying. She drives a big red station wagon with three bench seats "so the girls can bring their friends if they want to." She showed me pictures of the three children from the collection in her wallet. Marysue is ten. Denise is seven, and Laura is four.

Phyllis is in her mid-forties. Her hair is cropped close to her head and colored a warm sandy blond. Slender and tan, she was wearing a bright green blouse and one of those little golf skirts, green with navy seahorses on it. We sat out by the deserted swimming pool, under the shade of an awning.

She married late, and she says that the children keep her young.

> I had my fun first, and I would not trade it back for anything. I was glad I did not marry in my twenties. I could not have made a success of it—I know I couldn't have. I would have been, I'm sure, bored 'cause I see couples now that have been married that

long . . . people our age that have children in college and all, and they're lost. The woman's at the club—she's at the club trying to find things to do. Course her husband is happy with his profession, but she is lost. Her children are gone from the nest, you know.

Most of the girls my age, their children are in college or so. And here I am just still going to be in the PTA till I'm sixty.

The man guessed my age the other day at a little fair they had at the school. He thought I was thirty-two. I think it blew my husband's mind. We won a prize. Everybody was very excited. "Do it again, Mommy." Because I don't really feel my age, pushing toward fifty.

For the past ten years Phyllis has had at least one child at home all of the time, but now that her youngest is in nursery school, she has days when she is home by herself. The house seems empty then. "Tuesdays and Thursdays—really, I kind of say, 'Well, when are they coming home?' It's so quiet." We talked about the family's leisure time. How do they spend their weekends? "Everything centers around what the children want to do."

She didn't complain about the children at all until the very end of the interview, and then it was just an offhand remark. I had offered to walk her back to the car, and as we were getting up to go, she said, "Does that help you at all? I'm sure it's just been—well, what a dull life. You know, no excitement, no affair going on . . ."

"Do you really think of your life as dull?" I asked.

She thought about that for a minute, squinting into the noontime sun. "I do think one thing. I am not accomplishing. . . . That's why I just don't get involved in things, because you have to put so much of yourself into it—and you take away from what's at home. My children may turn out to be bank robbers, who knows? [She laughed.] You know, that could happen. I just am devoting an awful lot of time to them."

We said good-bye then, and I went off to pick up my year-old son, one sentence repeating in my head: "My children may turn out to be bank robbers." Well, yes, I guess they may. *Somebody's* children turn out to be the bank robbers. We mothers do what we can, but there's no guarantee. In spite of our best efforts, in spite of orange juice every day for breakfast and a special summer camp, in spite of accelerated reading or remedial math, in spite of expensive orthodontics, in spite of all we can do: Some children turn out bad.

And it's mother's fault. That's the thing. We put all of this time and energy and love into these little people, and we feel that whatever they become is our doing. When they turn out to be honor students and good parents, we feel like taking the credit. When they turn out to be bank robbers, we have to take the rap.

Listen again to Sherri, the mother of three-year-old Brett. What does she like least about parenting? "His tantrums. His showing off in front of people. You know, I feel like the way a child acts reflects on the parent. When I see Brett jumping on the furniture, I think: What will people think of *me*? Do I let him do that in my house? And I don't."

I looked through one of Brett's storybooks when Sherri got up from our interview to answer the phone: *Richard*

Scarry's Best First Book Ever. I read about a Daddy Cat who washes the dishes and vacuums the floor and about "police officers," including women and men. Just when I'm beginning to think that things are looking up in the world of children's books, I come to a story about good and bad manners. Two little boy pigs fight, interrupt, gobble their food, steal cherries off sundaes, and otherwise demonstrate bad manners. The end of the story says, "You will have to teach your boys better manners, Mrs. Pig." What I want to know is this: When do little pigs start taking responsibility for their own behavior so that Mrs. Pig can stop taking the rap?

Some of us can't get out from under it because we're hugging it so close. Another Birmingham mother, Jean Kreegar, talked about how hard it is to let go of her preteen daughter. "When Betsy gets up in the morning I direct her like a traffic cop. I have to tell her 'Brush your teeth! Get dressed!' This is terrible. It sounds awful. My husband says, 'Quit doing her thinking for her.' I cannot let go of it."

Jean had a good job that she liked, working as a sales clerk in a jewelry store, before her daughter was born. Her old boss has asked her to come back and offered to teach her the business, but she just doesn't feel that she can accept.

My daughter is not ready for me to go off to work and leave her, and I'm not ready to leave her. Having an only child is an unusual situation. People ask you, "When are you going to go back to work?" And you have a toddler or you have a preschooler so you think, when she goes to school, then I'll be able to go back to work. But there's no time when you can say "Okay. She's okay now. I can go back to work."

She needs me as much now as she did when she was a toddler or an infant, in a different way, of course. As she goes into her teenage years, I'm not comfortable thinking she would come home from school to an empty house when drugs and sex are so common today. I'm not ready for her to get into that. So I don't see a time when I can go to work and feel comfortable about leaving her.

At the same time, Jean feels that she doesn't have time for herself. And she recognizes that her attachment to her child is going to make more and more trouble for them all as Betsy grows up. "The thing I like least about being a parent is the growing up, the wanting to be independent—you know, I'm still like that general, still trying to direct everyone's life, and when she doesn't want that, when she wants to be her own self, that's hard for me to deal with." Mother's love—the fantasy that somehow we can keep them safe if only they will do what we say. It's harder to let go of that when there isn't anything else in our lives but the children.

And it's hard enough when our lives are full of other things to do. There isn't really any other occupation quite like raising children, and the love we feel for them is different from the love we feel for anyone else. It's a love that doesn't hold anything back. It's a love that never ends. The mistake of loving too much, of holding too close, comes easily.

So mother's love can turn—on us and on the kids. If we

didn't care so much, we wouldn't be so inclined to smother them. And mother's pride can also turn. When things don't work out the way we want them to, some of us take it pretty hard. Jerri Roland has two kids. The oldest, Kim, is nineteen. She has been a disappointment to her mother from the time the child was small. She was a nervous little girl; when she was in the third grade, the school nurse suggested that Jerri take her to a child psychologist, and Kim was diagnosed as hyperactive. She never did very well in school although everyone agrees that she is smart. She was expelled for truancy several times during five years of high school. Two summers ago Kim announced in the heat of an argument with her parents that she wouldn't be living at home any more because she was pregnant and planned to get married in a couple of weeks.

When I asked Jerri what she liked least about parenting, she said, "There are a lot of heartaches, a lot of heartaches. They don't . . . one just didn't pan out to my expectations. My daughter. I did not think she married like I would have wanted her to. . . . Her husband is just not that ambitious.

"I was a nervous wreck because I could not accept it. I just—you know, I had always had visions of having a perfect little girl, a little lady, and everything was perfect. I almost had a nervous breakdown over it."

I asked each mother that I interviewed to give herself a grade for being a mother: A, B, C, D, or F. An overwhelming majority of the women gave themselves good marks; 38 percent gave themselves A's and 48 percent gave themselves B's. Only 1 percent gave themselves the grade of F. Jerri wanted to split her grade because her second child has turned out better than the first one. As Kim's mother, she feels she has been a complete failure. "Grade for being a mother? How about an F? [She laughed.] How about an F on one and an A on the other? One has turned out great, and the other one—well, she's not so bad now. She'll probably snap out of it. She'll probably work out. [Under her breath.] Gosh, I sure tried though. It wasn't that I didn't try." [She laughed again.] But Jerri doesn't give herself any credit for trying. If the child didn't turn out right, the mother must have done something wrong.

Katharine, the congressman's wife, also feels that her grade for being a mother depends on what kind of children she raises. She gave herself a B, but she qualified it. "If you ask ten years from now, I'd have more results."

What about the fathers of these children? We mothers keep on taking the credit or taking the rap, and nobody even mentions dear old Dad. That's the way it has been, of course. Mothers have raised the children. Fathers have supported them. A mother who lives in a suburb of Chicago put it directly: "He pays the bills. That's his job. My job has been the kids."

This division of labor is the cornerstone of traditional domestic arrangements. It's the kids that keep a woman tied to her home. Barefoot and pregnant. A wife who is childless and employed outside the home may have a day-to-day existence that is not so different from her husband's. He works. She works. Perhaps they share the housework. But when the first baby comes along, her life is turned inside out. She stops working, at least for a little while. She stays home. She takes care of the baby.

The birth of the first child affects the father too, of course. But not to the same extent, not in the same way. Fathers who are working before the first child is born almost always continue to work after the birth. The way they spend most of their days is not changed by the coming of this baby. They can, and do, continue to have a significant life apart from the home and the child. Fathers come and go, much as they did before. Mothers don't.

For the first-time mother, the change is sudden and dramatic. Hour after hour, day after day, always that persistent and beloved presence. The new baby possesses her—even when she sleeps, even as she is making love, always when she is taking a shower or eating a meal. She listens with her face upturned at the foot of the stairs: Is my baby crying? The anxiety and the wish to respond quiver just under her skin. Her husband may listen too, when he is home, and get up from his dinner to answer the cry. "I'll go. You finish eating." Yet he can sleep through the midnight feeding and go off again to his job in the morning. Even if she goes back to a job outside the home, her attention will be divided now; part of her still listens for the baby's cry.

New mothers often feel a surge of closeness with other mothers—and a sudden distance from fathers. Sometimes it's tolerant amusement: "He *tries* but he just can't get the diaper to stay on." Sometimes the distance is full of bitterness. A friend once told me, when she was very angry about not getting any help from her husband with the children, "If men were the ones who had the babies, there wouldn't *be* any babies."

The distance is greatest when his job takes up most of his life. Katharine has been living with a husband who's never home all of her married life. As a member of Congress, he regularly works a sixteen-hour day, seven days a week. After more than twenty years of raising children without Daddy, Katharine is cheerfully resigned. "The children see their next-door neighbor's daddies spending weekends with them, and every once in a while they get a little rebellious, a little envious, perhaps. This is why—early on, when it was very evident that my husband was going to be gone a lot—I decided I was going to be the mainstay at home. That has been my role." Katharine and her husband have agreed that she will raise the children, just as they have agreed that she will manage the house. He earns the money. Their division of labor is sharp, well defined, and quite traditional.

But not every mother is satisfied to raise the children by herself. One December evening, two weeks before Christmas, I interviewed another woman whose husband's work schedule is as demanding as the congressman's. Polly Duncan is in her early thirties, a pretty woman with dark, intense eyes and a ready smile. There is something very ladylike about her, almost prim; she was wearing a soft pastel woolen dress and a neat pair of leather pumps. A little Christmas tree decorated with red velvet bows and old-fashioned ornaments sat in a corner of the front parlor. It blinked and sparkled as we talked.

Her daughter, Miranda, is just three, and Polly is expecting another baby in the spring. Christopher had come down with a bad cold that week while we were away, and I had called Polly to ask about a doctor, so she and I began by talking about our kids. I asked Polly what effect Miranda had had on her marriage. She hesitated and answered carefully. "I think sometimes I feel resentful. Although I know basically he understands what a hard job being a mother is, he's not here as much as I am, and I don't think he can really share with me what it's like to be with Miranda all the time."

We talked about how Polly spends her time. She's doing some volunteer work at the local hospital twice a week while Miranda plays in a neighborhood toddler program, but otherwise Polly is with her little daughter almost constantly. When Daddy doesn't come home for supper, the days get awfully long. "Miranda and I are just so tired of each other by six o'clock. Just to have another person to talk to or to have somebody else for her to focus attention on. That's what I'm desperate for. . . . Sometimes all it takes is a ten-minute break."

I had the feeling that there was something more going on there than just the usual mother's fatigue, but I couldn't quite focus on it. Finally, when I asked Polly how satisfied she was with her marriage, she raised her gentle voice in exasperation, and the story came flooding out. "I just don't know how to answer that. Suddenly I've been thrust into a totally different marriage. I'm married to the same person but it's not . . . it's a new life because it seems to me he's always away. And if he comes in, it's to dump his dirty clothes, repack, and run out again. I knew he would always have to travel some for his job and that I can handle, but it's gotten . . . he's gone seventy percent of the time, eighty percent lately."

I think I gasped out loud. "*Eighty percent* of the time!" She nodded miserably. Her husband's firm is opening a branch office in another city, and he is responsible for setting up the new office. Polly and Miranda have often been alone for four or five days at a time, and Polly is beginning to worry about the long-range effects. "I'm concerned about Miranda. He is really a very loving person, and he's just phenomenal with children. And because of that, Miranda's even more attached to him than most children are to their fathers. She goes to the window at night and says, 'Where's Daddy? When's he coming home?' And I'll say, 'He's on a trip.' And she'll say, 'Well, I'll check again.' She'll do it from four until she goes to bed at eight, looking for him, and it breaks my heart."

Neither Polly nor her husband accepts the traditional division of family roles by sex. He has always, up until his recent promotion, helped with housework and child care. But he is also ambitious, and she has always supported him in his efforts to get ahead. "I'm really confused because I'm delighted that he has a job he enjoys as much as he does. He's terrific at it. He's been very much in demand and well respected. And with this promotion, suddenly our income is going to double. We always had certain material goals. You know, we thought it would be great to make money, but now we both know that no amount of money in the world is worth living this way. I keep saying to myself, 'I'm coping fine.' And then I think, 'But this is not the life I want. This is not the life he wants. Why should we settle for this?' "

Polly's dilemma is compounded by her high expectations. She isn't willing to sacrifice Miranda's father to his job, no matter how well it pays. No, Polly wants it all: a daddy who supports the children and also helps to raise them. She doesn't want to go back to work herself yet, but she probably will in a few years, maybe by the time the kids are both in school. In the long run, having it all will mean having her own work outside the home as well, and this will complicate their lives even further.

More and more couples with children are facing this

conflict between work and home. The old expectation that mother will stay home indefinitely and take care of the kids is being replaced by new expectations for both mothers and fathers. We are coming to believe that raising children is not necessarily a full-time job for life. We are also coming to believe that all the delights and difficulties of raising children should be shared by their fathers.[5] This is a revolution if ever there was one, and it is happening right now.

When I asked the women I interviewed who does what around the house, I also asked who takes care of the children. Using the same five-point scale (1 = I do all or almost all of it; 2 = I do most of it; 3 = we split it fifty–fifty; 4 = he does most of it; 5 = he does all or almost all of it.), they rated their parenting for these three questions: Who does child care? Who disciplines the children? Who makes the major decisions about the children? The average of the three scores is called Kidswork; it's an index of who takes responsibility for raising the children.

Child care is part of woman's work; traditionally, the wife does all or almost all of it. But only 16 percent of the mothers in the *Wifestyles* study gave a score of 1 for child care. Thirty-nine percent—more than a third of the mothers—gave a score of 2; they do most of the child care. An even larger group said that they share the child care fifty–fifty with their husbands; a score of 3 was given by 45 percent of the mothers in the study. No one said that her husband did most or all of the child care; there are no 4's or 5's in the computer results. But the distribution of 2's and 3's is really quite remarkable: Taken together, 84 percent of the mothers said that their husbands are assuming at least some of the responsibility for the day-to-day care of their children.[6]

I chose the other two dimensions of Kidswork—making major decisions and disciplining the children—because they are often thought of as part of the father's job. I expected more husbands to participate in these two aspects of child care, and I was right. Only 10 percent of the mothers in the study said that they did all of the major decision making themselves; another 10 percent said they made most of the major decisions about the kids. A whopping 76 percent gave a score of 3— we split it fifty–fifty—for making decisions about the children. In only 4 percent of the families in the study does the husband make most or almost all of these decisions.

Making major decisions is not an everyday, day-after-day business, and it's not surprising that most fathers participate in the process. But the other area that I thought might be father's province, disciplining the kids, is much more of a daily concern. It's not surprising that 35 percent of the women with children in the study gave themselves a 1 or a 2 for disciplining the children; 5 percent said they did all or almost all of it; 30 percent said they did most of it. One mother explained her score of 2: "I have to do it. He's gone most of the time." Nevertheless, 60 percent of the mothers gave a score of 3 for disciplining, indicating that in more than half of the families studied fathers and mothers share equally in the disciplinary duties. Fathers alone did most or all of the disciplining in a little less than 6 percent of the families.

The average score for Kidswork as a whole (child care + disciplining + major decisions) is 2.6, about halfway between she does most of it and they split it fifty–fifty. This score is a lot higher than the 1.8 average score for Herwork, the housework traditionally done by women; it is also higher than the 2.2 average for all housework.* While some husbands have begun to do some of the housework, many of them are making a significant contribution to the work of raising the children. On the average, they come close to sharing that work equally with their wives.

Or at least that is what the wives say. I doubt, even among couples who are both working full time outside the home, that fathers are putting in close to an equal number of hours with their children.[7] Most fathers are away from home and their kids most of the time during the week, for one thing. But sharing the raising of the children can be measured in many other ways—making major decisions, for example, is part of the work, and it counts a third in the Kidswork score. And even if, as I suspect, the women in the study were being generous and overreporting their husband's participation, that in itself is important because it indicates that *wives perceive* equal participation by husbands in child rearing as a desirable thing.†

I know a man who has a fantasy about another life he could be leading if he weren't working nine to five and commuting a couple of hours a day. His fantasy is that he gets to stay home all the time, putter around in the garden, and

---

*My editor asks if I want to present these results in such a "low-key" fashion. Wasn't I surprised by the "high scores" here? Well, no, I wasn't. Pleased, yes, but not surprised. And not too pleased either. I don't see any good reason why the numbers can't all be 3's.

†There is still, however, no significant relationship between marital satisfaction and the Kidswork score. See Table 6 in the Technical Appendix.

spend lots and lots of ordinary daylight time with his three little kids. He calls it his Housewife Fantasy, but I think it's about being a parent. It has occurred to this man that his children are growing up, and he isn't getting to read them stories or make their lunches as much as he wants to. It has occurred to him that ten years from now his eight-year-old daughter will be a college freshman—*gone*. He doesn't want to miss too much of her.

Imagine what the world would be like if the fathers of little kids spent half their time raising the children. First, the mothers of those children would be free to do other things. Like rest. Like work at something else. Like talk to other adults about something besides the children. (The wife of the man with the Housewife Fantasy is often frantic and exhausted because she can't get away from the same kids he wants to spend more time with.)

Second, the children would have another adult person available every day to learn from, deal with, model themselves after.[8] We'd have to find another term for what we now call "the primary parent" because there would be two of them.

Third, the fathers would change. Some of them would become good at the skills we now call "mothering." They would become more patient because patience is what works with small children. They would learn to read nonverbal signals; very little children don't talk well. They would learn how to give in gracefully. And how to play. These skills are now learned more by women, especially women who are mothers, than by men. But men could learn them too.

Now imagine such a man as a husband, able to nurture his wife with the same skill that she nurtures their children.

You see what I mean by *revolution*. I wish that this would happen. I think it would be good for everybody, but especially good for fathers. And husbands and wives.

The Kidswork score says that we are on our way to different kinds of parenting, different kinds of marriage in which fathering and mothering will be more alike. But that kind of change doesn't happen in one generation.

Giving so much of herself, a new mother is bound to feel that the baby is more hers than her husband's. As the weeks and years go by, she will continue to be more involved with the child and to feel, reasonably enough, that she knows the child better than her husband does, perhaps that she loves the child more. It is going to be difficult to give those feelings up. One of the reasons fathers don't do more fathering right now is that the mothers are doing it all.

A woman who is the mother of two teenage boys told me that she and her husband, a high-school principal, had begun recently to quarrel more about the children; he wants them to be in earlier on the weeknights than she thinks is necessary—that sort of thing. She feels her husband's sudden interest as an intrusion. "So many of the years he was so busy with his work, and he's still out a lot at night so that I'm with the children so much more than he is. I guess I resent somewhat his trying to take as much a part in the decisions about the children as I do because so much of the responsibility is mine."

Phyllis Stair is not inclined to share her children either. Last Christmas her husband got one of the girls a battery-operated computer game that Phyllis thought was too advanced for the child. She explained to me that her husband isn't very good at picking out presents for the kids. "I think that comes from not being around them and not knowing them that well. 'Cause when you're with them every day—like he is with them, what? Two hours a day? If they're in school, they're at home with me two or three hours and then he sees them from about six o'clock to eight o'clock maybe. And then on the weekends. And you can't really tell what a child feels or expresses when you only spend a few hours a day with them." Phyllis is sure that she knows her girls better than their father does. Raising the children is what she is doing with her life. He couldn't possibly be as good at it as she is. She reminds me of the woman who does all of her own housework because her husband, who might be willing to help her, doesn't do it right. Except that raising children is a little more important than washing dishes.

So long as women are stuck with the children, they are bound to feel possessive of them. It's a vicious circle: *Because* she is raising the children, mother becomes good at it; because she's good at it, she's the "natural" one to raise the children. Things are starting to change, but we still have a long way to go.

And no matter how the work of raising the children is divided, kids make a lot of other trouble in a marriage.[9] Even couples who don't argue about anything else argue about the children. One woman, married more than twenty years, insisted, "We never never argue. We never had an out-and-out knockdown drag out fight." I was used to hearing that by the time I talked to her. It's hard for many women to admit that they fight with their husbands, so I coaxed her a little bit. Perhaps they had disagreements? "The main thing was raisin' the kids," she said.

They screw up your sex life, for one thing. Some women become disinterested in lovemaking as soon as they become pregnant, and every couple is disrupted sexually when there's a new baby in the house. I had a hilarious moment with one young mother when we were discussing all of the problems that babies bring to your sex life.

> Sexual communication was real difficult when the kids were little. Most of it was me. I think part of it was that I felt that mothers should not be sexual beings, should not have sexual feelings, that sort of thing. And I knew that should not be true, but there's that gut part that's hard to overcome. And also I nursed Rebecca for a year and then there was only three or four months until I was pregnant again. And I never felt—sex was just not an important part of my life when I was nursing or when I was pregnant. I don't know if it was psychological or physical or what. And then I nursed David—so there was a year, plus nine months of being pregnant, plus a year of nursing David so that was a long period of time.
>
> And I was *so tired*. And I also have leaky breasts. To me it was just not romantic to be squirting all over, you know. [She and I both burst into laughter, each with her own memories of this exquisitely unromantic event.] And I just hated after the lovemaking having this wet bed, and I never had the energy to change it. The bother of towels. . . . You lose the spontaneity too.

The memory of all those wet sheets—we had to either laugh or cry.

Phyllis also mentioned the inhibiting effect of the children. "We don't have much privacy, that's for sure. I told him I wonder how we ever had the last two children."

A mother whose children are getting to be teenagers complained about never being able to get away from them at night. "When we're in bed, I don't like the idea that they're still awake and listening to what we're talking about or doing, especially at the age they are now."

Beneath temporary difficulties (midnight feedings, leaky breasts) and logistical problems (the walls are too thin) there is another, more permanent stress that having children brings to a marriage. Katharine Lashley touched on it when she talked about the impact of her children on her sex life. "There have been times in our lives when sex was more important to him than to me. Perhaps when the children were younger, and I was more involved with them and they were more demanding, including at night. And they have to come first. Husbands don't always like to have someone come between you. And I think that carries over into sex life too. And as the children get older, we don't always have that opportunity to be alone as much as we'd like, even in our own bedroom. I took that in stride, I think, easier than he." The children have to come first. And husbands don't always like it.

The night that I talked to Alice Scott the rivalry between husband and children was a recurrent theme. A small, plump woman in a tailored silky shirt and neat gabardine trousers, she gave me a glass of wine, made herself a drink, and settled down for a good talk. "No holds barred," she said, smiling. I liked her instantly.

She is fifty, has been married for more than twenty years, and is the mother of one son, Justin, who is nineteen. Alice also raised her husband's three boys from his previous marriage; their mother was killed in an automobile accident when the youngest was two. About the children she said, early on, "I raised those kids, all four, and they're *my* children."

I asked Alice what she and her husband argue about. She said their only quarrel was about her son. "If we have a disagreement, *that's* the disagreement. Because—it's jealousy. (Don't play the tape for him!) My husband wants me totally, and he will not . . . you know. Justin is my heartbeat, and he cannot understand that. You can understand that, as a mother. [I said, "Absolutely."] But they do not understand it. They always think: *I* am number one. And he is. He is the sun, and the whole world goes around him. Except for Justin."

I asked Alice what grade she would give herself for being a mother, and she said a C. "I'm just about average." Then she paused and smiled. "There would be a dispute. I would say I'm not a particularly good mother. The children would say I am. I didn't spend as much time as I should have. I didn't neglect them, but my husband always demanded more time. [She sighed.] I have had to steal time to be with my children."

Who do you love the most? Who comes first? Another mother talked about the resolution of these questions as an important part of her own development. Cathy Saks is thirty-four, married eight years. She lives in a big, rambling farm-house at the end of a dirt road in Vermont, out in the middle of nowhere. There are pigs, chickens, guinea hens, and three

Raising Children

children—seven months, two, and a four and a half—all very much in residence here. Cathy is a tall, big-boned woman, about fifty pounds overweight, with long dark hair and a very pretty smile. When she was first married, she told me, she treated her husband like a king. "I was so happy to be married, so secure. I was very conscious of pleasing people and wanting things to be just right. No matter what he said, no matter what he wanted to do, we never hardly argued because I went along with everything. People couldn't believe it. He'd say, 'Honey, get me this, get me that,' and I'd jump, just like that. I just really—I didn't want any arguments. I wanted to be the perfect wife."

"How long did that last?" I wanted to know.

"A long time," she said.

"Is it still like that?"

"Oh, no. Not like before. I've become a lot more independent. It isn't the same as it was, only because I have children now. I couldn't possibly. . . . I don't have the time."

We came back to the effect of Cathy's children on her marriage when I asked her about the turning points in her life.

Those first few years, he had it made. Now that I look back, I think there were times when he took advantage of me. I was so good; the more I gave, the more he wanted. There were times when I felt a little resentment. I think probably he respects me more now than he did then because before I was like a little puppy dog.

But then when there were children in the home, I think I started changing only because he wasn't first.

I mean, when you have children, let's face it. I mean, he was like my baby, really, before we had kids. I just wanted to do everything for him. But then, of course, when you have children, the children come first.

If our idea of a perfect wife is a woman who takes care of all her husband's needs, there's going to be trouble when the children come. Especially if our idea of a perfect mother is a woman who takes care of all the children's needs.

Most of us wouldn't go that far in either definition, but the wish to be perfectly giving persists. Listening to mothers talk about their relationships with their husbands, I sometimes had a sense that the women live in two competing worlds: the world of the wife and the world of the mother. Cathy talked about it that way. She and her husband rarely go out by themselves, and she regrets not having more time with him alone. At the same time, she finds it hard to be separated from her three young children. "Once in a while I'd like for the two of us to be able to just go away. Sometimes you feel that your freedom is gone. Every once in a while, not often, but there are times when I'd just like to go away for a week. Now, we went away to Boston not that long ago for the first time, just the two of us, and his parents babysat. But I didn't feel free. I enjoyed it, but I was dying to get home. I missed them wicked."

Sherri Caldwell also complained about not getting enough time alone with her husband. "Our relationship is not two way. It's more three way—you know, with my son, Brett. And I think my husband should give it more of a me-and-you instead of a me-and-you-and-Brett. I want to spend more time with just him. And I want to do more things with just him. He's the one who says, 'Let's take Brett.' I feel like we need the me-and-you things. When usually the only time we have together by ourselves is at night when we're in the bed. And I just don't . . . I think we need time to ourself too."

Karen Baxter talked about children versus marriage too. I asked what effect she thought the kids had had on her marriage. "It's had good and bad things. I think in some ways it's brought my husband and myself closer together because there's that kind of common cause sort of thing where you have to work things out. [She sighed.] But I also feel like it's given us much less time together and in that way it's been alienating for us. I think because so much time and energy is put into the kids, you don't have as much time and energy to put into the marriage. And sometimes I think that if we had more time and energy for our marriage, it would be a better marriage."

Another woman who's been married more than twenty-five years said a similar thing: "If we hadn't had the children, maybe we would know each other better."

It's a paradox: She gets married because she wants to have a family with this one special man, and then when the children come, she never gets to spend any time with him. The potential for conflict increases as the expectations do, and these days women want a lot. We want marriage to include both intimate sharing between the couple and devoted attention to the children.

Fortunately the presence of children also enhances most marriages. Sometimes the pros and cons come out in the same breath, as if to balance one another. Asked the effect of the children on her marriage, one woman replied: "The few times we've argued seriously in twenty-three years of marriage, it's been over the children. But they've added a great deal to our lives—satisfaction and pride."

Another veteran wife and mother said she sometimes thinks about what her marriage would have been like without the kids. "How delightful to have my husband all to myself, to go and do as we please! But then I think of what we would have missed: the chance to see how kids could be raised in a happy home life, the chance to give to them. Overall they've enriched our marriage. There's more to it than there would have been if it had been just the two of us."

"Like the frosting on the cake, the children make our life complete," crowed one mother, now the grandmother of two. In spite of the complications that children bring, many mothers feel that the kids add more to the couple's relationship than they take away. Polly Duncan could certainly accommodate to her husband's demanding job more easily if they didn't have a three-year-old. But she still says that having Miranda has enriched their marriage: "We both adore her—it's such a pleasure to share that pleasure with him."

Another mother mentioned the common goal she and her husband have bringing up their children: "To give them good values and love."

And even Katharine, who has raised the children pretty much by herself, talks about their positive influence on her marriage: "That's what it's been all about; we have worked together for the children. If we hadn't had that to work for, I don't know what. . . . It would have been very different."

I asked every mother, "What do you think the effect of having the children has been on your marriage?" It's an open-ended question; I was casting for a wide range of answers, both positive and negative. But almost a third of the mothers in the study (30 percent) responded in much the same way, often using the same words. They said that their children had increased the bond or the closeness between them and their husbands.

Several women said that the children had kept their marriage together. "The kids really saved my marriage," one told me. "There were times when I might have left, but I felt I had this other life to contend with. I had to bring them up."

A thousand miles away, another mother echoed her. "I think kids help to hold the marriage together. You know, had it not been for my children, I think I would not be married to the same person today."

And in New Orleans, a woman who has been married almost forty years and is the mother of eight children explained why she puts up with her husband, who drinks and runs around and doesn't come home for weeks at a time. "I'm a woman who worries about my children. I want the best for them, y' understand? And instead of me takin' off, you know, saying I'm going to leave here, go live somewheres else—I'm leaving my home when I do something like that. There's a lot of things when you've got children that you have to put up with, y' understand? In order to make things go on right, you have to put up with that stuff." So some still stay married for the sake of the children.

It may be that being parents makes us better people too. Raising children provides a lot of opportunity to put somebody else first. Asked if she would have her children again, one mother said, "I can't imagine a marriage without children. I would think the people would be extremely selfish." Well, maybe. I was more moved by the testimony of Dorothy Hunt about her early hard times during the depression when her coal-miner husband was disabled and there were three little kids at home. "It used to be when I was working so hard and no one to help me, I thought, well, if I could just get $300 then if any of my kids got sick, I'd have money. I could take them to the doctor. You know, I thought $300 sounded like a lot of money years ago." What impressed me was that she thought of putting that precious $300 aside, not for her own safety and comfort but for her children. I suppose we take it for granted—I'm sure Dorothy does—but the way parents give and give and give to their children is just extraordinary.

Even today, when public displays of putting oneself first have made adult selfishness almost chic, parents go right on thinking of their children's needs before their own. Cathy Saks and her husband are in terrible financial shape right now, overextended in their credit, with barely enough money coming in to cover essentials. She needed a new winter coat this past year, but she decided she'd go without. Telling me about it, she said, quite matter-of-factly, "We will buy for the kids before we buy for ourselves."

There's something about being a parent that makes a person irrevocably *grownup*. A New Orleans woman told me how her husband has changed since the birth of their children. "He would still love to be totally independent. If there weren't children, he'd go sailing every weekend. He'd probably still have a race car. He also fully realizes that he probably wouldn't have a marriage. The children force him to be responsible." Couples without children may feel as if they're in a different league—more frivolous, perhaps; not so settled as their married friends with kids. A childless woman explained that she and her husband enjoy different kinds of recreation and often go their separate ways during their free time. "We don't have any children, so there's no responsibility."

A woman and a man are just a couple. There's nothing wrong with being a couple, especially the first few years, but having children adds a whole other dimension. The children make a family. And all the racing cars and sailboats in the world can't hold a candle to a good family. Children complete us, linking us to the future and to the past. They give their parents a kind of immortality that you can't get anywhere else. After all, those little people *are made of your DNA*. (Well, you can't say I didn't warn you. I told you at the beginning that having a child is a miracle to me.)

Raising children gives us another chance to remember our own beginnings and to understand our own parents. One mother told me that the best thing about being a parent is "remembering the pleasures of my own childhood from watching my kids." It isn't always the pleasures you remember, of course. Another woman said her least-favorite parenting job is "confronting my teenage daughter and remembering how I felt when my parents said no."

What are children for? To keep us from loneliness, especially the loneliness of an old age alone. Asked if they would have their kids again, several of the women I talked to echoed one who said, "When you look at people who have not had children, they lead a very lonely life."

Another mother spoke of the security that having children provides at the end of a person's life. "My husband has a sister that has no children, and when I think of later years in life when I'm older, I just can't imagine not having my children to help me through those years. I think that's why my dad and I have such a close relationship now. I know that I have helped him through some rough times, and I would like to think that when I get to be that age I'll have someone to help me through."

It's not always easy, but that's what families are for: to help with the hard times. Joanna Albright's father was a difficult person all his life—domineering and tyrannical, he managed to alienate most of his other children. But she stuck with him. He lived in the house next door to hers for more than fifteen years after he retired, and she was able to provide for him. "Dad always until he died had a place in our home, a place at the head of our home. We allowed him to have it. And our kids grew up to love their grandfather and respect him very much. My youngest brother said, 'How do you handle that?'

"And I said, 'We understand where Dad is and we accept it. It makes Dad feel like he has a place in this world, a place to go and a place to be responsible.' And I said, 'That's what a family is. My kids are going to be benefited by seeing their grandfather and by us honoring him.' " Joanna felt the obligation to teach her children "what a family is" by her own example.

Our children can also give us a natural way to be involved in the lives of other families and in the life of the community. One woman whose kids are grown up and gone

Raising Children

still has friends from the early days. "Some of our best friends come from the time when we lived in the apartment complex. We all had babies. We all wanted to buy houses but couldn't afford them yet. We had a lot in common. It's nice to have neighbors and have things in common." Several other mothers now in their late forties and early fifties remembered those early, struggling years of their marriages as a time when lasting friendships were formed.

Sandy Lord is raising her two children in the same neighborhood she grew up in. They live in a rundown, ramshackle house in Oakland, California. (This house was the site of my first great failure of nerve, the one with the dog, which is described in the introduction.) It's a poor inner-city neighborhood, not what you usually think of as a desirable place to bring up kids. But there is a strong sense of community here.

Sandy's youngest is five. He and his older sister are surrounded by extended family every time they walk down the street. "They play next door—and a lot of times they have dinner over there. 'Cause, you know, we just like a big family 'cause people on the block is—ah—when I was comin' up, we grew up together. And now our children are growing up together. So we are very close. And a lot of times my kids might not eat home. They might eat next door. They might eat down the street. And then the kids down the street come over here and eat dinner here—you know." I do not mean to romanticize Sandy's poverty. I am grateful that I do not have to struggle with that particular burden. But I wish that I could raise Christopher in a neighborhood where he was so well known he would be asked to dinner just because he happened to be there at dinnertime.

I also wish that my parents and my sister and brothers all lived close enough to visit all the time and enjoy my son as he grows up day by day. (To appreciate that wish, you need to know that I spent my adolescence and early adulthood trying to get as far from my family as I could.) My parents are a five-hour drive away now. Most of my siblings live more than a thousand miles from here. Like so many of my generation, we've been scattered across the country by our upward mobility.

But in a few lucky families that I visited, there are three generations all right there together, living close enough to influence each other every day. Esther Jonas lives in a red frame house right across from the railroad tracks in a small mountain town near Parkersburg, West Virginia. Her mother-in-law lives next door. Her daughter Susie and her family live down the street. Esther was born in another little house in the same town; you can just see it from her back porch.

Susie works days at the post office and Susie's husband works nights at the factory. Esther keeps her two-year-old granddaughter every day from about four o'clock when the husband's shift starts until Susie gets home from work at six. And then Susie usually stays and has supper because there's no point in her going home and cooking for just her and the baby. I asked Esther if she minded being tied down to the babysitting chore every afternoon, and she said, "Oh, no. I just love holding that grandbaby."

In June I was in Iowa, driving along mile after mile of cornfields, everything lush and orderly and spacious. Grain elevators punctuate the horizon. Otherwise it is green and flat as far as you can see in every direction. I talked to Birdie

Tucker here, in a little green house with white eyelet curtains and yellow daffodils on the wallpaper. She is sixty and has been married for thirty-five years. They've always lived within twenty miles of the house they're in now.

Once a week Birdie gets together with four other neighborhood women for a morning of handwork and talk. She learned how to tie quilts from her mother, and she has her mother's old quilting frames, so she taught the others to do it too, and lately they've been tying a quilt for their morning project. One of the women finishes stitching the top of the quilt, and then the rest of them get together and help her tie it to the backing. They meet in each other's homes, tie the quilt in the morning, have lunch together, and then go home.

I asked what becomes of the quilts. "We give them to our children." Birdie has made two, one for each of her daughters, and now she is working on another for her older daughter's hope chest. "I don't know of anyone who has kept her quilt." What a precious legacy!

Then there's Dorothy Hunt, whose second husband was her high-school sweetheart twenty years before they were finally married. She had been married and widowed in the meantime. After her first husband died, her old beau just came around and started courting her. When he finally asked her to marry him, she talked it over with her mother, who said, "You fought with that boy all through high school; I don't know why you're thinking of marrying him now." She also talked it over with her first husband's parents. (His father thought it was fine; his mother thought it was too soon.) She asked her own three children what they thought too. All of these people have known each other all of their lives.

After Dorothy married again, her second husband's father came to Thanksgiving dinner from the nursing home where he had been living. When the meal was over, he said he wanted to speak to his new daughter-in-law alone. "He asked if he could come and live with us. He said, 'I know I've got to ask you first.' And I said, 'Well, if it's all right with your son, it's all right with me.'"

The spun-sugar fantasy of a family that you see in the telephone company commercial on the television has almost nothing to do with real families like these. They are infinitely tougher, less sweet, and more nourishing. They are also a perfect place to raise children.

And raising children may be the most important work in the world. It's a perfect part-time, lifetime job for two grown-ups—a mother and a father—with lots of assistance from assorted relatives and friends. What the commercial tells us is how much we yearn for family closeness, the warmth and joy and lasting pleasure that raising children can be. It's time for mothers and fathers to share the pleasure.

Four

"WORKING"

Superwoman gets up in the morning and wakes her 2.6 children. She then goes downstairs and feeds them a grade-A nutritional breakfast, and . . . then goes upstairs and gets dressed in her Anne Klein suit, and goes off to her $25,000-a-year job doing work which is creative and socially useful. Then she comes home after work and spends a real meaningful hour with her children. . . . Following that, she goes into the kitchen and creates a Julia Child 60-minute gourmet recipe. . . . The children go upstairs to bed, and she and her husband spend another hour in their own meaningful relationship, at which point they go upstairs, and she is multiorgasmic until midnight.

—Ellen Goodman

My own mother never worked. She had five children and worked all the time.

I have worked for pay since I was seventeen, perhaps sixteen. I guess it was sixteen; the summer I was sixteen. In a Friendly Ice Cream Shop in Springfield, Massachusetts. The first day, before I went out on the floor, the assistant manager who had trained me said that I wasn't bad looking and should do all right, even if I didn't fill out the front of my uniform. But I was more charming than either of us knew. Dealing with the public brought me out, and several summers later, when they had a contest for the friendliest waitress, I won the first prize: ten silver dollars. I sewed them in the hem of my first wedding dress, to give it weight. Don't know what happened to them after that.

I worked as a high-school English teacher during my first marriage and went from being so scared I could hardly get up enough volume to reach the back of the classroom to being very very sure of myself and very very good. Then my husband left me. (I wonder if that's a cheap shot. It probably *is* a cheap shot. He would have left anyway.) When it got bad between us, I brought papers home every night. As a matter of fact, my desk was in our bedroom.

After I got married again, when we looked for a house to buy, there had to be a separate room for my office. Now when my husband goes in and gets a pencil off my desk to do the crossword puzzle I wonder what the hell he's doing in there, and unless I've got myself in better-than-usual hand, I say something too. He gave me a little porcelain sign with pink flowers around the border for my office door; it says "Dawn's Room."

I am one of those women who needs to work. (I mean more work than keeping house and taking care of the kids. My "work" is writing books.) Right before and after Christopher was born, there was a period of about six months when I did not write at all (I was, of course, busier than I had ever been, and it was a splendid, golden time) but that's the only time I've stopped working for that long. My self-esteem plummets when I'm not working. This is an inconvenient attitude and doesn't fit my philosophy, which says that the housework and child care I am doing are just as valuable, but there it is.

I feel lucky—no, more than lucky—I feel what I used to mean when I said "blessed" because I have such good work to do. I realize that I could not do it if my husband were not willing to support me and our child. I still would rather support myself, which is also inconvenient, since I don't.

Every so often I wonder if I'm serious about my writing since I only work about twenty-five hours a week. And I *know* that I'm serious about my writing.

I met Helen Beal on a warm June evening at her home in New Orleans. We sat in a little back bedroom upstairs. When Helen's eighteen-year-old daughter, Suellen, moved into her own apartment last May, Helen decided to take Suellen's old bedroom for herself. She needed a place to put her books and spread out her sewing, a place to go when she just wanted to be by herself. She grinned as she explained how she had taken possession. "I knew I had to move fast, so I got the sewing machine set up in here the day after Sue moved out. Nobody else really had a chance."

It's a tiny room—maybe nine by nine—and full of stuff. An old green sofa, early imitation leather mended with silver duct tape, takes up the back wall. There is a small shabby bookcase overflowing with paperbacks and magazines; the sewing machine is open on a makeshift worktable; up against the wall by the door are a couple of gray metal folding chairs. Nothing matches anything else. Suellen took the curtains with her, and the windows are still bare.

The rest of the house is color-coordinated and neat as a pin. Helen ushered me through the living room (good solid American pine, beige-and-red calico prints, a bunch of wild-flowers in a basket), past her husband and their two towheaded boys watching television in the family room, and up the back stairs to the room she had taken for her own. I felt funny not stopping to speak downstairs, but Helen assured me that it was okay. She had told them this was a private visit.

Helen is in her late thirties. She plays racquetball three or four times a week, and her body is trim as an adolescent boy's. She keeps her short hair in a simple face-hugging style; it's ash blond with lighter highlights, obviously not her own color but subtle and attractive. A light makeup, carefully applied: soft coral lipstick, neat penciled brows. She had on a terrycloth shorts set, matching top and bottom, green and white plaid. The effect was offhanded and pretty, like the living room we had just walked through.

She curled up in a corner of the sofa and began apologizing for the state of her room. And then she stopped herself. Helen has been trying to spend less time on her housework and to worry less about it. "I used to be really fussy. But that seemed out of balance to me. There should be more important things in my life than cleaning house. It used to be *all* I would do—I would like wash the floor every day. I mean, *now* there's a lot of dirt. You wouldn't used to find dirt." I said I hadn't noticed any, and she grinned again. "I'm not apologizing for it. I like . . . I'm better. It took me a long time to learn to live in my own house. I would not sit down and read a book or do handwork or anything. It was like I always had to be cleaning something. It was *constant*."

Last spring, for the first time in twenty years of marriage, Helen did not do any spring cleaning. She has her own projects now, activities that have nothing to do with the house or her family: a Bible study group, the racquetball. Sometimes she thinks about getting a job. Helen worked as a secretary after high school until she got married, but she hasn't worked outside her home since then. "When we got married, he said I didn't need to work unless—how did he put it? 'The only time I want you to work is when I don't need you to work.' There's probably a little ego there. He'll kind of look around and say, 'Well, I don't know about all these other men—with their wives working. You don't have to work.' We married very young, and it was like he had to prove that he could handle everything."

Back then, in the early sixties, staying at home was fine with Helen. She was very happy just keeping house and raising the children.

> I grew up wanting a little house with white tie-back curtains and a cat and rocking chairs and braided rugs. I guess I grew up in that period when you were going to marry and have children, have family and you'd reached it.

> And then, I would say about three years ago— I suppose when the kids were in school all day—it was like I was saying to him, "What am I going to do with the rest of my life?" And I can remember thinking: When I was young, you know, all the things I wanted, I have them. Yes, I am where I dreamed of being. And now what?

And I am not the norm, I guess, in that I really enjoy being home. I want to can. I want to wear my apron. It's like mother should be with the cookies and the milk. But society is telling me that's wrong. So I have some of this guilt complex. As far as women around me go, they're all out in the working world. It's hard to find women who are where I'm at and happy about it.

She turned restlessly and rubbed at a worn spot on the sofa arm with her thumb. "I used to enjoy cleaning. I used to get—I used to be satisfied to do those things. What happens along the way that that's not enough any more?" She wasn't really asking me, and I didn't say anything. The air conditioner rattled and hummed. After a minute she looked up at me. "I wish I could go back to being happy with just keeping my house. It seems like it's not enough, I think, because other people are telling me it's not enough, or it shouldn't be enough. If other people around me were still at home, still in that same place, I'm not sure if I wouldn't be just as happy too."

It's really lonely in her neighborhood during the day, she said. The kids are all in school. The women are all out working. Ten years ago the place was swarming with mothers and toddlers. Now it is like a ghost town. "And when you were a little girl?" I asked. "What was your neighborhood like then?"

Full of children, she said. Full of mothers and children. Except her own mother. "My mother always worked. And I hated—I resented that. I think it's partly why I don't work myself. And yet now my kids are saying to me, 'Why don't you work like other mothers?' You know. 'How come you're the only one?' Where my mother worked and she was the only one, and I resented that. So, I don't know." Helen raised her eyebrows in mock exasperation and laughed. "Twenty years later. . . ."

Helen Beal graduated from high school in 1959, the same year that I did. In 1950, when we were in the third grade, more than three quarters of the married women in the United States were not working. Of all the wives "with husband present" (as the Department of Labor puts it), only 24 percent had a paying job of any kind. Among these employed wives, 28 percent were mothers of school-age (six to seventeen years) children.

In 1960, the year that Helen got married, 31 percent of wives with husband present were employed; 39 percent of them were mothers with school-age children. By 1970, it was 41 percent of the married women, of whom 49 percent were mothers of kids six to seventeen.

In 1980, the year that I interviewed Helen, she had become a part of a new minority. For the first time in our national history, more wives were employed than not (September 1980: 50.5 percent). Almost two thirds of these women (62 percent) had children of school age.

That much change in such a short period of time has upset a lot of expectations. Helen Beal could laugh about the irony of it all: She wanted to be a good, stay-at-home Mommy, and her kids are pushing her out the door to get a job. Some of the other women I talked to were less amused. In a suburb of New York City, I interviewed a woman about Helen's age who has not worked outside the home since her first child was born twenty years ago. Asked about the effect of the women's movement on marriage, she was bitterly clear.

> I think it's had a bad effect. I think it has—and this has nothing to do with women working or anything else—but I think that it has taken the role of the wife and the housewife and placed them in the role of like being a dummy. That it really isn't important. That to really become worth something yourself, you must have a fulfilling job.
>
> Now, I think that the most difficult role in the world is to be a mother. And nobody ever prepares you for it. And I think as time goes on our country is going to suffer more and more because of this: No one wants to be a mother anymore. Or very few people. They want to be part-time mothers or surrogate it to somebody else. I am not saying that some women shouldn't work, and I'm not saying that some people can't combine both. But I think it's time that the wife, the woman who stays at home and raises children and is just a housewife, should not be looked down on.

And so the lines are drawn: professional women with careers on one side, housewives and mothers on the other. Another full-time housewife articulated exactly those extremes: "The women's movement made me aware that I don't know who I really am. I don't think that I'm a happy homemaker. But I'm not an aggressive woman that would want to go out and be completely independent from a man, or in my own way do my own thing, utterly and completely independent."

One of the women who helped me set up my interviews in New England responded to my first request for contacts by saying "Sure, but I don't think I know anybody you'd want to talk to." Why not? Well, she didn't know any married women who had jobs, she said.

And my feminist friend (who is married, has two school-age boys, and works full time) says I can't call this chapter "working" because if I do people will think that *I* think the only wives who work are those who have paying jobs. She says when I call paid employment "working" I suggest that keeping house and raising children are somehow "not working." My friend is haunted by the housewife stereotype—that mythical woman who sits around the house all day watching soap operas and eating bon-bons while her poor husband slaves away at the office to pay her many bills.* She wants to make sure that people, especially men, recognize and respect the vital work that women do at home every day without pay.

I, of course, agree with her. I agree that woman's work is worthwhile; I think it's so worthwhile that men should do it too. I certainly agree that the words we use make a difference. But I can't help thinking that the *best* way for men to learn the values of keeping house and raising children is for

---

*There must be, somewhere, a real woman who does sit around all day watching television and eating bon-bons, but I have never met anyone who will admit it. I can't even get women to admit that they watch television during the day. Only 13 percent of the women I interviewed mentioned watching daytime television as a typical weekday activity, although more than 50 percent of them are sometimes at home during a weekday.

them to keep house and raise children. When they are doing that in large numbers, I expect the distinction between "working" and "not working" to change.

In the meantime, what Betty Friedan called "the problem that has no name" is still with us. Women who are not working still say they "stay at home" no matter how many trips they make to grocery stores and girl scout meetings. And some of them still despair because they are "only" housewives. One said to me, "I wonder if people know my name. Nobody addresses me by my name. My husband doesn't call me anything; he just starts talking to me. And my daughter, of course, just calls me Mommy or Mother, whatever pops out first. And there are times when I think—Well, doesn't *anybody* know my name?" She sounds just like the housewives in *The Feminine Mystique* twenty years ago.[1]

But the economic and social landscape has changed considerably in those twenty years. *Half* the wives in America are working now. Nobody is quite sure what to make of that, least of all the women themselves. And since there is no longer any consensus about what married women ought to be doing with their time, each wife is vulnerable to defensiveness about whatever her own choices have been.

For every housewife who attacks the working mother, there is another wife in some office putting the housewife down. One woman in the *Wifestyles* study who works full time offered this evaluation of the housewife's role: "I mean, staying at home all day, what would you do? You become a bore. Whereas going to work, you meet different people. There's a reason why you should get dressed, kinda comb your hair, try to look decent so you can face the day. I think it's very important. It's like a therapy. All people should go to work, especially women. Because women who don't work have nothing to speak about."

There she is again—mute and slovenly. The nightmare of the housewife. Like her counterpart, the nightmare of the working woman ("aggressive"; "completely independent from a man"; "our country will suffer more and more"), this caricature expresses anxiety: Is it all right for a woman to go to work? Is it all right for a woman to stay home? Why does anyone care so much what her neighbors do with their time, except she needs to judge them to reassure herself?

There are dozens of options in the new landscape, and the way you see it depends on where you are. Pat Hinton grew up in the mid-sixties, when most wives and most married mothers were not working. She always planned to go to college, get married, and stay at home. "As an adolescent, I just really felt like I would go to college—my parents could afford to send me—and I wanted to go to college. I wanted to expand my horizons, but I didn't want to learn how to do anything. I imagined that I would find a lovely U. Mass. boy and just marry him up and be a housewife in Amherst somewhere and live happily ever after. That's just the way I thought it would be."

By the time she graduated from college in the early seventies, many of her peers were getting jobs and delaying marriage or childbirth or both. Pat found a job she loved, as a money-market analyst. Five years later she was still single and head of her department. Now, at thirty, she is married, pregnant with her first child, and ready to stop working. But she's not at all sure how she feels about being a housewife.

My husband *says* that if I stayed home all the time he would consider that very important and very meaningful and as meaningful as doing what I do now. Whether that would be really true, I don't know. We've never tested those waters. He's traditional enough to . . . he's just traditional enough to believe that possibly . . . if I stayed home, I was having a good time for those eight hours a day that he was off working and that therefore he was contributing more to the marriage or to the family—that he was losing out. That may be unfair to him, but that's a possibility. And I think that *I* would go through a period of feeling that same kind of guilt—some guilt about it if I stayed home. Even though cognitively I know that that's just not true. Emotionally it would be hard.

I admire Pat's clarity. She first expresses her ambivalence in terms of her husband's opinion, but she is quickly able to say that she too is concerned about becoming "just" a housewife.

Since I work at home and only some of the time, I can pass for housewife or for working wife. I have certainly felt the contempt of the kid behind the counter in the drugstore who keeps me (in my jeans with a baby under my arm) waiting while he gives newspaper change to several men in business suits. I have also felt the coldness of the other mothers at nursery school, where I am one of the few career women around. I imagine that they envy me because I am running to my desk as soon as I drop off my kid. But I also feel like the new girl in the neighborhood who doesn't have any friends. I want to apologize for not being able to go out with them for coffee—and they're probably not going out for coffee anyway.

The signals that cross between women who work outside the home and those who don't can reach epic—and comic—proportions. When I was making the transition back to work after Christopher was born, my first business trip was a day-long excursion to New York City to attend a conference on the Future of the Family sponsored by the National Organization for Women. I was three months postpartum, still nursing, quite lumpy in fact but oh so pleased to be doing something about my book again in this shiny New York hotel among all these nicely dressed, dynamic career women. There were workshops and panels to register for, genteel jostling at coffee breaks for the places close to the famous, television crews coiling yards of extension cords for their cameras.

During the lunch break I had to express some breast milk, a tedious twenty-minute chore that requires partial undressing and a fairly relaxed atmosphere. There were long lines in front of all the rest rooms in sight. I appealed to a woman behind the information desk, who said she would get me a key for one of the hotel rooms being used by the conference staff.

As we waited for the key, it occurred to me for the first time that I might have brought Christopher with me to this conference. Was there any child care here? The woman behind the desk smiled. Well, yes, there was. Sort of. They hadn't planned on it, and then some women had asked for it, so they had made some last-minute arrangements.

Could I see them?

Oh, sure. She led me to a small conference room off the main hall. Wood paneling, a blue carpet with large gold medallions on it, a big table and a dozen or so chairs pushed off to one side. In the middle of the room under a crystal chandelier sat a young woman in a white uniform; beside her, asleep in his stroller, was one small toddler, still crammed into his snowsuit. He looked hot, and his caretaker looked bored. No toys; no diapers; no cookies and juice. "It's a good thing you don't have twenty-five," I said.

Well, the key came and I went up in the elevator, unlocked the door, went past the unmade bed and into the blue and beige bathroom where I crouched over the sink and pumped Christopher's milk down the drain, thinking sad and angry thoughts about the feminist movement. I was missing my baby. I was hoping for a world in which women could have babies and also have work. I had learned to hope for such a world from the women's movement, and here we were at a conference on families only nobody had thought to provide decent child care.

I was late for the conference luncheon, but I got there in time to hear Betty Friedan declare that the women's movement really was on the side of marriage and mothering. No one had intended for women to have twice as much work as before, she said. We thought we could have it all, but now we see that it's more complicated than we knew. It's time to say No More Superwoman. Thunderous applause. A standing ovation. My breasts were still sore and I was still mad, but I joined in the ovation anyway, not only because Ms. Friedan is irresistible but also because she is right.

The solution to the problem that has no name is not simply for every woman to go to work. Women who have jobs are not automatically happier or more satisfied than those who stay at home. Indeed, among the women in the *Wifestyles* study the opposite seems to be true. Women who don't work at all are more satisfied with their marriages than those who work either part time or full time. Fifty-eight percent of the nonworking wives gave their marriages the highest (9–10) satisfaction rating, while only about a third of the working women gave the highest score.*[2]

About the only thing you can be sure of is this: If a woman is married, keeping house, raising children, and working, she is going to be tired. Gwen Nielsen looked exhausted the Saturday morning that I interviewed her. She had worked the three- to eleven-shift on Friday and was going back on Sunday morning for an eight to three. Gwen works the nurses' swing shift at St. Mary's Hospital. If her husband is still at the warehouse when she goes in, she drops off their five-month-old daughter, Natalie, at her grandmother's on the way to the hospital. ("That's been a lucky thing, having my mother right there and willing to keep her. We haven't had to have a sitter once since she was born.")

Last September the Nielsens bought their first home, a little brown-shingled house in the middle of a street lined with old trees and other little houses. The street was full of children the morning I was there. Shouting and laughing, they rode their bicycles up and down, up and down in the summer sun. Out behind the house Gwen's peonies were in fullest flower, impossibly fragrant, white and pink. Green leafy shoots pushed

---

*See Table 7 in the Technical Appendix.

up in tidy rows in the vegetable garden. The railroad runs right through the backyards here. From time to time a train would clatter by.

She met me just inside the screened-in porch. It was dim and quiet, almost chilly after the sun outside. We sat there on an old loveseat. It smelled of upholstered furniture left out in the rain. Gwen looks like a nurse, even in blue jeans and a T-shirt. Compact and sturdy, not pretty but pure and self-contained. She moves the way she talks: directly, without flourishes. Her eyes are brown and steady and she looks straight at you. Her hair is the surprise—an oversized halo of pale, frizzy curls. A nurse's cap would tidy it, I thought. It seemed so out of place with those eyes. She will be twenty-eight next month, and she looks both older (the eyes) and younger (the hair).

We started slow—the coffee, the peonies, the upstairs bathroom that her husband was painting. And then she let go of whatever was holding her back, and it all came out in a rush. Gwen stared at her plain strong hands and talked about being four people: a wife, a mother, a nurse, and herself. "I feel so divided up, so torn—husband, child, job, self just pulling at me, all in different directions."

Her husband shares the load. He cooks, washes dishes, gets up in the middle of the night when Natalie is sick. "He's always been like that—helpful, you know? We're the kind that just pitch in and get it done. I could never stand people who expect to be waited on." Nevertheless, their day-to-day life is a blur.

We just feel like we're in a mess all the time. We get home at five and then he tries to fix supper while I feed the baby. And we eat supper. And we wash dishes. And we fix formula. And we don't have a washer and dryer, so we go to the Laundromat sometimes. And we're not using disposable diapers, so we do, you know, eight or nine loads a week just for her. Our Monday-through-Friday routine is basically: Eat, sleep, go to work. Eat, sleep, go to work. Or, in between that, go to the Laundromat.

And our weekends have really changed since Natalie was born. We spend a lot of time messing around with her, talking to her and stuff. You know, it goes back to we don't have a lot of time with her, so the time we do spend, we want it to be quality time. And there's *never* enough time left for the other things that need to get done.

We talked about women who seem to manage better, the ones in the magazines and on the television, women who have children and careers and unchipped fingernail polish. Gwen has considered them, and she knows how they make it work. She looked up at me suddenly and spoke with deep conviction. "They have to be rich," she said. "That's the only way."

Her husband has been in and out of work for the past two years. He got laid off the last job he had. Now at least he's working again, but they have lots of debts. She said it's "a combination of bad luck and bad judgment." She also said she didn't mind. Gwen believes that a husband and wife should both earn money to support their family. That's what women's liberation means to her. She knows that he is capable and sincere, and she is sure that it will work out. She is happy to have work herself so she can help him get back on his feet financially. "It's not really, to me, women's rights. It's human rights. Before it was always the man that had to be the bread-winner. And in many cases—well, I'd say most cases, yet—that's still the way it is. At least in the environment we're in. And I don't think any man should have that burden."

But still, it seems that having a little more money would make a lot of difference right now, and sometimes when she's really hassled, when all the diapers are dirty and the baby's bed is wet and she has to work the late shift again, Gwen is not as understanding as she wants to be. The other day she said to him, "Why don't you get a $20,000-a-year job? Then I could stay home and do the things I want to do and make our house a real home." It was one of those half-joking cruel things a person says when she's feeling torn.

In every interview there were questions whose answers had become obvious by the time I asked them. I knew what Gwen was going to say when I asked her, as I did every woman, "Do you have enough time for yourself?" "Never," she said. "Not since the baby's been born."

More than half (56 percent) of the women in the *Wife-styles* study said that they did not have enough time for themselves. But it isn't working that makes them so busy. It's raising children. Seventy-seven percent of the working mothers and 62 percent of the nonworking mothers whose kids are still at home said that they had too little time for themselves.* In sharp contrast, only 28 percent of the working women

---

*See Table 8 in the Technical Appendix.

without children at home said that they had too little time. And, if you want to be sure to have enough time, I'd suggest that you get rid of both your kids and your job. One hundred percent of the nonworking women without children at home said that they had enough time for themselves.

Gwen Nielsen's mother quit her job when she had her first baby and stayed home until her last baby was in the first grade. Even now, up and down this little street there are mothers who stay at home. So why is Gwen still working? I asked every woman I interviewed who had a job this question: Why are you working now?

Gwen smiled, a smile that was almost a shrug. She looked at me again with those steady eyes.

Well, first of all, I'd really *like* to stay home. Those five weeks that I stayed home when the baby was born, I enjoyed them even though it was winter, and I really didn't get out that much. I enjoyed staying at home.

However, I did become bored. The fifth week I was home, I was bored. And I needed that week to be bored, to know that's why I like to work. I became lonely. I missed the contact with the public and the sharing of ideas with others in the same field. I missed all that contact.

And money has a lot to do with it too. There's no way we could survive on his salary. There's just no way. There's no way we could survive on my salary alone. His father lent us the money for the house, but we couldn't keep up the payments if I wasn't working.

(I love this answer. It has something for everyone: She'd really like to stay home, but she became bored and lonely at home, and besides they need the money.)

Sixty-one percent of the women in the *Wifestyles* study said that they were working because they needed the money.[3] It was mentioned more often than any other reason and often in a voice that said the answer was so obvious she wondered why I had to ask. "I have to work," one woman said. "I have bills to pay."

I interviewed a woman whose husband is permanently disabled and unemployed. She earns about $8,000 a year as a nurse's aide and is also going to nursing school. She said she was working and studying "because I want to start a good income for my family. I want my kids to have a good future. I don't want to be dependent on nobody. Welfare—I don't want to be on welfare."

Another woman who comes from a poor family but has a very comfortable income now said simply, "I think things are always better when you have more money."

Many of the women gave more than one reason for their working. The second-most-common reason, after money, was "personal fulfillment," a phrase used by an astonishing 48 percent of the interviewed wives. (What's so astonishing? That so many women would use exactly the same words.) The third-most-often-mentioned reason was "to keep busy" or "to get out of the house." Thirty-four percent of the *Wifestyles* women mentioned it. One put it this way: "I would do it [my job] for free. I think I would pay them to do it. I gotta get out. That's five hours a day when I'm not home. If I didn't work, I wouldn't know what was going on [in the world]."

"Working"

Some wives mentioned self-esteem and a sense of their own identity as important benefits of being employed. A woman who had worked as a legal secretary to pay for her children's education found that she wanted to keep working even after her income was no longer needed. "I always thought, well, once the boys had their college, there's really no need for me to work any more. And then when you stare that right in the face after you'd worked for seventeen years and there's nobody at home—well, what are you going to stay home for? I think more than anything my work really has let me have my own identity. I know people that my husband doesn't know and my children don't know either."

She was echoed by another woman who has also been employed for many years. "That's the only time that I can really be me. When I'm here, I'm somebody's mother or somebody's wife. In my work, I'm me. I'm not considered somebody else."

There were lots of other reasons mentioned—everything from a woman who was working temporarily in her husband's new business until he could afford to hire someone else to several women who went to work on doctor's orders to relieve their depression. Married women, like other people, have many reasons for working, but there is a difference. A generation ago most mothers didn't work. Today almost half of the wives in this country are not working. So it seems reasonable to ask a married woman why she is working, although that's a question one would never ask a married man. Work is something adult men do—they leave the house and go somewhere else and earn money. Nobody asks why they have to do that. But a woman who works, especially a married woman, may still be seen as someone who needs to explain herself.

In *Kramer vs. Kramer,* the novel that was made into an award-winning film, Joanna abandons her husband, Ted, and their four-year-old son, Billy, because she feels suffocated by motherhood. Soon after she leaves she sends Billy a letter in which she tries to explain. She says, in part, "I have gone away because I must find some interesting things to do for myself in the world."4 There's something terribly cold and dry about that explanation, and yet it is certainly the reason that many people, women and men, leave their warm beds every weekday morning and go off to their jobs.

Some people excuse a woman's working by saying "she has to work," which means that her salary is needed to help pay the family's expenses. But nobody ever says that a man "has to work." Nobody parses a man's motivation into "personal fulfillment" (read: self-indulgence) and "earning money." It's taken for granted that a man will have a job and for many reasons—because he needs the money, because he has to make his mark, because he must find some interesting things to do for himself in the world.

Gwen Nielsen doesn't question her husband's despair when he is out of work. She just asks him to call before he goes out drinking so she won't be waiting supper if he isn't coming home for a while. But she wouldn't feel justified getting drunk herself if she lost her job. It doesn't mean the same thing to her. A part of her would really rather be at home, anyway. And she is not alone. Many of the working wives that I talked to expressed ambivalence about their jobs.

The mothers of small children are especially torn. Sherri

Caldwell's son is three and a half. She went back to work when he was six weeks old, and she expects to work the rest of her life. But part of her wants to stay home. "I work because I have to and because I like my job, but I would love to stay home and raise Brett instead of have some babysitter raise him."

Cathy Saks has three children and works part time. "I don't want to work. . . . If I had my choice, I wouldn't work at all. I've had it with my job. I worked for fourteen years, and to me being a mother is full time, as far as I'm concerned. That's my personal opinion. I went to Europe for six months before I got married. I did some traveling. I've done an awful lot, and I was ready to settle down. It's not going to be that many years my kids are going to need me."

Another woman, pregnant with her first child, expressed a similar readiness to "settle down" after years of working. "I feel very grateful and gratified that I can support myself and that I can make a meaningful contribution. I feel like that's very important to me to know—and I know that about myself. I proved it a long time ago. Now I'm at a point in my life where I wish I had the choice. And economically I don't have a choice."

For Mara Jackson being a working mother has been harder since she left her night job and began working days. She has more time with her husband now, but her children were used to having her home during the day. "Billy said to me, 'Mommy, you're the only mother that didn't go on a field trip this year.' " And I've always been like a teacher's aide since Lucy was in kindergarten. I live right close to the school. Now it's 'Mommy, you're the only one that doesn't come after school to meet me.' In nursery school, I was always a mother that drove. So I think that kind of . . . I say, 'Billy, I know. But it's better this way.' I feel bad because I have to work."

Ted Kramer said that "feminists will applaud" his wife's decision to put her own needs above those of her family. The last time I heard feminists applauding, it was for a new slogan: not Me First, but No More Superwoman. I interviewed a woman in Minneapolis who has spent most of her married life trying to balance her need to be out in the world working with her need to be a good mother. Marcie Shannon is thirty-two and has been married for ten years. She is a pretty, slender woman, dark eyes in a young, sharp-featured face. We sat in the kitchen at a small breakfast table next to a wall full of children's drawings. Her son, Michael, is nine; daughter, Melinda, is four.

Marcie was pregnant when she got married. After she gave birth, she went right back to her full-time teaching job. "I was always determined that I would not become 'just a housewife.' I was educated. I was going to do something with my life."

Michael was five months old when the school year ended, and Marcie decided to request a half-time placement for the fall. "I really started to feel torn between staying home and . . . between the child, taking care of my child, and working. It was just getting to be too much—to work full time and take care of him the way I wanted to."

When her son started walking, she gave up her job altogether. But the next year, in the spring, she took another part-time job, just to get out of the house. "I really felt like I needed to get back into the world. I'd been isolated here—alone with a child in a Minnesota winter, you can get very isolated. I really felt like I had to take some steps to get more contact with other people again.

"In the fall I went back to school and kept that job. And then in the spring I quit. It was not a good year. I think we were all trying to do too many different things: full-time school and part-time work. We were sick a lot. It was just too much. So I quit."

Marcie finished her master's degree and got another job as a substitute teacher, working two or three days a week. When Michael went to kindergarten, she took a full-time teaching job for one year. Then she and her husband decided to have another child. The school year ended in June. Melinda was born in July. "And then I stayed home two years. I wanted to stay home."

When Melinda was two and a half and eligible for the local daycare center, Marcie got another part-time job, again as a substitute teacher. She has been working ever since.

I still feel something about being home full time, that it's not enough. And that's at one level, I think, perhaps a social level. Where I'm getting a lot of messages that say that you're not enough if you just stay home. Another part of it is kind of a survival thing—that if I stay home a long time, I won't be able to go back to work when I want to. Because you'll have this big chunk of time when you didn't do anything. And you have to keep your hands in, you have to keep doing something so that you have that on your record.

Another element is the money. I like to bring in money, some money. It doesn't matter how much you talk about it, how liberated you are, how liberated your husband is, it still is—the reality is, the money you make is yours. And if you don't make it, you don't feel free to spend it.

I think another element that is more prevalent right now in my life is just the boredom of staying home all the time. At first it's kind of challenging and they really need you a lot, but when they get to be three and a half or four years old, they need to be with other kids their own age a lot.

Why are women working now? Like Marcie, many have half a dozen reasons.

Earlier that spring I visited with another woman who has been through years of struggle as she made her personal transition from full-time housewife and mother to full-time worker. Marjorie Barnes teaches seventh grade and is the curriculum coordinator for social studies in her school district. It had rained for most of the week that I was in Vermont interviewing, the soaking April rain that finally washes the snow away and starts to thaw the ground. Although it was almost Easter, Marjorie had a fire in her woodburning stove the afternoon we met. She had just come home from school. The tea water was boiling when I arrived and there was a tea tray waiting by the stove: real china cups with saucers, a plate of lemon slices, a dish of fancy store-bought cookies.

I was so tired that I had almost canceled this interview. It was the last day of one of the first interview trips, when I was still trying to talk to two or three women every day. Marjorie was tired too. It's not so easy to keep up with a classful of thirteen-year-olds when you're almost fifty, she said.

She is a tall, handsome woman with a headful of gray curls and gold-rimmed aviator glasses. Her body is easy in the chair—a woman who is frankly middle-aged and comfortable with herself. She was wearing a soft, pretty shirt dress that day, a little blue and violet print, and navy-blue pumps, which she kicked off as soon as she brought in the teapot. We propped our wet feet up by the fire and sipped and talked.

Marjorie got married when she was seventeen because she was pregnant. ("It was just awful. Every time I saw his mother, she burst into tears.") His parents wanted to give them money so that her husband, who had just graduated from high school, could go to Middlebury College as he had planned, but the young couple felt that they really wanted to be on their own. So he got a job, and she had the baby and set up housekeeping in a tiny apartment above a store. And then he started to go to night school, and there were more babies, five in all. It took him almost ten years to get his degree. Marjorie remembers those early, difficult years with fondness now. "A long struggle. It really was. But, you know, when I look back at it now it was a good time. I was busy with the children. He was busy with school, but yet I was happy. I was not . . . I think now, how could I ever have done it? But, of course, the world was different then. Women weren't expected to go out and have careers."

The day of her husband's college graduation it poured rain. She was determined that all of the children would go to the ceremony, and so they did, from ten-year-old Christie to Brian, who was barely two. Five pairs of boots, five little slickers, everybody so excited they were practically exploding in the backseat of the station wagon. "That's when it seemed like everything we'd worked for was going to happen."

He got a promotion and a raise. They were able to have supper together every night for the first time since they had been newlyweds. But it seemed as if the time hung heavy on their hands.

> When you get that piece of paper and all the excitement's over, it's like that song "Is That All There Is?" Here we've worked and we got it and where are we? What was it really all about? And I think we both kind of—we'd both gone at it every minute—and here we were, finally, with nothing to do evenings. *He* had nothing to do evenings. Just kind of lost.
>
> And that's probably when I decided that I should —it's my turn. I will go and get—take some courses anyway and try. Not really having a degree in mind but just because I sat home so long. I figured it was his turn [to sit home]. I really think that was the reason.

For ten years Marjorie had taken care of everything so that her husband could finish his education. She had cooked and cleaned, washed and ironed, taken care of their five children, scrimped and saved the money for tuition and books. Now she wanted her education—but he was not so willing to sacrifice for her. "Of course I went through all those years that he was in school without a car. But the minute I went to school nights, it became very important to have two cars. And I just think the male point of view is so different—when they're actually involved in it. When the tables were turned, then suddenly he could not be tied to the house every night I went to school. He had to be free to go out, even if it was just taking the kids with him somewhere. I wasn't two months into school and we suddenly could afford a second car."

There was trouble between them almost at once. It was, after all, 1959 and most wives and mothers were still staying at home. Besides, as Marjorie sees it now, she had been teaching her husband ever since they got married that she would take care of everything.

> Of course, I'd spent all these years catering to him because he was busy—you know, no question. And I was home all the time. But suddenly things were not the way they had been. The wash wasn't done. . . . What I would do is get the supper for them and tear out the door. I really didn't have time to eat, or I would eat while I was preparing it. So this meant that he had the responsibility of seeing that the dishes got done and the kids got to bed. And this was new. He never had time before.
>
> And there would be times when I might not . . . I would get behind in the wash, and he wouldn't have his clean underwear in the drawer. And he would just go into a tantrum because his underwear wasn't in his drawer. And his socks. You know, like it was the worst crime in the world. Or the buttons weren't sewn on. We really had some terrific battles about that for a period of years.

It was worse when I was going full time during the days. And, of course, I had a lot of schoolwork to do when I got home—as well as housework. We had some real battles to the point where I thought either I'd have to give up school or we were going to split up.

It got to the point where he would almost want to assault me physically he would get so angry. I can remember one time I had all the wash done and folded, and I put the stuff on top of his bureau—his underwear and his socks—and it infuriated him that I had left them there. And he threw them across the room. He actually took them and threw them across the room because I hadn't got them in the drawer. You know, like a spoiled little kid. And I thought, My God, I really *have* spoiled him. All those years of catering to him, and he can't cope with this not having everything just the way it was. So . . . I don't know how we got through that. I really don't.

"And yet," I said, "you persisted. Why?"

"Yes, I did." Marjorie nodded thoughtfully. "Well, I suppose because I just felt I had to. For two reasons: I did not like the position he was putting me in as far as just being his slave. And I really loved going to school. This was something where I found myself. You've been a housewife and a nothing and you're not even sure you've got any brains left. [She laughed.] I really felt that this was for myself. I had to do it no matter what. And he came around. Gradually. We worked it out. But it wasn't easy."

She and her oldest daughter graduated the same spring—Marjorie from college and Christie from high school. Marjorie has been working ever since. She's earned the money to put four of her five children through college. When the last one is finished, she'll be about ready for early retirement, she says.

It's tempting to cast Marjorie Barnes as a sort of prerevolutionary feminist, but she resists the role. She doesn't quite approve of working mothers, for example. "The woman is almost required to work today, which I think is too bad. As far as the children go, I can see the difference. They've not had the care that we gave our kids when they were growing up."

She still does most of the housework too. (Her workscore is 1.8, where 1 = She does all or almost all, and 2 = She does most of it.) She doesn't think much of these modern arrangements where husband and wife share the responsibility for keeping house. "I'm not all that keen about that. You know, when I see that my married son has to do the laundry. . . . [She made a disapproving face.] Now his wife is perfectly free to set it up anyway she wants to, but I think it kind of takes away."

When I asked her about the effect of the women's movement on marriage, Marjorie said the movement had had both good and bad effects. "But—I think women are kidding themselves when they try to get on an equal footing with men. We're not the same. Women are much more emotional than men. We don't make decisions as well. We're not as strong physically."

Things have mellowed considerably between Marjorie and her husband. Most of their children are grown and gone. She's usually finished with her job before he gets home from his, and often she has time to fold the laundry too. He hasn't had a tantrum over his underwear in a long time.

In other two-paycheck marriages, the battles are still brisk. For one thing, young working wives expect more from their husbands in the 1980s than Marjorie ever dreamed of asking in 1959. A twenty-five-year-old woman in Cambridge, Massachusetts, has temporarily abandoned her own graduate education to support her husband while he finishes his schooling. She expects him to do the same for her. "I feel determined that he will become the breadwinner when he's completed his graduate program, and I will return to graduate school."

This couple has an ongoing argument that is a lot more common today than it was even five or ten years ago. She described it to me, blow by blow, as if it were a tennis match. First she says to him, "Suppose you got an appointment at Harvard and I got an appointment at Stanford, what would you do?" He replies that "he would not want to have to be separated but if he had no alternative, for the sake of his career, he would choose to move away [from her] and hope that it would be temporary, hope that with time, a career option would arise for both of us that would be geographically compatible."

This is not, I remark, what she wants to hear. "No. What I would like to hear is that he would turn down a more favorable position to enable me to get a more favorable position since I have turned down opportunities to be with him during his graduate program."

"Who brings it up?"

"I do," she confessed. (We both laughed.) "The quarrel is always begun by me and it always stems from defensiveness and feeling potentially threatened by the dominance of his career choices. And I will lash out and assert that my career choice deserves as much priority as his. And along with that defensiveness I'm sure is my own frustration with an upbringing, a traditional societal upbringing that states that because I am a woman, I should be more willing to compromise."

When both a wife and her husband are serious about their work, whose career is more important? Underlying the argument here is a new hard-nosed attitude: Some wives are saying "I am willing to give to you, but then you must give to me." The traditional wifely virtue of putting one's husband first is more easily eroded when both partners pursue the same kinds of achievements.[5]

Toni Roberts also lives in Cambridge. She has been working full time for several years to support herself and two children. Toni and her husband have been separated, but now they are trying to negotiate a reconciliation. She too has her terms. "My main stipulation if he and I are going to live together is that he supports me until I finish school. And that's a condition of us getting back together again. That he understands that I cannot work and go to school at the same time. And if I don't get that, I don't think I'll ever forgive him. Because I did the kids, and I did everything so he could get his MBA when we were still living together. And our *deal*, our contract, was that I would go back to school. And he hasn't done good by that. And I'm pissed."

Talk about "deals" and "contracts" is very far indeed from the romantic ideal of a relationship founded in mutual trust and selfless giving. This new talk is the language of the marketplace; it says marriage is an exchange in which the wife needs to watch out for her own interests since members of her sex have traditionally given more than they have received. Such a view of marriage is commonly attributed to the women's movement, and in this case that's where the language comes from. Toni Roberts has been an active feminist since the early sixties.

But feminist ideology is not always at the root of this conflict. Even the most traditional wife may feel the balance of her marriage shift because she has gone out to work. Adele Stephens works two days a week as a dental hygienist and still does almost all the housework, which is just the way she wants it. A slight, dark-haired woman in her early thirties, she was shy about the interview and visibly uncomfortable for the first half hour or so. She sat on the edge of her chair in the living room, which is dominated by a huge color television and her husband's Barcolounger. Although she does not like television, she sits in here with him most evenings while he watches it. Hardly a feminist, Adele believes that the women's movement has had a bad effect on marriage overall because "it has made women more concerned about themselves than what's good for the family as a whole." She is a devout member of a Christian church that emphasizes the submission of wives to their husbands. But when her husband was laid off and she had to go to work full time, Adele felt justified in asking for some more help at home. And now she complains when she doesn't get it.

> I crab a lot. I get mad. I say, "I'm not cooking supper because I worked all day and you didn't do anything all day and I asked you this morning would you please

have the supper started and the dishes done, that's all I ask."

[And does he do it?]

Oh, no, he won't do it then. He'll just say, "I'm sorry. I didn't get to it." He's very apologetic, but it happens again. He doesn't really mean that he's sorry, obviously.

[So then you wash the dishes and make the supper?]

Oh, yeah. I'll do it, but then I'm mad just the same. And I say that I'm not going to go back to work if he's not going to help. It's just like I say, if I have been working and he's home, it's just like if *he* was working and he came home, he would expect dinner ready, and I do have dinner.

Adele is renegotiating the traditional marriage contract just as much as Toni is, although the rhetoric is different. She has changed, and she wants him to change too.

When a woman talks about the difference her working makes in her marriage, she often talks about the money she earns. A wife who brings home part of the bacon may feel less dependent on her husband. Some recognize a change when they stop working. Marcie Shannon's view ("It doesn't matter . . . how liberated you are . . . if you don't make it, you don't feel free to spend it.") was echoed by another young woman who is also the mother of two preschoolers. "When I was working I think I spent more easily. Sometimes it's real hard for me now. He doesn't consider it 'his' money, but sometimes . . . I mean, sometimes I would just like to go ahead and buy something and I feel like—well, I guess I can get by without it." These young women who have earned their own money since they were old enough to get a job feel less independent when motherhood puts them temporarily out of work.

Conversely, wives who work relish the freedom to spend without consulting their husbands. One two-paycheck couple has three bank accounts: his money, her money, and their money. Each pays a fixed amount into the joint account for all of their household and child expenses: mortgage, groceries, utilities, phone, baby clothes, baby doctor, babysitter, and so on. The rest is kept in the account of the person who earns it. "He has his account that he's always had, and I have my account that I've always had. They are not joint accounts. They are independent—very independent. How much either of us make or what we do with money that is not the community money is nobody's business. . . . I have no idea how much money he has in his personal checking account, and he has no idea how much I have in mine. . . . We're very very happy with this arrangement. We simply do not have arguments in terms of spending. It's great. If I feel like running myself into debt to buy eighty-dollar shoes, I can if I want. And nobody's going to tell me I can't go shopping this month. It's my conscience. I have to live with it."

Some three-way division of two incomes into "mine, his, and ours" is not unusual among *Wifestyles* families, although few are this systematic. Most couples do not restrict each other's access to and information about their individual incomes, as this couple does. Almost two thirds of the women in the study (62 percent) reported that all of the family income is deposited in joint bank accounts or otherwise accessible to both husband and wife. Where the wife is working, her income is often earmarked for specific household expenses (groceries, child care) or it is saved for large, one-time expenses (a new washer), special luxuries (a vacation trip), or the children's education.[6] Almost no one in the study, husband or wife, simply hands over the paycheck to the spouse.

As a matter of fact, money does not seem to be the focus of power struggles among *Wifestyles* couples. Sixty-five percent of the wives say that they don't fight about money, and only about 10 percent report that their husbands restrict their spending in any way. Even fewer wives (8 percent) restrict their husband's spending. It isn't that everybody in the study is rich—a wide spectrum of family incomes is represented here, and many of the women complained about rising costs and working hard to make ends meet. There just isn't much struggling between husband and wife about how the money is to be spent or who is going to spend it. This absence of conflict must be due in part to the fact that most of the wives in the study are working women. Since they are helping to earn the money, it seems fair to both them and their husbands that they be able to make decisions about spending it.

Some of the working women I interviewed have what seems to me to be a double standard about their family income. Few women feel, as Gwen Nielsen does, that the wife ought to relieve her husband of the burden of being the breadwinner. Indeed, some of the working women want to have their cake and eat it too. "I expect him to support me," said one, a woman who has been working for almost twenty years. "We're old-fashioned enough that we hold to the traditional values of marriage that he married me for better or for worse, and he's going to support me. . . . What's mine is mine and what's his is mine too."

"Her" money, the money she earns, can be the way around him if he's difficult. A farmer's wife in Iowa buys for herself and for the house from the income of her own garden produce, which she plants, tends, harvests, and sells herself. She was contemplating some new furniture the day I visited. "This is where the idea of having your own money is. You just can do it. You don't have to ask him. Like that chair—if he doesn't fix it, it's going out. A new one will take its place.

"I don't buy anything on credit. For myself. Or for the house. I use my garden money. That's what it's for. I even bought my new car out of it. Then I wrecked it. And I had people say, 'Well, didn't he get mad if you wrecked the car?' And I said 'Well, it's mine. I paid for it. How could he get mad about it?' "

There is more at stake here than buying a new chair or taking responsibility for your own car. Every woman who earns her own money is a woman who can be on her own. The difference was articulated directly by a working-class wife in West Virginia. "I think marriage has changed because more of the women are working women now, and I think that has changed a lot. Because when I was little, my mother didn't work, and I think that has a lot to do with it. It gives the woman, you know—I don't know how to say it—she can be more independent, and it gives her a way to show that if things don't work out she can take care of herself. I really feel that that's important to a woman."

Her husband understands the difference too. He would

prefer that she quit her job. "He wants me to depend on him all the way. He wants me to lean on him, where right now I don't. I'm an independent person."

Some people say that the trouble with marriage these days is that wives don't stay home where they belong. If all these married women would just stop working, all would be well. I myself favor the opposite solution; I think marriage will improve when *husbands* stay home from work more often to attend to domestic affairs. But the first theory does acknowledge an important fact: A wife who has a job may need her husband less—for tangibles like spending money and intangibles like self-esteem—than a wife who doesn't. A working woman has more options, at least theoretically. If she doesn't like the way the marriage is going, she can think about leaving.

I talked to a woman who is thinking about it. She has been married for twenty years and has worked full time for fifteen.

My husband and I have grown apart. Our difference of work is a great big problem. He knows nobody that I work with. He doesn't know anything about my work. He doesn't care to. . . . He spends his time with other people all the time. The time we have, or the time he has, with his family is so little compared to the time he has with other people.

It doesn't scare me anymore. It used to frighten me. I would never, never have thought of anything like that because I was completely dependent upon him. But not anymore.

[You mean emotionally dependent?]

Security. And just having a man there. But I don't feel that anymore.

[You feel if you had to you could be on your own?]

[Softly.] Yes.

[Do you sometimes wish you were on your own?]

[Softer.] Yes.

[Ever think of leaving?]

[Softer.] Yes.

[A lot?]

[Barely audible.] Yes.

Of all the women I interviewed there were a few, maybe five or six, who were in marriages that I thought would not last much longer. This woman was one of them. I don't know what the problem is between this couple—she didn't say much about that—but I would guess it isn't just the fact that she has a job.

Nevertheless, somewhere in their bones a lot of people feel that a wife's job represents a threat to the stability of her marriage. And some of the people who feel that way are married to women who work. There are certainly more divorces now than there were when fewer wives had jobs. No one can say exactly what the relationship is, although several authorities note that women who were once trapped in unhappy marriages because they had no economic alternative now have more of a choice. When Helen Beal and I first sat down in her little room at the top of the back stairs, I asked the standard set of demographic questions: age, length of marriage, number of children, education, and so on. When we got to her occupation, it went like this:

ME: And are you working right now?

SHE: Other than the piano, I'm not employed right now.

ME: Okay. You're a musician? A piano teacher? How would you describe your occupation?

SHE: [Thinking about it for a minute.] I guess I don't feel like I have an occupation.

ME: Okay. [Pause.] Well, I'll write . . . [I just can't let it go at that.] Oh, I don't know. If someone said to you, "What is your occupation?" you'd say, "I don't have one"?

SHE: I'd say "homemaker," I guess. I don't know. I do a little bit of everything.

ME: Okay. I'll write "homemaker" and then I'll put "music teacher" here in parentheses, so that will cover both. And your husband's occupation?

SHE: [Quite sure of this.] He's a registered pharmacist.

A few minutes later I asked Helen to give her own personal income by choosing the best category from a numbered scale (1 = no income, 2 = less than $5,000, etc.). "My income?" She said. "It would be 1 [no income]." She looked again at the card. "Or, I guess it could be 2 [less than $5,000]. (She laughed) "I guess it would be 2 because of my lessons. But it's not steady."

By the time the interview was over, I had learned that Helen had worked before she was married as a music teacher, as a telephone operator, and as a store clerk. She has also been teaching both piano and organ in her home for most of her adult life. You will recall that Helen's husband takes considerable pride in the fact that his wife is not working. And she seems to see herself as not working too, even though she *is* working, part time.

The impulse of a wife to downplay her own work surprised me every time. Even after I had done a lot of interviews and should have seen it coming, I sometimes missed it completely. In another interview much later in the year, I talked with a woman who has been a foster parent for almost fifteen years. In this time she and her family have provided a temporary home for over fifty infants and small children. Nevertheless, she said that her occupation was housewife and that she had not been employed since she got married more than twenty years ago. We were about halfway through the interview when we discovered that we had overlooked an important part of her employment history. She was talking about money—how she and her husband decide what to spend on Christmas presents.

SHE: Last year, I did take care of a little girl daytime and so I was able to buy our Christmas presents with that money. That's the first time I've ever been able to do that.

ME: You had a job last year then that we didn't get on this sheet?

SHE: [Flustered. Am I scolding her?] Oh, but I . . . Oh, well I guess that is right. I didn't even think of it because it wasn't outside the home.

ME: [Sympathetic. Understanding.] Uh-huh. Is that the only other part-time job you've ever had?

SHE: Yeah. Because, see, I didn't get paid for fostering. [Pause.] Well, I got paid. But then foster care doesn't qualify as a paying job really.

ME: [Finally I see it. Deadpan. Best professional neutrality.] Why is that?

SHE: Well, I guess . . . I don't know. [Bright laugh.] I guess it really is, but I didn't think of it like that.

ME: [Tactful.] I think we should go back and make this a little more complete. You've been a foster parent for . . . years and years.

SHE: [Obvious pride.] Fourteen.

ME: [Filling in the chart.] Fourteen years. That's a . . . I suppose it's a kind of part-time job, isn't it?

SHE: Well, sure. I mean it's twenty-four hours a day, but. . . .

ME: [Rebuked and I know it.] I guess it's a kind of full-time job, isn't it. Okay. [Moving on, embarrassed.] You were married then, you had children then. You were working at home.

SHE: Right. I didn't really stop to think of it like that.

ME: Yeah. [Relieved to confess this.] Me, either.

One could argue (though I would not) that taking in foster children or teaching a few piano lessons is not really working. Perhaps these women do not think of themselves as working because what they do is not regular, full-time employment. Perhaps. I think there is more to it than that.

I talked to a couple of women in Birmingham, Alabama, who also make light of their jobs. Each made clear her own stake in doing that. Roberta Myers lives in a sprawling, expensive-looking ranch-style house in a suburb of Birmingham. They have a pool and a big yard with lots of nice old trees. We sat on the patio at a small white table with a huge red-and-white striped umbrella over it. She is short, a bit heavy, deeply tanned. Her three school-age boys trooped in and out of the house during the interview.

Roberta said that her occupation is "basically a housewife." She earns between five and ten thousand dollars a year working at two jobs—as a real-estate broker and as a library aide in one of the community colleges. Reporting her income, she said, "Mine would be just number 3 [between $5,000 and $9,999.00]." Reporting her husband's income, she commented, "He keeps us going. Mine is just like a bonus."

Roberta enjoys her work, especially the real-estate job. She has always been employed, at least part time, because "it keeps me in the know, a part of things." Her husband would like her to quit at least one of her jobs now, but she says she would miss the stimulation.

Nevertheless, she puts herself squarely on the side of the housewife and mother.

> I had a friend come over. . . . This girl is very much into ERA. She doesn't have any children, and she's not sure she wants children because she feels that the husband and wife have to share everything totally equal. And I told her, well, I think if you both have the same profession and the same type of hours that you can do that. But I have enjoyed the financial independence of my husband's job, and I know that if I had been the type that said, "You've got to be home at five o'clock and you've got to do this and I'll be home at five o'clock and we're going to do this and this" that he couldn't have progressed like he has.

> And, on the other hand, after I got my real-estate license, I saw right off that it was going to be extremely difficult for me to pursue that right now because you just don't tell a customer that you're out showing houses to "I got to go get my kid now." I don't know—maybe the time will come when men and women share more equally with household and childrearing. But on the other hand, I don't know but what there are certain things a woman's more inclined to do. I'm glad my children didn't have to be raised by somebody else.

> Sometimes I think the professional woman—that

they're the ones you're hearing from, more than the housewife or the homemaker or whatever you want to be called—domestic engineers. [She laughed.] I went to my twentieth high-school reunion last year and one girl put "domestic engineer." I have sometimes just wondered if those that were being most vocal, if maybe it wasn't a little one-sided. I think there are a lot of women beginning to speak out more —ones that have been just housewives and mothers.

That's the way it seems for me, but I think everybody needs to do what works out for them. And that's what I told her. That . . . um . . . that there's no way that you can do all of the things. And I suppose that's why a lot of couples are deciding not to have children. I think it's where you put your priorities.

What strikes me about Roberta is that she is not "just" a housewife and mother. She's a working woman too. She makes well over $5,000 a year. She has gone to school to prepare for the licensing examination so that she can practice her chosen profession. She has had at least one job for years and plans to continue to work.

But, clearly, in her world there are two kinds of women: the professional woman on one side, and the housewife and mother on the other. (This, of course, is where we started.) And since she sees professional women as selfish people who put their own careers ahead of their husband's and leave their children to be raised by somebody else, there's not much question about which side Roberta wants to be on. When I asked her about the women's movement, she articulated her own strongest grievance again, admitting also to some of her ambivalence. "I straddle the fence. I am for women having more advantages. I mean, I would not want to be the woman fifty years ago or however many years ago that didn't know anything except the home. But on the other hand, I still think that it's awfully important that there be a father or a mother around for the children. I think the more natural instinct is that it would be the mother, but I don't think it has to be."

During that same trip to Birmingham I visited with another woman on the other side of town, very much on the other side of the tracks. Missy Montgomery has been married nineteen years, since she was fifteen, to a man who is chronically unemployed, alcoholic, and abusive. They have five children. We met at an all-night diner after Missy finished her shift. She drives a cab at night—it keeps her out of the house when he's most likely to come home. The kids are old enough to clean up after supper and get themselves to bed now, and their father doesn't beat them, just her.

He's been out of work this time for more than a year and there are no more unemployment benefits. Missy has been supporting them all with her cab job, barely making it from one paycheck to the next. Last fall when her youngest fell out of a tree and broke his arm, her mother gave her some money to pay the doctor. Missy would never go on welfare, she said. "Too proud."

When she and I were going through Household Jobs index, she said that "earning the money" was a 3: "We split it fifty–fifty." If I could go back to that moment, I would ask her why she said so, since he hadn't earned anything in the past year. That night it was all I could do to listen to her story—there were so many things that I wanted to say and knew I shouldn't. But she did offer one other comment about her economic situation. "I'd like to, one day, be self-sufficient," she said, "where I didn't have to depend on his paycheck. I mean, I didn't have to swallow 'The hell with you' to pay the bills on the first of the month. I mean, there are times when you'd like to say 'The hell with you' and you can't, you can't say it, because there's no way you can support yourself and five kids." Again I kept my mouth shut, resisting the impulse to point out that she had already been supporting herself *and* her husband *and* their five kids for more than a year.

It's easy to condescend in the face of such obvious discrepancy. But Missy is not the only working woman in the *Wifestyles* study who seems confused about her financial contribution. What answer would you give? The scale is the same as for keeping house: 1–5 where 1 = I do all or almost all, 2 = I do most, 3 = We split it 50–50, 4 = He does most, and 5 = He does all or almost all. Rate your own marriage right now: Who earns the money?

A surprising number of the *Wifestyles* women who have jobs and make money nevertheless give their husbands most or all of the credit for earning the money. Fourteen percent of the *working* wives said 5, He earns all or almost all, and another 42 percent said 4, He earns most of the money.* Of the women with jobs who say he earns it all, most are part-time and occasional workers who earn less than $5,000 a year. But one

---

*See Table 9 in the Technical Appendix.

woman who makes more than $10,000 a year also said that her husband earns all or almost all of the money.

The difference *between* the two incomes turns out to be the most important factor. Most of these women earn considerably less than their husbands do, of course.[7] And their answers reflect the dollar difference between the two incomes. In families in which the wife earns a modest income (up to $10,000) and the husband earns much more (at least $15,000), 53 percent of the women say 5, He earns it all, and another 34 percent say 4, He earns most. Only 13 percent of women in families with a large income difference say 3, We split it 50-50. But when the couple's earnings are more equal in dollars (both earn between $10,000 and $25,000), 39 percent of the wives give a 3, We split it. Only 15 percent say 5, He earns all.* The most equality in earning is reported by working women in modest and middle-income families.

The overall pattern adds up to a curious phenomenon. In this so-called liberated era when more married women are working than ever before, a number of working wives from many levels and circumstances give their husbands much more credit for earning the money than they give themselves. Why? From what they have said, I think some are reluctant to think of themselves as working women because they believe that women who work are by and large more self-centered and aggressive than women who stay at home.

An even larger group seems to underplay their own working and earning role out of deference to their husband's

---

*See Table 10 in the Technical Appendix.

feelings. One woman put it this way: "A man, I think, likes to be the one that earns the most money. If the woman earned more than the man it would make the man feel inferior to his wife. I mean, maybe I'm wrong, I don't know. I know my husband would feel that way because whenever he was on his unemployment, he felt good because his unemployment check was more than my paycheck. He was still bringing home more money than I was. I don't think a man likes to feel like he's second in his wife's life. He's the one who brings home the bacon."

And, of course, all of these working wives are juggling their responsibilities at home and at work—trying to be wife, mother, worker, and person all at once. This means that they are constantly setting priorities, constantly having to decide what is most important. There is no question about how most of these women choose: If it's between their families and their work, the family will come first. Their husbands, their children, and their life at home are more important than their jobs. They say so in many different ways. For some it's the answer to "What's your occupation?" Fifteen percent of the women in the study who earn money said they were housewives. Asked to describe a typical day in her life, a working wife generally talks more about housework than she does about her job. Wives who work commonly answered the "typical weekday" question by running through their morning routine, then saying something like "I go to work. Then when I get off, I go pick up the baby and pick up my husband and we all come home," and then describing the preparations for dinner and the rest of the evening's activities. Her job is in another, less important world.

Several employed women expressed the feeling that their life at home would be better if they weren't working. Some, like Gwen Nielsen, are overwhelmed by their multiple responsibilities. Others said that their work prevented them from giving their children or their husbands the necessary attention. "If I wasn't working, I feel like we could be a lot closer. Because when I come in from work he wants to tell me of his tales from the office, and I come in and I want to tell him mine. Whereas I could give him a lot more attention, you know, and we'd have . . . I could tell him things that happened at home and tell him things about the baby. He can relate more to them than he can with me working."

Another woman quit her job when they asked her to travel more. "I was real good—they wanted me to stay on there, but I said, 'There's no way. I just am not going to do it. I don't like being shipped all over the country at your beck and call whenever you want me to go. I have to be home.' I'm basically a home person. And I think that my husband suffered. It just wasn't that good. Everybody suffers when Mom's gone . . . and especially Dad. He really doesn't make it when I'm gone."

This sense of her attention as essential to the couple's harmony was echoed by another woman who had also abandoned her own work temporarily so that she could devote more time to her husband. "I think that things go better when I am not as involved in my work or in an activist cause. I think that he does better if I spend more time with him. . . . We were having a bad time, so I've stopped working for the moment. It just seems to me that it goes better when I pay more attention to him, as they say. It's like a child. You have a child. It's probably like—I've never had children—but if you don't spend time with them, then they become fractious and they don't know why and you don't know why. And then if you spend more time with them, or some adult spends more time with them . . . And I think that's probably part of it." Somebody else—the husband, the children, the household—comes first, before her self and before her work. Not grudgingly or bitterly but with a clear sense of her own priorities.

Such a choice may even be made by a superwoman. I did interview a few women who are at the top of the employment scale, successful professionals who earn handsome salaries and enjoy the power and prestige that comes with their rank. One of them lives in San Francisco and, predictably, asked me to meet her at her office, which is in Oakland.

It was so hot that day that everyone just stayed inside with the blinds drawn and the air conditioner blasting away. Walking from my cab toward the stone-and-glass facade of a downtown office building, I could feel the heat through the soles of my shoes. The sidewalk shimmered in the noontime sun. Inside the building it was suddenly cold, and by the time I got up to the twelfth floor I was shivering. The secretary in suite 1220 was on the phone, but she was expecting me; she smiled and gestured the way to Ms. Alvarez's office.

Maria Alvarez is a handsome Chicano woman with snappy black eyes and strong features. She looked up from her desk, took in my goosebumps, and got up to get me a sweater —a beige cashmere cardigan, very soft, very warm. It smelled of some rich musky perfume. Her heavy dark hair is pulled back into a high chignon. She is taller than I expected, and her body is lush—full and round. She was wearing a creamy white linen suit and a black-and-cream print shirt with a soft fabric tie at the neck. A wide gold bracelet cuffed her right wrist. As soon as I got the sweater on, she smiled and introduced herself. She speaks softly with a barely discernible accent.

Since we were meeting at her office, I started with some questions about her work. Maria has been employed by a large, West Coast manufacturing concern for eight years, first in community relations and now in personnel. She worked herself up, from administrative assistant to middle management, and is now the highest ranking Mexican American of either sex in the Oakland office. She developed the company's first Equal Employment Opportunity outreach program, a program that is still used as a model for noncomplying businesses in the area. Some of her friends, teasing, say that all she really wants to do in her own career is prove that her program works.

She is almost forty years old, and she is not sure how much further she will advance here. There are younger women coming in, women with advanced degrees in business. She's taking some graduate courses herself, but. . . . She raised her eyebrows and shrugged, as if to say: Who knows what will happen?

Maria sees herself as having come a long way. She got married at eighteen to her high-school sweetheart, a young man from a wealthy and established Mexican-American family. Her mother was delighted with the match. Maria was one of eleven children, and it had been a struggle to provide for them. The wedding was in June. The first grandchild, a boy, was born nine months later. Maria had three more children in the next five years.

And then she started taking the Pill. The kids got old

enough for kindergarten, and Maria went back to work. She began to take night courses at the local community college.

> When I started college, I did it because I had started to work, I had the children pretty well in school, and had a very comfortable home. And there was a lot of leisure time there. I don't know if a lot of wives go back to college because they're bored, but I was very bored at home. I had nothing to stimulate my mind.
>
> My husband and I couldn't talk about my work. He had nothing to tell me about what he did. The kids just needed basics. So when he'd come home, he'd be tired. I'd make supper. We'd sit there and watch TV, this is from six until ten or eleven. That's all he'd like to do. I was terribly bored. He just didn't like what I liked. So I said, "Well, I'll just find me something I'd like to do."

She loved being back in school and having grown-up friends again. But her husband became more and more silent, more and more distant. "When I started to work, and started having my own friends, he would get. . . . I couldn't even talk about it."

Finally he came to her and said that they had to talk. He complained about never spending time with her. He said he was worried about the children. And he was getting a lot of pressure from his family. "His mother was always questioning, you know, 'Well, why is it different with you? Who's taking care of the kids?'

"And his brothers were always saying 'We keep our

women at home. What is your wife doing?' I realized that I had just blindly gone on my merry little way without considering what he was going through."

Maria dropped out of school for the summer term and stopped going out alone with her business friends. She and her husband took tennis lessons together and went on long family picnics. Things eased up somewhat between them. But in the fall she got a promotion at work and went back to school. She was just six credits short of being halfway to her degree that year, and she was afraid she'd lose her momentum.

I asked if she had considered just giving it all up and staying at home. "Not then." She paused and thought for a minute. "No, and not now, either." She shrugged again.

I have a career and I have ambitions. [Another long pause.] I think he feels threatened sometimes by my ability to do things. We have gone through times when he says that he's just going to have to leave because I can do better without him. He says that sometimes.

Other times he'll say that my ambition is so overwhelming that it's making me a very unreal person, not a caring kind of mother that he wants me to be or a wife. And then he says—it's conflicting—he says, "You can go to school. You can do whatever you want to do. I've already learned to do the wash on my own." But say the day comes when I'm going to enroll in school. We have two cars but that day one is not working, and suddenly he needs the car.

The conflict continued over the years, a low-grade, chronic uneasiness. Maria pushed ahead, changed departments at work, finished her undergraduate studies. The kids started high school. Her husband got a new job. Gradually their time together seemed more important to them. They looked for interests they could share and cultivated friends they both like to see.

Maria has learned to set more realistic standards for herself. "When I started working and when I started school and I had this career, I used to try to do everything perfectly. And that left no time for myself. And just recently—there'll be a day when I just indulge. I'll read or I'll work on my hair or I'll just take a nice, long shower. I won't answer the phone. Just take the time to be alone."

Every once in a while she feels as if it would be good for her to be at home more. It's partly that some things around the house never get done. "You know, I was home for a while and one of my big things was to keep my house really clean. I don't worry about it anymore to that extent, but if I had more time I would like to just stay home and do what I used to do. I kind of sometimes just want to go back to being home."

Sometimes it's worrying about her teenage children. "It's like the boys are doing okay this year, but the girls aren't. My fourteen-year-old is having problems in school. I keep thinking, well, maybe I'm spending too much time away from them."

And sometimes it's just wanting to be with her husband, to spend time with her family. "I don't know what's changed. I don't know if I've mellowed. But suddenly—I want to do things with him and suddenly I want to be home. I want to do these other things that I always figured, well, there'll be *that* to do tomorrow. But these kids are not going to be around forever. And he and I will grow old together. We have a lot of things we share. We love to travel. We like to be out in the evening with friends. I don't want to sacrifice that."

Later, as we were finishing up the interview, Maria's secretary put her head in the door to say that an afternoon meeting had been postponed. Maria sighed. She had spent most of the morning getting ready for that meeting. Then she sat back in her chair and stretched, moving her head to relax the neck and shoulders. "I wonder if I can get that husband of mine to buy me a drink before we go home tonight." She smiled. I left Maria as she was picking up the phone, the consummate career woman calling to make a date with her husband.

Being a wife and keeping house have had so much bad press that professional women are sometimes actually surprised by the pleasures of domesticity. I spent a delightful time with Susie Patterson, sharing a joke she cracks about her late conversion to the domestic life. Susie was first married, at age thirty-five, after fifteen very productive years in public relations. When I asked what her occupation was, she broke into a broad grin. "Well, I'm in the home, as we say. People say to me, 'What do you do?' And I always think, well, I work in the home, and it sounds as though it's an institution. There's this Home and I'm *in* it. There's a place for people who don't fit elsewhere called The Home. 'We've had to take her to The Home.' "

"So how do you like being in The Home?" I asked.

"I tell you, I just love it. It's one of the best jobs I've ever had in my life. I worked for so many years, to me this is just heaven."

Being a married lady who stays at home hasn't always seemed like heaven to Susie. When she was first married, she kept her job. She didn't realize that housework and her new stepchildren would demand as much from her as her profession did. The crisis came when they bought a house and one of the kids moved in the same winter that Susie took on a new and demanding account at the office. By Christmas she was exhausted and irritable, but she couldn't understand why.

Finally I realized what was wrong: I *have* a job—at home. Being here—in The Home—is a job all onto itself. If some woman I'd never laid eyes on walked up to me during those days and said, "I stay at home," I would have said, "That's your job." But I couldn't do it for myself, somehow. Until I realized: No wonder I'm dying. I'm working two jobs.

And my husband said, "I really don't want to do part of the housework. I know it's not fair, but that's where it's at for me."

So I said, "Well, gee, I used to work all the time when I was single, and I had a cleaning woman. What am I doing to myself? I'm now working, and I don't have a cleaning woman, and I have a husband and a kid—and a dog—and a house and a yard. But I didn't assess any of that until I was lying on the floor glassy-eyed staring off the wall saying, 'Why does this seem so hard?' "

So she quit her job and has been in The Home full time ever since.

Another woman who is working full time spoke almost wistfully about the pleasures of her home life. "A lot of times I feel like—Gee, I wish I could be home more often. Gee, I wish I could work half time. I'd like to have more time to dig up more of the yard and plant more things in it. I enjoy doing things around the house, and it would be kind of nice to do those more leisurely. Sometimes I feel like I'm pretty busy. If I had more time, I think I'd do more gardening in the summer. I really do enjoy homebody kinds of things. I'd probably bake all our bread, you know, and things that if somebody had told me ten years ago that I'd be doing, I'd have said they were crazy. I enjoy domestic things much more than I thought I would." She told me later in the interview that she thought she would never be able to stop working because "I'm still too much into my own money as power." But she is twenty-nine and would also like to have a baby, so the next few years are going to be full of hard decisions.

One way or another hard decisions are becoming a part of many women's lives. A generation ago there were fewer choices for married women. Most wives stayed at home, kept house, and raised their children. Most people thought that was fine. Now, no matter what a woman does, she is likely to feel overworked or inadequate or both. A young woman from California who has a demanding job talked about the way things have changed.

I think the women's movement has put an awful lot of pressure on women to be superwomen. A woman is not only supposed to be a terrific mother but is also supposed to work and is supposed to be terrific in bed and be gorgeous and. . . . If you look at social movements in terms of pendulums, you know, before there were very few expectations for women, and all of a sudden we're under all of these expectations. Hopefully at some point it will come back and be somewhere in the middle. But I think women as a group just have a terrific amount of stress right now.

Somebody once asked Sigmund Freud what he was trying to achieve with his technique of psychoanalysis. What would a healthy personality be like? Dr. Freud is said to have replied that the person would have two capabilities: He would be able to love and able to work. In the traditional division of labor by sex, women have done most of the loving and men have done most of the working, and neither has been a fully realized person. The great opportunity of our time is for women and men to break out of these narrow roles, for women to learn more about working and for men to learn more about loving.

Anyone who tells you it will be easy hasn't tried to do it. There are two great dangers: intolerance and overwork. If a woman is not secure in her own decision to work outside the home or to remain in the traditional role, she will be tempted to think less of those who make other choices. If she feels that she herself has no choice, she is likely to be angry about the women who do. So long as any of us insist on there being only one Right Way for everyone to live her life, we will continue to witness the disheartening spectacle of women attacking other women. We need a world in which there are real choices.

And we need a world in which men assume a significant domestic role, moving away from their traditional single focus on work. A husband who takes on some of the responsibilities at home opens himself to a new dimension *and* frees his wife to do the same. Whether she chooses to work or to study or to nourish herself in some other way, their family will be enriched. It's a world worth working for.

Five

LOVING AND HATING

I used to think . . . that women were masochists. Not now. Now I think that most of us were raised to suckle, to make other people happy. When we cannot, we feel guilty, because we cannot distinguish between what we are responsible for and what could not be helped. It must be, one says, my fault, thereby both taking the blame and asserting power.

—Mary Cantwell

There may have been a sexual revolution in the sixties. There certainly was a lot of talk about it. They say that premarital and extramarital sex increased geometrically. The Pill became the most widely used contraceptive. Masters and Johnson established that women and men are sexual equals. Nena and George O'Neill suggested that marriage become open to what used to be called adultery. Down at the corner drugstore the owner started putting the condoms out on the counter where everybody could see them and the pornographic novels right in with the other paperbacks on the shelf. In 1973 the Supreme Court ruled that abortion in the first trimester is a private matter between the woman and her physician.

The last decade has seen some significant backpedaling. Dr. Masters divorced his wife and married Mrs. Johnson. The O'Neills found that most marriages, including their own, can't tolerate infidelity. The book racks in the supermarket feature romance—*The Thunder of Love, Love's Quest, Hidden Love*—with wide-eyed, full-breasted heroines, embattled virgins all. Parent committees comb the school library for "obscene" books. In 1982 a resolution that proposed to strike down the Supreme Court abortion ruling so that the individual states would be free to pass more restrictive measures was reported out of the United States Senate Committee on the Judiciary.

I'm talking about history because I'm not comfortable talking about sex. I thought when I began the *Wifestyles* study that, of course, there would be some questions about the couple's sexual relationship. You should have heard me trying to ask them. This was one of the squirmiest times:

> ME: Is it, ah, a very touching marriage? Are you very physical people?
>
> SHE: I wouldn't say *very.* . . .
>
> ME: [Encouraging interviewer's noise.] Uh, uh?

Loving and Hating

SHE: I'd say probably . . . about average.

ME: Probably about average. [Helpless silence.] Ah, do you have . . . um . . . is your sex life frequent? Do you have sex frequently?

SHE: [Apologetically.] I don't know if I want to get into that. [She laughs.] [I laugh.]

ME: Oh, what are we going to do about that? [The doorbell rings.] We're going to be rescued, that's what we're going to do about that! [Her husband comes in with bags of groceries.]

HUSBAND: Hi. Am I interrupting anything?

SHE: No, we're just finishing up. [He goes into the kitchen and bangs around in there, putting stuff away.]

ME: [Whispering.] It's all right.

SHE: Huh?

ME: It's all right. If you don't want to.

SHE: I think I prefer not to.

ME: Okay. That's fine, really.

HUSBAND: [Leaving.] See ya.

SHE AND ME: Bye.

And then he got back in the car and drove off to get the kids, and she said, "Well, why don't you try a couple?" So I ran through the questions about sex real fast, and she answered them all—yes, no, yes, no. When I finished, I said, "That's it." And we both laughed again. For the rest of the interview I felt quite close to this woman, as if we'd shared an ordeal.

Sitting across from a stranger and asking her about what she does in bed just isn't very much fun for me. I'm too shy, and besides I really don't care to know. I don't feel like telling anybody about my sex life either.* (I sound like the woman who told me that she had been a virgin on her wedding night and she wasn't ashamed of it either—a little defensive.)

Everyone was waiting to be asked, though. I finally decided to put the questions about sex in the second hour of the interview so that I would be more comfortable asking them and the women would be more relaxed about answering them. The next woman I interviewed looked at me quizzically after about fifteen minutes. "When are you going to ask me about sex?" she demanded. "Oh. Well. Right now," I said, growing pale. Most of the women who talked with me expected to be asked about their sex lives, and only one woman in the entire study refused to answer any of the questions about sex.

There is, among the *Wifestyles* women, an infinite variety of sexual appetite and sexual experience. There are women

---

*Telling these stories could be seen as methodological suicide. Researchers aren't supposed to have trouble asking questions because their trouble influences the way the question is answered. But part of the point I'm trying to make, here and generally, is that the researcher's bias *always* influences her results anyway, and the best any of us can do is to acknowledge the bias. I think this is especially true of studies about human sexual behavior—mine and everybody else's.

who hate making love and women who love it, women who always initiate the lovemaking and women who never do. Some of the wives had had many different lovers, usually before they got married. Others have never made love with anyone except their husbands. Many of the women I interviewed were able to talk easily about sex. A few could manage the conversation only in whispers with downcast eyes. There were a fair number of complaints (56 percent of the women mentioned some kind of problem with sex), but most of the women (73 percent) said that they were satisfied with their sex lives.

Some were sure about their sexuality; others seemed uneasy. Stella Hopkins was one of the most self-assured. I talked with Stella in the little diner she runs with her husband. It's a low, one-story building at one end of Main Street in a small town in rural Texas. It was Sunday morning. Stella goes to early services so she can come back and get the store set up, but she doesn't open until noon. People might think she was being irreverent on the Lord's Day if she did. She is short and heavyset, like a wrestler, with large firm arms and hard-working hands. Her hair is tinted a brassy blond that doesn't quite cover the gray, and her face is lined and sagging. Stella is sixty-five and has been married to the same man for more than forty years.

She has a low, growly voice and a short bark of a laugh. We laughed a lot that morning, drinking iced coffee and finishing off yesterday's doughnuts. Stella is a blunt woman, and she enjoys making speeches. When I asked how important sex was to her, she climbed right on the soap box.

My husband always called me the second refrigerator in the house. And I said, "Well, as long as I meet your desires, that's all you should worry about."

Sex never meant as much to me as I've seen other ladies. I worked with a lady one time, and she would come to work in the morning and remark about their sex life. To me—now this again shows that I'm getting old—but I always thought sex life was people's private affair. And I thought—you don't have much privacy—but I thought that was one thing that should have been private. But she would tell me about how she woke her husband up at three o'clock in the night, that she just could not wait.

And I said, "You have *got* to be kidding."

And she said, "Do you mean that you have never asked your husband?"

And I said, "No, siree, I never have. In fact, lots of times I hated to go to bed at night because I knew what was going to happen. But I felt that that was my duty and that was what I was supposed to do."

And she said, "Well, I just don't believe it."

And I said, "Well, that's right." I said, "Sex to me has never been important. I could have married and lived all of my life without it."

And she said, "I don't believe it."

And I said, "Well, remember. All ladies are not alike."

Everyone is not so self-accepting as Stella. Along with bare breasts in *Vogue* magazine and best-selling books about how to make love, the sixties brought us new and higher standards for sexual performance. Some of the *Wifestyles* women feel that they don't quite measure up. A young New Orleans woman who has been married only a couple of years expressed her reaction to this pressure. "Sometimes I wish that I wanted more sex than I really think I do. Sometimes I feel like—oh, they say that when women are thirty they're supposed to be at their peak, and how come you don't want to be in bed every night?" Another woman who is involved in a demanding professional career nevertheless feels that she ought to be making more time in her life for lovemaking, even though neither she nor her husband has much interest.

> Usually by nighttime I'm too tired. . . . Sex is not a really big important part of our marriage. Okay? I think we were more sexually oriented before we were married. I think we probably have less sex than a lot of people who've been married a year . . . once every two weeks. I don't think either of us feels frustrated or anything. . . . We've talked about it, and we think we need to have more sex. [She laughed.] I really think sex brings people closer together and you become more involved with that person . . . beyond just the superficial aspect of it, I think we become more in tune with each other if we have sex more often. I think it would be better for our marriage if we had it more often.

Sounds more like duty than pleasure to me.

A few of the women I interviewed are bitterly unhappy

because they are not as sexually responsive as their husbands and the latest magazine articles say they should be. Mara Jackson was practically in tears when we talked about her love life.

> Sometimes I know that I go to bed early just to get away from him. He has said this to me: "It's been ten years of the same thing over and over."
>
> I say to myself, "You've got to be more responsive." And then I say to myself, "Tonight I'm going to be a different wife." But I'm not.
>
> I'm not really that "with it." I really do love him as a husband, as a father, as a lover, whatever, but it's like it's just not important to me right now. He's always saying, "You have changed so much. I don't know what's happened to you." And I don't say anything. I turn over and go to sleep as he rubs my back.

I also talked with some women who have chosen to resist the imposition of an outside sexual standard. Helen Beal has been involved in several group discussions of marital sexuality through the adult education program at her church. When I asked her if she and her husband could discuss intimate things, she flushed and made a face.

SHE: Ah—no.

ME: That's an issue for you?

SHE: No. It's not an issue. I just—when we were with this minister who had these great classes.

There's some book—I don't know—long time ago, we read. _Art of Making Love_ ? or something like that. And it ruined lovemaking for us because that's all we could think about. Do we do this? Should we do that? It made it too scientific to me. I know I listen to those programs or read different things about how you could say exactly what you want, but to me that would take away from it. I'd rather not.

ME: How does your husband feel?

SHE: I don't know. I never asked. I will tonight. [She laughed.] It's always been enjoyable for both of us.

A few weeks later another woman said a very similar thing. "He doesn't . . . and I don't either believe in buying books to tell you how to have sex. I mean, I feel like we can find it out between each other. If we don't like it, we'll say —Hey, I don't like that, or whatever. I just don't think I need a book to tell me how to make love to my husband or him, me."

It's hard to tell how much new sexual attitudes are influencing behavior in the marital bed. Certain traditional ideas are being challenged—the notion that men want sex more than women do, for example. Forty-three percent of the wives in the study said that sex was more important to their husbands than it was to them, but almost as many (37 percent) said that it was equally important to both of them. There is practically no difference among younger and older women in these two responses: 42 percent of the forty-and-under women and 43 percent of the over-forty women said sex was more important to him; 36 percent of the younger wives and 38 percent of the older ones said it was equally important to both. Some difference is apparent in the other two responses to the question, however. Eleven percent said sex was more important to her than to him; of these, only one woman was over forty. The rest, another 11 percent, said it wasn't important to either of them; more of these were over forty.*

Everyone pretty much agrees that married sex becomes more mellow after a while. Many of the women mentioned a change in their sexual perspective over time. A twenty-year-old married less than a year said, "When I first got married, my thought of being married was going to bed with my husband and having sex and it being an all-time thing and really the number one. And it's not."

Another wife who has been married for twenty-five years put it this way: "Now it's comfortable and not any big, pounding . . . you know, heart pounding or whatever. Because it's so comfortable after so many years."

A woman in her thirties who had been sexually active before her marriage said that married sex is different from single sex. "Once you've been married—or *been*—with anyone for a long length of time, sex is different. It will never be that exciting feeling you get with a new person. Now the sexual act may be better than it could be with anybody else, but it doesn't have that same excitement. And it never can."

Another woman said that the intimacy of marriage is

*See Table 11 in the Technical Appendix.

sexually inhibiting for her. "During the period in my life when I was a single woman, I had a very different sex experience than I do as a married woman. I liked it—the romance of it—and it's harder for me to be free sexually with my husband because we know each other so well."

But there are also advantages to sharing a bed with the same partner for many years. One wife said that both she and her husband could ask for whatever they wanted from each other when they were making love. I wondered how they had achieved such open sexual communication. She grinned and said simply, "We practiced."

Some of the women spoke of a quietness that they treasured in their loving. The romantic excitement had given way to something more comfortable and sure, a slower pace, the tenderness that comes from knowing another person very very well.

Others have maintained or renewed the sexual excitement of their courting days. A woman in her mid-forties who had been divorced and then married again reported that her second husband brought a whole new dimension into her sex life. He had been a bachelor before they were married and, she explained carefully, "There had been women, you know. So he's learned me a lot. I had a very sheltered life, you know, and he's taught me a lot of things I didn't even know. And I thought I knew a lot." Another couple, married since they were in their teens, insist on their own intimate time now that their children are teenagers. They have put a lock on their bedroom door and established a clear do-not-disturb policy for weekend mornings.

A woman whose children are all grown up said, "You

know, it's rather nice having all those kids gone because now we can make love whenever we feel like it." She looked at me in mock sternness over her bifocals. "Having sex was not invented by the young, you know." Nor is sexual pleasure the sole preserve of the single population. Some married people have quite a lot of fun in bed.

There is a significant relationship between sexual satisfaction and marital satisfaction among the *Wifestyles* women.[1] Those who say they are dissatisfied with their sex lives tend also to rate their marriages at the bottom of the 1–10 satisfaction scale. And those who say their sex lives are satisfactory tend to give their marriages a high score for overall satisfaction.* A similar pattern is found among those who say they have no problems with sex: Most (52 percent) rate their marriages 9–10 for satisfaction. But among those who do report sexual problems, there is little difference in marital satisfaction: 38 percent rate their marriages 1–7; 32 percent rate them 8; 30 percent rate them 9–10.†

I did get better at asking the sex questions. One of the tricks I learned was to phrase them more tactfully. When I was first doing the interview, I used to introduce the questions by saying that they were about sex. One day it finally occurred to me that some people would find that threatening. After that I said that the questions were about "loving." Everybody knew what I meant, but the impact was a lot softer. By the end of the interviewing time, when I had listened to more than

---

*See Table 12 in the Technical Appendix.
†See Table 13 in the Technical Appendix.

a hundred women, I began to see that the change was more than a sleight of hand to increase everyone's comfort. When you come right down to it, the sex isn't the most important thing. What matters is the loving.

What a woman and a man do for each other in bed matters less in the long run than what they do for each other day after ordinary day. Every couple works out its own personal equation for giving and taking. Each wife and husband has an unwritten, usually unconscious, agreement about who is to take care of whom under what circumstances; their day-to-day married life is the arena in which this agreement is played out. A wise friend put it this way: "Marriage is a trade-off, and it all comes down to who's feeding and who's getting fed."

Traditionally, of course, it is the woman who feeds. Both wife and mother are seen as nurturing roles. The home the woman creates is shelter from the storm or, in Christopher Lasch's famous phrase, a haven in a heartless world.[2] Taking care of others is the woman's traditional job—and the source of her traditional power. Perhaps the greatest revolution in the entire ideology of the women's movement is the challenge of this tradition. Feminists have suggested that women learn to put their own needs first and that children and men learn to take care of themselves. This challenge to the traditional woman's role has been easily misunderstood, probably because it threatens the way things have been in such a fundamental way. Putting your own needs first is not the same as being selfish; expecting others to take care of themselves is not the same as abandoning them.

In any case, I do not know of anyone who is married and

has achieved this transformation, either within herself or among the members of her family. I know a lot of people in some stage of transition away from the old ways and a few who have dug in their heels to stay where they are. Among the women I interviewed there were those who complained about their husbands' dependency and those who were angry and begrudged what they gave, but there were very few who had abandoned the nurturing role altogether. Most of the *Wifestyles* women assumed that part of a wife's job is to take care of her husband.

There were, of course, many different ways of loving. Elena Kirby feeds generously, with both hands. She settled me in front of a crock of good cheddar cheese surrounded by whole-wheat crackers and poured me a generous glass of bourbon and water before we started our interview. At the end of it she insisted that I stay for dinner with her and her husband, who was just coming in from work. She gives easily and fully, and she was a joy to interview. The stories just came bubbling out.

Elena reminds me of a little Bantam rooster—she struts a little and likes to crow. She's small and round and utterly self-sufficient. "I treasure my own company," she said. "And I've never been lonely." Her husband works for the international division of a major corporation. He is gone for several months at a time on business throughout the year. When their three children were still at home, Elena filled her days with the kids and their needs. Now that they're gone, she works full time as an administrative aide in the local district office of a United States senator. "It's a lot of nursemaiding and handholding," she said. "I'm very good at it."

I asked how she felt about having her husband gone so much of the time. "You know I hear these women say, 'Ralph and I have never been separated.' And I think, 'Oh, my Gawd, isn't that awful.' I always had plenty to do. I sewed. I did hobbies. I cleaned house, raised children. I did a thousand things. When he got the assignment in Saudi Arabia, he'd been doing it for so long that my flippant statement was 'He was gone for three months before I noticed!' "

But she and her husband enjoy each other's company immensely when they are together. They both like to work on big projects. Two years ago they bought a piece of woodland about an hour north of the city and cleared more than five cords of wood off it, just the two of them working together over a summer. He gave her a new chain-saw that Christmas. Last year they started putting up a little house on the property. They dug the foundation for the crawlspace under the house by hand, two shovels round and round in the hole until it was deep enough.

I tried to imagine working with Elena—she seemed so independent to me—so I asked, "When you and your husband are working on a project, who's the boss?"

She threw back her head and laughed. "He would say he is. And he *is* the boss. I'll say something very racist. I'm his nigger. I carry things and pick up things and fetch things. I'm a Step 'n' Fetchit."

I was astonished. "What made you choose that role? Because it complements him?"

She laughed again. "It gets him to do what I want done. I mean, if I want that building. . . ." She paused and shrugged.

When her husband is off on a trip, she spends her time

doing "just what I like." She works late at her own office, has dinner with friends, goes to the opera (which she adores and her husband hates). When he is home, she organizes her life around him. He often stays late at the office, for example, and she always prepares a meal for them to eat together when he comes home. "I never eat without him. I don't like to eat by myself."

Talking about the effect of the women's movement on marriage, Elena was characteristically blunt. "I think it's a bad effect. And—oh God help me, the women will just kill me— I think when the woman takes herself down off the pedestal that the man prefers to have her on, and when the woman says 'This isn't the most important thing in my life,' they have both lost something. Because the better I keep him, the better he will keep me. I don't need to say 'I am wonderful' because I know damn well I've been able to handle it all these years— manipulating it." Elena claims the traditional woman's power of manipulation, making the marriage work by doing what her husband wants so that he will do what she wants. Feeding him so he will feed her. She insists on keeping the pedestal, and yet she is hardly a fragile female. Her own power is so substantial it's hard to believe that her husband doesn't notice it.

The American psychiatrist Harry Stack Sullivan has defined love as the state that exists "when the satisfaction or security of another person becomes as significant to one as is one's own satisfaction or security."[3] For all her insistence on quid pro quo, Elena Kirby exemplifies this kind of loving. She doesn't hold out on herself or on her relationship. She has found a way to give to her husband without taking away from herself. I asked her how satisfied she is with her marriage. "I don't think it could be any better," she said. "Yeah, he's a ten. He's an eleven." And what does she think the advantage of being married is? "Well, the advantage is to be able to come home and have somebody that's gonna talk to you about some trivial thing that you've done all day that nobody else would give a rat's ass about."

On the pine coffee table in Joanna Albright's living room there were three books: *A Guide to Breeding Collies,* a copy of the revised standard version of the Holy Bible, and a history of abortion whose cover warns that every civilization that has legalized abortion has perished in flames. The room seemed small and dark after the bright Idaho sunshine outside. She was making coffee when I rang the doorbell and went back to the kitchen to finish, so I sat for a couple of long minutes in front of those three books. Finally I picked up the one about collies, and Joanna reappeared with two steaming mugs. She does indeed breed dogs. Later that morning she took me to see the kennel—cages full of fluffy puppies, sable and white and black.

She is a small woman with clear-rimmed glasses and heavy gray hair in a single fat braid down her back. She was wearing work boots, blue jeans, and a red plaid flannel shirt. Her face and hands are deeply lined and deeply tanned. She looks as if she could ride a horse bareback across rough country for a long time without getting tired. It's hard to tell her age —she could be forty-five or sixty.

Joanna's story is about personal transformation, about a profound change that came over her and her marriage. She and her husband had struggled together in the early years to establish a home and get their own family underway. There had been a lull when the kids were small, but as each of the four boys became a teenager he grew more and more rebellious. By the time they had four teenagers in the house, their life had become almost unbearable. One of the kids was always in some kind of trouble; she and her husband were fighting all the time. Joanna has been a devout Christian for many years, and in her despair she cried out to God: "Why are my children rebellious? I have done all the things that I know to do before You. Yet I have rebellious children. Why?"

Gradually she began to understand that the problem in their home was not the children at all. The problem was in her marriage.

> And I remember one time we were having a real terrible time over our oldest son's discipline, and my husband had one opinion and I had another. I was really judging my husband—this is important for you to hear—I was standing in the way of my husband's being the head of the family. And my kids—I tell you they hated me for it. They didn't know what was happening, but if you look at my kids during this period they had far greater respect for their father than they did for me. All they were getting from me was hate, hate. . . . I'm doing all the right things. Your father's doing all the wrong things.
>
> [She sighed and sipped her coffee.] We women are so stupid. The Bible says we're "deceived." I think *stupid* is a better word. You can use whichever one you want. I began to be real sensitive about

women and about their husbands and about what happens to them because—see—he wasn't able to talk to me. So I began to leave myself open to really contemplating my role as a woman and my role with my husband.

God has a structure for marriage and for life and for our world. God is an authority figure. He's the father. And in our families the father is the head of the household. And the woman, because she's deceived, she's not to act independent of this Adam. You see, if Eve had dialogued with Adam, she never would have taken of the fruit. . . . A woman, so often, she will come out from under the husband, and she makes a decision about right and wrong. And the decision isn't what causes the mayhem because she could be right or she could be wrong, but it's because she has come out from underneath the head.

And the man. He wants to be mothered so he doesn't want to make the decision. And he lets the role be released. Instead of being a man, he's a little boy. And the woman's up here, and she's doing right and wrong. And then you have all the other things—the rebellion of the children.

And when I saw this, I went to my husband and I said, "Can you ever forgive me for the pain I've caused you and the kids by the way I've been acting?" I wept. I was broken. I knew I was wrong. And then I went to each one of my youngsters and said, "Hey, look. This thing was real wrong. And I promise to start from now to get things healed."

Since that day, she says, everything has changed. The boys have straightened themselves out. There is peace in the Albright home, and new warmth between Joanna and her husband. "When Mother's Day came on, the florist came with an orchid for me. And here, this man, for the first time in our marriage was treating me like a woman. See, I had never been treated like a woman because I wasn't acting like a woman. I was a person who used her mind, figured all these things out, did things very quickly, I can think faster than you can; I can see a thing faster; I'm smarter than you are. Now I don't make decisions, whether they're right or wrong. That's not important. What's important is to know where he is."

Joanna no longer goes to meetings or social events without her husband. "Our pastor called last week. They had a thing at the church on Thursday, and he said, 'Are you coming tonight?'

"I said, 'No, my husband's not here. I don't come without him. If we come, we'll come together.' I said, 'You don't want me there anyway because if he's not there, knowing my big mouth, I'll be taking over the meeting. I need the covering of my husband. If he's there, I'm quiet and peaceable.' See the change in attitude?"

I asked her what it was like to be changed so fundamentally. "I have a peace that I have never had," she said. "I feel for the first time like a woman. I feel loved. I feel protected. I have all the things that I always wanted. More and more. Not a dishrag or anything like that. I just have what I always wanted. He could never give it to me before—how could he?"

Listening to Joanna was like riding an emotional roller-coaster. I was alternately drawn to her and put off by her. She is so very sure of what she says and so obviously sincere. Yet transformations trouble me—I'm always listening for the crash that comes when the high is over. And submission is not my style. Joanna wouldn't put it this way, but her story suggests to me that the way to love your husband more is to love yourself less. I prefer a less self-sacrificing arrangement.

And perhaps what Joanna is advocating isn't submission at all. Perhaps it is just a different kind of exchange. Elena Kirby plays Step 'n' Fetchit for a little house in the woods. Joanna Albright has traded her independence for some peace at home. But she hasn't really let go of all the power. There were times as she talked that she still sounded very much in charge.

> One time my husband was on the phone, just cursing and screaming and just so angry. And—whosh—here it comes up in me. And at that point, inwardly, it was like a voice saying "Are you going to reverence and honor your husband right now at this minute because he's your husband?" And my spirit came down like that, and I said, "Yes. I reverence and honor him." And it was like a miracle taking place. His language began to change. He hung up the phone and came and sat down.
>
> You can't believe how a man is influenced by the spiritual attitude of a woman. When he's held in honor and reverence, he has the power to be the authority. He has the power to care for and tenderly give to a woman what she wants. But never until she reverences and honors him.

In the end I found that I was not worried about Joanna, however hot and cold she made me run. The new rules that she and her husband have made seem likely to nourish them both. Joanna is taking care of herself too.

But there were other arrangements that troubled me long after I had turned off my tape recorder and said good-bye. I talked with some women who have given too much of themselves away, women who are bullied, women who are beaten. I used to think that loving and hating were totally different, but more and more I see that they're at opposite ends of the same continuum. These women seem to me to suffer from a basic confusion: The only way they can love their husbands is to hate themselves. Their interviews are striking because they are full of stories about the husband. He does this; he says this; he won't let me do this. I asked one abused wife to tell me about a typical weekday in her life, and she ran me through her husband's schedule. It was as if she didn't exist without him.

Missy Montgomery, the taxi driver who works the night shift to stay away from her husband's fists, talked about how he controls her. If they sit down with the children for a meal at home, everything must go according to his rules. The milk carton may not sit on the table; it must be put away again after each glass is refilled. The serving bowls must have covers so that the food stays warm. The meat platter must go back in the oven after it has been passed. And the rules are always changing—one week everyone should have paper napkins because cloth ones have to be washed; the next week paper napkins are wasteful.

I asked Missy what she would like to do if she had more

time for herself. She frowned and shook her head. "I don't know. . . . I don't know. . . . I don't know how to bowl."

I persisted. "Well, suppose you had one night a week when you didn't work and you didn't have to go home. What would you do with yourself?"

She thought about it. "I'd like to do probably what other women do, but I have no idea what it is. . . . They go to Tupperware parties and women things. . . . That's probably what I'd do." She sighed heavily and looked into her coffee cup. Another cab driver came in and said hello to her. She waited until he had gone and then she sighed again. "If I could do one thing I wanted to do a week, I'd go out with my friends on Friday night and not have to catch hell for it. That's one thing I'd really like to do. It would make going through the week worth having gone through. Where I can say what I want to say. Talk to whoever I want to talk to. And not have to run every sentence through my mind before it comes out my mouth to make sure it's not going to upset him." Missy's husband is easily upset and entirely predictable. When he is angry, he bludgeons her. Whenever she is with him, all of her energy is devoted to preventing his anger.

The pattern of coercion and compliance is found in other, more subtle marital arrangements. Hannah Brown's husband uses his anger alone as the instrument of control. She is pregnant and often feels too tired after supper to clean up the kitchen, but her husband insists that she should do the dishes before she goes to bed.

Most of the time I give in and do what he asks because he has a way of giving the cold shoulder. And I can't stand it. It's like I'd rather do what he wants me to do, no matter how much I don't want to do it, than to face the attitudes he's gonna have. He'll just kind of be ugly. Not really say anything—but he won't say. He won't talk to me. And I can't stand that. So he's like a child in a way, you know, children learn real quick the ways to handle people, I guess. But I mean he says what he wants me to do and if I don't do it, then I know that I might have a consequence. And I can't always live with the consequences.

He has never hit her, but Hannah remembers vividly the day he came close to it.

One time I just drove him up the wall. And see—this is it. I can nag and, you know, really there's a point where if he's in a mood or if you can't reach him logically with something, there's really no point in talking to him because you're only just going to make him mad, and the madder you get, you don't think reasonably. And one time—I'll never forget this—I don't remember what the circumstance was but he got really mad, and he put his fist right in my face and said, "I want to bust your fucking head." And he turned around and walked out of the room as fast as he could. And that's the closest I've really been to being hit.

And the minute he said that, I realized that I probably deserved to have my fucking head busted. [She laughed.] I pushed him too far. I hammered at

him and hammered at him until he was showing remarkable restraint not hitting me.

Assuming the blame is one way of keeping some power for
herself.

Irene Walker and her husband have hit each other in
anger throughout their nine-year marriage. She talks about her
physical abuse as if she were in charge of it. "I don't know,
I talk to other women about this and they say, 'You should
never have to take any kind of physical abuse' but if I know
what will set him off, it's my responsibility, I feel, to not set
him off as much as it's his responsibility to learn to control his
physical temper. In my equality of mind or of marriage, I don't
feel a man should never hit a woman because I think women
sometimes tend to provoke."

Two years ago Irene and her husband had a terrible
argument that ended in blows so serious they both landed in
the emergency room. They talked about splitting up then.
"We discussed about how we really, maybe we're not good
to each other. Maybe we do not bring out the best in each
other. Maybe we should separate for a while. But then we
think of the years we've had together and what we've been
through. And neither of us want to be alone. So I guess it's
really never gotten bad enough. I . . . during the years when
it was real bad all the time or a lot of the time, I used to say,
'If it's bad four days out of the week, that's more days than
it's good and that's when I'll leave.' And it never got that way.
'Cause I guess I would never let it. At the end of the week
I'd say, 'We had three bad days and four good days so I'll
stay.' "

Recently things have been better between them. And, again, Irene attributes the peace at home to a change in her behavior. "We don't argue anymore like we used to. I think I've done a magnificent . . . I think I set a goal for myself to see if I could behave. To see if I could mind him when it was important to him. To see if I could give up my own self for him. And I was able to do it. And most women do it without ever thinking about it. You know, they mind their husbands because they made that commitment that they would be that kind of wife. But it makes me real proud that I can do it, so it's easy to do."

Both Hannah Brown and Irene Walker give their marriages high ratings for satisfaction, 9 on a scale from 1–10. Missy Montgomery gives hers the lowest rating, a 1.

Valerie Reed gives her marriage an 8. "My daughter says I may as well tell you the whole story," she said as soon as we sat down to talk.

I nodded and switched on the tape recorder. "Okay."

Three months earlier Valerie and her husband of more than twenty years were sitting across the table from each other having dinner on a Wednesday night. Their one teenage son who is still at home had gone out to a baseball game, so it was just the two of them. Valerie chatted away. "The man who came to clean the gutters said the house really does need painting this spring. . . . Elizabeth called from school to say she'll be home a week early because she just has to get a job this summer. . . . Old Mrs. Williams came by today and gave me some more begonia cuttings—should I put them in the front or on the side?" Her husband seemed preoccupied. He answered her in monosyllables. He'd been awfully quiet lately.

Suddenly he looked up at her, started to say something, and burst into tears. Valerie sat in silence, stunned, until he could speak again. Then he said, "I can't go on like this."

Valerie's husband has been having an affair with a woman in his office for more than a year. All those nights when Valerie thought he was staying late to finish up his new accounts, all those early mornings when he told her he was going to play golf at the new public course across town, all those weekend business trips—he had been with this woman. And all he would say to Valerie that night was that he couldn't keep up the deception anymore.

Since then they have both lived a kind of double life. He spends most weekday nights "away on business" at a local motel. Weekends he is at home with his family. They go to the movies, to baseball games, out for a hamburger together. (Valerie's voice quivered. She took a deep breath.) "We still lead an absolutely perfectly normal life together other than we don't have sex any more."

He says he doesn't want a divorce. He also says that he can't give up his new love. Sometimes he and Valerie will talk a little about what happened to their marriage. He says things like one of her problems is that she didn't grow with him.

Valerie has confided in two of her close friends and in her oldest daughter. She also sought help from her parish priest, who has arranged for her to be in therapy with a local counselor. No one else knows. Her son does not appear to be suspicious. Her neighbors have not noticed the change.

I tried to imagine what it must be like to be Valerie, alone most nights under the powder-blue puff in the king-sized bed upstairs. Talking to her fourteen-year-old about his homework. Smiling and chatting with people after church on Sunday. I asked her how she was doing. She smiled bravely. "I spend a lot of time crying."

"Well, what's going on with him?" I asked. "Any idea?"

Oh, yes. She's thought about that a lot. "He really is a good person. I think he's terribly confused. It's—a lot of things have happened to him in his life, and I think they all came together in this. He's running from problems he doesn't even know what they are. I think he's definitely scared of getting old. He's getting a pot. He's starting to get bald. He's stooped shouldered. I look at him, and I think, 'It's not yourself you see in the mirror.' "

I asked Valerie what she thought was going to happen.

> I'm going to fight it out. I don't know if I'll win. I don't want him to go. I love him. Now I ask myself: How can I say that? My head says one thing, but my heart says the other. It seems to be very old-fashioned to say that you believe in your wedding vows.
>
> But you see, I also feel that running is the easy way out. It's easy for him to walk out that door and support me. All he's gotta do is bring me the money. He doesn't have to worry about the kids.
>
> I really feel that if I can just get him in therapy . . . I know what it's done for me in two months. If

he'll really go. And that's going to be the thing to see. I can see all this because I've had the therapy.

The three hours that I spent with Valerie Reed were among the most difficult in the entire *Wifestyles* study. I was so furious with her husband. And I wanted to shake her and shout at her, "It's not worth it! Give him up!" But she was trying so hard to keep herself together and tell me the whole story, and I wanted to respect her judgment even if I didn't feel like it. So we went through the long sad business together. My voice sounds cool on the tape. I remember holding back tears to help her get through it since that was what she had decided to do.

"Would you marry again?" I asked her.

"Yes."

"Would you marry him again?"

"Yes."

"How satisfied are you with your marriage, right now, today? Do it on a scale from 1 to 10, where 10 is high."

"Today?" (She sat for a long pause.) "Believe it or not, I'd still have to go for an 8. Through all the pain and through all this hurt, he still basically has the values and needs that I wanted. He's sensitive. He's . . . I enjoy him. We enjoy each other's company. At least I enjoy his company. He's basically still the person I knew except that right now he's very confused."

There was only one time in the entire interview when Valerie sounded angry. When we were finally through all the questions, I asked her if there was anything she had left out, anything else she wanted to say. She closed her eyes and leaned back against the sofa. Then she opened them.

I don't think that I'm alone in my age group—say the early forties—of what marriage was, what we thought it was going to be. I think we all believed we were going to get married, have children, and live happily ever after. And that was all there was going to be to it. We never asked, "Gee, are we going to be fulfilled?" We just automatically figured: You had children; you kept a house; you were fulfilled.

I think that our country has lost so many values because of me-ism. It seems that all of a sudden everybody wants to fulfill themselves—you read *Passages*. You read *Your Erroneous Zones*. You read—any of these. And everybody says, "You *must* be fulfilled." Well, that's fine, and I agree, to a point. But when does it become narcissistic? And when should your needs overwhelm somebody else's needs? Because you cannot live just unto yourself, I don't care what anybody says, and survive or be happy or be anything. Because you're living an unreal existence. To completely fulfill only yourself, you have to step on a lot of people.

Her voice got louder and it started to quiver again. "I'm tired of being blamed for twenty years of something that I did not contribute to entirely." Then she dropped her head back against the sofa. Her voice was soft again. "Anger will have to come out in time. I'm holding it back very well. Simply because I'm still trying very desperately . . . I realize that my husband is in deep need of help."

There's a long silence on the tape. Then she said, "I think you did a really good job with this."

And I said, "I think *you* did a good job."

Missy Montgomery's husband has been running around with other women since he and Missy first got married. Missy says it's a universal condition. "I know now that all men will go out with a woman if they can get by without getting caught. All of them. I don't think there's any exception. The right time and the right place, they will."

Among the women in the *Wifestyles* study, only 13 percent reported any experience with infidelity in their present marriage. That's about half the number usually given in studies of marital fidelity.[4] "If he cheated on me, I'd leave him . . . or kill him!" The wives who volunteered this information were mostly older women whose husbands had, in fact, always been faithful. Often the women made the threat and then took it back. "Oh, I used to say that. Now I'm not so sure. We'd probably survive it now."

The younger wives—those who grew up in the sixties or seventies—were less clear. A few rejected the whole concept of marriage as a sexually exclusive relationship. Because Toni Roberts is a smart political activist, she had the words to express this rejection. When I asked Toni about her own marital fidelity, she said, "I don't like the word *unfaithful.* To me marriage is not somebody owns somebody else. *Cheating* means you're cheating on somebody you own or want to own." She also said that she has had many "affairs"—her word of choice—both before and during her separation from her husband. "I'm just much more highly sexed than he is. I always have been."

Anne Morgan is also a feminist and living in a liberated marriage, but her feelings about infidelity are quite traditional. When I asked if her husband had been faithful to her, she said, "If he hasn't been, I don't want to know about it. If I knew about it, I'd be upset." Even so, she wonders if her feelings are reasonable. "When we were living together, he was going out with other women. And I knew it. And this was part of the his I-don't-want-to-be-attached thing. And I was *terribly jealous*. Really, maybe unreasonably, but I was terribly jealous. But there's just something psychological that I feel about, you know, if you want sex, I'm here. You really shouldn't need anybody else. And I'm aware that that's not always true. Maybe theoretically men would like varying types of partners, but that's not where I'm at."

Jody Kovar, the California woman who got engaged on April Fool's Day, started her marriage with the agreement that they would be faithful to each other for a year. "On our first anniversary, I said to him, 'Well, I've been married a year, maybe I need my freedom again.' Maybe we do. I certainly am attracted to other men. But I think that for me it would be very hard to have a double relationship or a triple relationship. I tend to really give so much of myself in a relationship that it would really hurt him and me if I was seeing someone else. And it would also, I think, not be fair to the other person because I'd want to give more and therefore take more away from my husband."

Had they ever discussed the possibility that their marriage

would include a permanent commitment to physical fidelity? "Yes. We both just said that we wanted to try this relationship with one another and right now it seemed like it would be a good thing. But we were unable to say that in a year or so maybe one of us would have a need to be with somebody else."

Jody looked out over the mountains and the bay and the bridge far below. "I think I'd be hurt, if that happened," she said. "I think he'd be hurt too. A lot of my friends that are married have open marriage, or whatever. I don't know how common it is. But, I mean, it is there. And the more I hear about them—at least all the people that I know that have had open marriages—it starts out kind of being cool and then things get very confusing, very confusing."

Nancy Simons and her husband have a very modern understanding about fidelity. After they'd been married about two years, he said that he wanted to be free to have sex with other women. Nancy was horrified.

So I said absolutely not. And then he said, "Okay. I'll be faithful to you. But I'll hate you forever." So I thought about it some more. He's the type of person that I do believe needs to feel that he has the freedom to do it. And I think I finally realized that. And I think that was the turning point of our marriage. And I said, "Okay. I think I finally realized that it's not fair. You're your own person. I have no right to control you. And therefore I'm telling you that though it would hurt me—and I do not think you should have an affair in that you should get emotionally involved. I think that would be detrimental to our marriage. But if you have sex relations, or whatever, with someone else then that's not really wrong. But the thing is— I know myself well enough—*don't tell me*. Whatever you do, keep it from me."

"And you know," she dropped her voice to a whisper, "I don't think he ever has."

The arrangement is simple: "Don't tell me, and I won't tell you." And it was Nancy who finally set the rules. "He says that he would like to know, but I refuse to tell him anything. If I had an affair, I am not going to tell him because I strongly believe: I love him and he loves me. But I think telling each other about affairs that happen now can only plant little harmful seeds."

Nancy likes to go out to bars, but her husband doesn't. Since they've reached this new agreement about sexual freedom, she's been going out by herself or with a group of friends. Often she meets men who buy her drinks and ask her to dance. "I'm right up front. I say, 'I'm happily married. My husband doesn't like to go out. I do. That's why I'm here.'" Then she goes home and tells her husband all about it. "He shows a slight discomfort. Just a slight. But I think he's fair to the point that he wouldn't really push the issue. You know what I mean? Intellectually he realizes he doesn't have a right to tell me not to do that if I want to do it."

Bobbi Webster has had one brief affair in her three years of marriage. She lost a lot of weight one spring, and she said, "I guess I got a little sassy." He was someone she met at work, an attractive man in his early fifties. But he was terrible in bed, and she didn't want to see him again. When I asked Bobbi how she thought marriage had changed in the last twenty-five years, she talked some more about her experience with infidelity.

> The world has changed so much. I think the world is so much more liberal. Well, for instance, my feelings about "cheating." If you ever told me four years ago that I would have, I would have said you're crazy. But now when it happened to me, I just thought of it as an experience.
>
> I think people today are more free with their sex. I don't think it's very good for marriage. There's married women and married men having affairs with each other, and it just gets to be a vicious circle. I don't think you can trust anybody nowadays. You really can't, you know. You asked me if I thought my husband had cheated. If you asked him, he might say, "Yes, I have, but I don't think my wife has." You can barely trust your mother these days. It's really sad.

Sara Corey sat on an old wicker rocker on her back porch with the tears running silently down her face when she told me about her husband's affair. It was many years ago, and he has said it will not happen again. "But since then I have always worried. It's always right there, and you're always worried about it."

And the one woman in the entire *Wifestyles* study who said she was having an affair now wouldn't talk about it at all unless I turned off the tape recorder. She insisted that I agree to special measures to preserve her anonymity. I was to change not only her name but the name of the place she and her family live and several other details. I decided afterward I couldn't tell it at all without risking that her husband would recognize it. When she told me about the affair, she assured me that it was the perfect solution: Her husband meets her economic and social needs; her lover meets her sexual and romantic needs. We were talking behind closed doors and the tape recorder was off, but still she whispered.

We used to talk about "the double standard" when I was a young woman and just beginning to think about such things. It meant that boys could have sex before they got married and still be considered decent people, but girls couldn't. I remember puzzling over how it could possibly work—who were the boys going to have sex with?

When I talked with the *Wifestyles* women about loving, they explained to me that wives and husbands express their love in different ways. "How does he show you that he loves you?" I asked.

He's not real lovey-dovey. You know, I asked him that one time, and he told me, "I'm still here."

I said, "Yeah. That's true. Is that how I know that you love me?"

He said, "Yeah."

He doesn't say that he loves me, but I tell him all the time. All the time. I know he gets tired of hearing it. I feel like I'm a very affectionate-type person.

I know that he loves me because he comes home to me every night. His main thought is his family.

He tries to give me what I want. He's very close to the children.

He shows me he loves me when he takes care of his kids.

He does a lot as far as the money deal of it goes. As far as owning things, property-wise, he does a lot of that.

And how do you show him that you love him?

Oh, doing all the old wifey things.

Keeping the house neat. Cooking the things he likes to eat. Doing the things he likes to do.

I try to make him comfortable and make sure he has everything he needs. Buy him things that he likes, you know, little food things. And cook things that he wants, you know, his favorite things.

I really try to tell him and show him by having the house clean and fixing his meals and having his clothes ready and all of that and being willing to go with him every time there is something to go to.

Cooking what he likes. You know, certain things he likes—that I really don't like and maybe the children don't. But because he likes them, I'll center everything around what he enjoys.

A good wife feeds her husband. She gives him food, attention, affection. A good husband comes home to be fed. (I exaggerate for effect.)

I do not mean to diminish the importance of coming home every night. Coming home every night, or being there when the other gets home if that's the way you've set it up, is the essence of the marital commitment. Everything else follows from it. Nor do I mean to diminish good old-fashioned responsibility for children or for bringing home the money to buy the children and the wife what they need—if that's the way you've set it up. I mean to say that being responsible and making money are not the same as nurturing, which is more subtle and more personal. Putting money in a bank account is not the same as knowing where the pain in the back from the day's tension will be and rubbing it away without being asked. Any more than doing another load of wash is the same as getting everybody together to walk over for ice cream after supper and sending the children ahead so you two can hold hands and talk.

I also mean to say that wives generally expect more giving from themselves than they do from their husbands, and that this limits both of them since it prevents him from feeding and her from getting fed.

Women also have a special responsibility to make the marriage work, they told me. "It's the woman who makes the overtures after a fight. And it's hard, you know, and you give in when you don't think you're wrong, but you give in because it's too miserable and because you love him too much to waste any more time like that."

"I always try not to take my mad to bed. I always had a kind of a rule: Don't go to bed mad. Even if it means apologizing for somethin' you don't think you should apologize for. If I go to bed mad I can't go to sleep. He does. [She laughed.] He just goes right to sleep. But I can't go to sleep. I wake up with guilt complexes next morning."

And it's the woman who makes love when she would rather roll over and go to sleep.

> I'm not that interested in sex any more. And I don't feel badly about it but it bothers me that if it continues how he will react to it. I think sooner or later I'm going to have to—if I don't come around—I'm going to find it enough of a bother to have to say something to him, and I don't think he'll take that that well. I never have turned him down since the one time—when he reacted so strongly. That was a rejection to him that's very hard to take. So it's easier for me to go along with it than to go through the real rejection that he feels. You know, deeply wounded.

> Frequently we make love in the morning when we get up. Sometimes he will wake me. I try to be nice when he does. [She laughed fully and sweetly.] But I have to because if I'm not nice, that upsets him. And it doesn't really bother me.

I asked the women I interviewed, What do you do when your husband talks to you about something that you're not interested in? More than half of them (56 percent) said that they pretended to be interested and heard him out. I also asked what the husband did when she talked to him about something that he wasn't interested in. Less than a third (31 percent) of the men returned the favor. "He turns me off with one ear," said one wife cheerfully. "Sure. I know he doesn't listen. I think I have his full attention, but if I ask him a question. . . . [She laughed.] And it's my fault, not his, because I chatter about something. I think a lot of the time his mind is on business. And I'm chattering at the wrong time. I have learned never to chatter at breakfast, for instance. He doesn't wake up until about ten o'clock in the morning, down the road by that time. So you don't make any decisions in the morning. See what you learn after forty years?"

At the end of each interview, I asked the question outright. "Who gives more to your marriage—you or your husband?" Thirty-six percent of the *Wifestyles* women said that they gave more. But almost half of the women (48 percent) said, "We both give equally." It's separate but equal as far as I can tell, a double standard if ever there was one.

There's a wonderful song in the Broadway show *My Fair Lady* called "Why Can't a Woman Be More Like a Man?" A handful of the younger wives who talked with me wanted to turn the question around. They want more emotional equality in their marriages. They want their husbands to take care of them the way tradition says a wife should take care of a husband. One complained that her husband was not as quick to help others as she was. "He's not thoughtful about other people. I'm the kind of person that if I see an opportunity to do something for someone, I will look for the opportunity and do it. And he doesn't do that. I don't know why he's like that, but he is." (I thought: He's like that because he's a man.)

Another said that she was more willing to sacrifice for her husband than he was for her. "I will do things just to be with him. He won't do things just to be with me—sometimes he will—but most of the time if I have a business banquet to go to or something else like that, he says, 'Do I *have* to go?' And I get so angry with him because I resent that unwillingness. To me marriage implies a willingness to help the other partner even through the bad times—you know what I mean? Even if there is an unpleasant task and we haven't seen each other, let's at least be together. That's the way I look at it. He doesn't always look at it that way."

A third young woman drew a fine distinction between two kinds of support.

What he considers support is something different from what I consider support. When I need support I feel like it should be free, gratis, for nothing. That it should just *be there*, available to me when I need it. And I shouldn't have to ask for it. He has always been just the opposite. He'll give support, willingly and lovingly, but he's always asked for it when he's needed it, and he's always felt like I should ask for it. That it's okay for me to say, "Listen, I need you for this and this and this. This is going on in my life—and will you come through for me? Will you do this specific thing?" You see what I'm saying? Whereas I just always felt like I wanted him to understand almost implicitly.

These are high standards, lofty goals. But if women and men are going to come into full maturity, men need to learn nurturing even as women need to learn independence. And the best place for learning to nurture may well be with one's own children. That's where women refine their caretaking skills. As more fathers become involved in the daily care of their children, it seems reasonable to hope for a generation of husbands who will be able to love their wives as fully and tenderly as a good wife is supposed to love her husband.

Six

MAKING THE BEST OF IT

I suppose it is like marriage, that when you get into it, you find it is the beginning, not the end, of the struggle to make love work.

—Flannery O'Connor, The Habit of Being

accommodate . . .**1:** *to make fit, suitable, or congruous* **2:** *to bring into agreement or concord* **3:** *to furnish with something desired, needed, or suited* . . . **4:** *to make room for* . . . **5:** *to give consideration to, allow for* . . . *to adapt oneself.*

—Webster's New Collegiate Dictionary

The summer that I was finishing this book I spent a lot of my Sunday afternoons sitting with some good friends on their deck drinking rum punch and complaining. My friends, a couple in their late thirties with three little kids, had read parts of the manuscript, and we used to talk about it some. The husband liked to imagine that I was harboring some rabid feminist rage beneath my suburban Mommy facade; he teased me about the book's being too "soft." When it came time to write the conclusion, he said, "You'll never do it. You're too objective." He suggested that I visit one of the remaining bastions of male supremacist power—the Knickerbocker Club in New York City, perhaps—and work up a good lather and then come home and finish the book.

I was bemused. I certainly don't think of this book as soft or of myself as objective in it. But what he meant is that I'm not mad anymore, and he is right. Something happened in the three years that I was working on the book. Maybe it was that I became a mother. Maybe it was that we celebrated our fifth wedding anniversary and I realized that I never think about leaving anymore. Maybe it was that I spent three hundred hours talking to women about their marriages. In any case, I'm more settled than I used to be.

As for conclusions, while it's obvious by now that I would rather tell you a story than make you a list, there are certain strands running through the stories collected here that ought to be drawn together. For all the diversity of the *Wifestyles* women, certain themes are constant.

1. *Women have more choices than they used to, and this makes their lives more difficult as well as more rich.* A generation ago most women in this country got married, stayed married, bore children, stayed home with their children, and kept house. Now more women can choose to do other things, and the questions are endless: Should I get married? Should I stay married? Should I wash the dishes? All the time? Should I have children? Should I have more children? How many more? How long should I stay home with them? Is it okay if I get a job? Is it okay if I don't get a job? Not every woman is faced

with all of these questions. Many must work to help support their families, for example, but since working women are not as universally accepted as working men, a woman who works may still feel torn about it.

Having lots of choices is stressful by definition. It can leave a person feeling uneasy, incomplete, on the line all the time. Some women look back wistfully to an earlier time when wives seemed much more sure about what they should do and be. When these women were little girls, for example, most of their mothers stayed home without asking why.

It's also very hard to feel sure that you're doing the right thing when there is no consensus in the larger community about what the right thing is. Many women live with a low-grade, nagging anxiety about whether or not they have made the best decisions for themselves and their family, no matter what their decisions have been. Being able to choose is what separates the children from the adults, and I would not be willing to give up any of the choices I have. But I can't help thinking sometimes that my life would be a whole lot easier if I didn't feel quite so responsible for it.

It is in the context of the stress that comes from having many choices that I finally understand what I heard in my interviews about the women's movement. I think that the anger and ambivalence the *Wifestyles* women express about feminism comes from the tension created in their own lives by so many choices. The women's movement is not the only or even the primary reason for the social changes that have occurred in the last twenty years, but the movement is taking the rap for the fact that the world will never be the same.

When a woman can choose to put her own needs first,

the equilibrium of the family is inevitably disturbed. One wife who talked to me had watched several of her friends go through painful divorces in the last few years, and she was angry about the women's movement.

> I know a lot of women who have decided that they are more important than they thought they were prior to reading about the women's movement in the newspaper. And they could not handle the submissive relationship in the marriage. They were not willing to be submissive or cooperative in *any* way. And it came down to the point where they would not give in on *anything*. They just couldn't handle marriage any more. And so they all have gotten divorced. . . . And it wasn't a matter of—it isn't that they had a bad marriage or that they were particularly unhappy. And in the three or four years since then, I can't say that the children are better off because they were in a bad marriage, and I can't say that the woman is happier or that the man is happier. But in all cases it was a miserable thing for them to go through, and I don't think they're better off for having done it.

In every marriage both partners find a balance between giving and taking. But the balance seems more precarious these days. If women are no longer willing to give as they remember their mothers giving, then everything else must change. And who's going to take up the slack? Another woman I interviewed sees wives as more selfish now, and she blames the women's movement. "There has been too much emphasis on

Me First. I don't think a marriage can work unless both people are willing to give 90 percent. Now, maybe the women's movement has caused men to be more willing to give than they were previously. [Her voice says she doubts it.] I don't think it's caused *women* to be more willing to give. . . . So I think it's had a more negative effect because there are many more women who are now *not* willing to give than were before. And I don't think there's been enough of a balance of men willing—or able—to give [more]."

Women are making more choices to satisfy their own needs than they used to. Some of them are choosing to break up their marriages. A woman who has chosen to remain married or to put the needs of others before her own may feel her behavior as a challenge. At the heart of the anger about the women's movement lies an uncertainty about oneself—it is simply more difficult to feel secure in one's own decisions these days. And the temptation to think less of those who make different choices is strong.

Feminism and marriage are often uneasy partners at best. Among the *Wifestyles* women there is a strong inverse relationship between marital satisfaction and positive feelings about the women's movement. Wives who feel that the women's movement has had a bad effect on marriage are more satisfied than those who think the effect has been good.* Sixty-seven percent of the women who have only bad things to say about feminism rate their own marriages 9 or 10, while

---

*This relationship is apparently a function of age. A higher percentage of the over-forty women (51 percent vs. 34 percent) rate their marriages 9–10 for satisfaction, and 60 percent of the women over forty say that the effect of the women's movement on marriage has been bad. See Tables 14 and 15 in the Technical Appendix.

only 46 percent of those who have only good things to say give their own marriages the highest rating. But the least satisfaction of all is found among the women who can't make up their minds, those who had both good and bad things to say about the women's movement. More than half (57 percent) of these undecided wives gave their marriages the lowest (1–7) satisfaction ratings.

Among the younger women in the *Wifestyles* study were several who found that getting married had changed their feminist convictions. One woman in her early thirties confessed, "I think when I first got married that equality to me was—let's do everything my way. And now we get along much better if he says, 'Please don't buy this. We don't have the money.' And I say, 'Okay.' Instead of arguing or pleading or getting mad."

Another young woman, still a bride, experienced the opposite development. She expected to play the traditional role as a wife, but she found it didn't suit her.

I've disagreed with a lot of women's libbers before because a lot of times they come off as crass and aggressive. I do not want to be labeled that. I have always *thought* that I thought that the man should be the head of the house. I always felt like the man should take care of the woman. These are things I have been raised with and felt, that the man should open up doors, be very chivalrous, you know.

But then I get to my marriage, and I feel as if I have just as much say-so in what goes on and I do not look at my husband as the head of this household.

I feel like it's split fifty–fifty down the middle. I'm not sure how I feel about that. I get mad. I defend my rights. When we first got married and he bitched at me about cleaning the house, I thought, "Gosh, I'm going to be a maid-servant to him." And I refuse to be that. I didn't know I had that fighting instinct, you know, because I will raise hell with him about it. And I think one reason why is that I've come of age, so to speak. I know a lot more about myself than I did, and I make no apologies for myself.

But there are times when I feel "Gosh, I am the one who is hustling around to make more money and he is sitting on his butt." I do not feel taken care of a lot of times. I would love the luxury of not having to work. But then, I'm thinking, if I want this career and I want all these equal rights, then why should I feel all this resentment toward him? That he doesn't feel so protectively toward me. Sometimes I feel like something's missing there, and I'm confused as to what I want because I think I want [to have] my cake and eat it too.

So I'm confused about what I expect and if what I expect means that I can't have certain things. But I do feel like we share equally in this marriage. He is not a male chauvinist. He thinks I am smart. He thinks I have just as much say-so as he does, and I feel like that's very good. But there's still some times I wish I had that sense of security that some women feel that stay at home and have their husbands take care of them.

All of that turmoil and disagreement make for a less satisfying marriage. She gave her marriage a rating of 7, which is lower than 74 percent of the women in the study.

I too struggle with being married and a feminist. One week last spring we had a terrible time at our house. First my husband was sick in bed for a couple of days, and then Christopher got the bug and couldn't go out to nursery school or to his babysitter. I was supposed to be writing, but somebody had to stay home with our son and since my husband had already missed two days of work, he felt that he had to go in to his office. I simmered along, feeling more and more resentful, and finally I just exploded one night right after he got home from work.

Afterward I felt sorry and puzzled. I thought we had these things worked out. Why had I been so angry again? Suddenly it struck me. The week before I had reread a collection of essays from the first *Ms.* magazine, writing full of fine fresh feminist anger. Reading it again had rekindled some of my old rage, and when the opportunity arose I was ready to be angry. The anger that the feminist movement has focused for women is a useful and powerful political tool. The energy of that anger has generated much good for me and for all women everywhere. But at that particular moment in my life, it was not helpful to be so angry. I just can't stay married if I'm that mad all the time.

I hope that the conflicts that have been focused by the women's movement will become less intense in the next decade. If feminism can mature and move toward the second stage outlined by Betty Friedan, the issues that most women care about most—home, family, children—will become more closely identified with the women's movement. At the same time, the younger women who see good in what the women's movement has already done for marriage will grow older. Their daughters will become the brides of the next generation. A woman who grew up and married in the sixties and seventies faced a world that was quite unlike her mother's world, but for her daughter the world of many choices will be a more familiar—and hopefully less threatening—place.

2. *No matter what lifestyle a married woman chooses these days, she is likely to want more from her life than her mother did.* This is a time of high expectations, especially for married women as they try to preserve the best of the old values and enjoy new opportunities.

Some struggle to balance their freedom with the commitment that marriage requires. They want to preserve a strong sense of personal identity and also to enjoy sharing their lives with their husbands and families. Toward the end of the *Wifestyles* interview, I asked, "What's one advantage of being married?" Young and old agree that the main attraction of marriage is the commitment to share a lifetime with another person. Fifty-four percent of the over-forty women and 44 percent of the forty-and-under women said that one advantage of being married is companionship.[1] "I can't possibly imagine being single," said one woman in her forties who has been married for twenty years. "I think that it's a great comfort to know that you have somebody else that depends on you and that you depend on."

Several of the women responded to this question by raising the specter of the single life. A wife in her fifties said,

"A single life is a lonely life. Women that are single are always looking for something."

A wife in her twenties who had been single herself only a few years before said that she felt marriage was less superficial and lonely than living alone. "I like being married a lot better than being single. I really do. 'Cause it's having someone there all the time, you know. Like I said he's my best friend, and I tell him just about everything, and you've always got someone to be honest to."

Another young woman said the chief advantage of being married is "not having to worry if I have a date on Friday night." And then she laughed and added, "It's knowing that I'll always have somebody to talk to and he'll always listen whether it's good or bad that I have to say."

Both the younger and the older women acknowledge the importance of a shared history, the value of having days and weeks and years of living side by side in good times and hard times. A thirty-year-old wife whose early married years had been full of quarrels and problems said that their shared history had bonded her and her husband together even though it was a painful history. "I think that love is as much a connection as it is an action. It's not: I stand back here and love this person. It's like: We're bound together and that's love as much as what you think love is when you're first meeting somebody and you're thinking you're in love with them."

It's not surprising that married women continue to cherish the quiet comforts and tensile strengths of a lifetime commitment. But now they want more than companionship. I also asked about the main disadvantage of being married, and again the older and younger *Wifestyles* women agree. The one disadvantage most often mentioned by both groups was loss of freedom—22 percent of those over forty and 28 percent of those forty and under talked about being confined by their marital state. A wife in her thirties said, "Well now, you gotta be back on time. You gotta get on home. You can't take longer if you want to. There's somebody you gotta tell. It's more or less like back when I was a child. You know, 'Mama, I gotta go to the store.' And she says, 'Well, you gotta be back by four o'clock.' And I rushed to get back. That's one of the disadvantages of marriages."

Another woman echoed her. "A disadvantage of being married is not being able to just pick up and go. That's a big disadvantage when you're just right in the middle of things and—uh, oh, you've got to consider someone else."

Some wives have fantasies about what they could do if they were not married. "If I were alone," said one, "I could spend more time by myself and do what I wanted to do and not have to worry about how's this person going to think about what I do. How's he going to handle this or that."

Another woman dreamed of having some time at home that was just her time. "Sometimes now I feel when I get off of work that I'd like to go home and just get in bed, look at television, not eat or do anything. But you can't do that. You have a husband that wants dinner so you gotta go home and cook dinner."

Among the younger women, some expressed a feeling of being confined by the need to work out the problems that arose in their marriages. When they were single, they could just break off a relationship when things got tough. Now that they're married, they have to resolve their differences. A wife in her twenties said the main disadvantage of being married is "the need to make things work when you disagree. If you have friends or relatives, you can walk away from the problem, but being married, you have to work it out. You cannot walk away. Sometimes it would be a lot easier just to—you know —walk away, ignore the problem. Do things your way all the time."

And a forty-year-old woman who has been married for five years said the hardest thing about being married for her was "having to stick it out. You know, not just moving on and doing it easy. It's hard instead of easy."

Henry David Thoreau once remarked that if you travel alone you can begin today, but if you want to travel with someone else you must wait until the other person is ready. It's a trade-off—you give up some of the opportunity to set the pace for the pleasure of another's company on the road. The women in the *Wifestyles* study told me that the advantage of being married is companionship and the disadvantage is loss of freedom. Put side by side, these two answers reveal a paradox. You can't have companionship without giving up some freedom. A man can't expect his wife to come home at night if he's never there. A woman can't expect her husband to fix supper unless she sits down to eat it when it's ready. Everybody knows you have to be willing to give if you want to get.

Except lately self-sacrifice has gone out of style. For the past two decades, people have been testing the limits of these old assumptions as never before. Self-fulfillment is all the fashion now. And the expectation for marriage is that somehow you can have it all.

Making the Best of It

The wish to have it all is also expressed in the current multiplication of a married woman's roles. As they combine the traditional work of keeping house and raising children with the new work of "working," many women find themselves caught in the Superwoman trap. They want to be good wives and good mothers and still put in a forty-hour week away from home. They want their kitchen floors to be as clean as their mothers' were. They feel bad because they don't have time to make spaghetti sauce from scratch. But they also want to be paid a decent wage at work. Some of them even want the work to be fulfilling. It's no wonder that these women are exhausted and frustrated; they have too much to do and they expect too much of themselves.

Married couples are under new pressure from another source: the expectation that the honeymoon can go on forever. The sexual revolution of the past two decades has raised an impossible new standard: Married people are supposed to continue to be as close and intimate as new lovers. Even people with little children feel deprived if they can't find the time and energy for their own relationship too. One *Wifestyles* woman in her late thirties told me that she and her husband expect to feel close to each other all the time. "And mediocre isn't okay. If you know what that feels like, to really be in synch with another person, when it's not happening, that just doesn't work anymore. It's not enough. And both of us have high demands —we like to know what's going on with the other person and we like to feel intimate and close and we have worked very hard all the way through this marriage to get that."

All of these new demands can be so exhausting that they are self-defeating. I think the era of the Superwoman is already passing and that women will gradually be able to give up their wish to be perfect in everything as it becomes clear how much it costs to try to do that. Several of the women I interviewed talked about the need to become more realistic and mature in their expectations about marriage in general. One said, "We look for too much in other people. I think we expect the other person to produce a miracle to make us happy, and that's not the way it works. We need to come down off our high horses, so to speak, and give a little. I think that marriage can be happy if we aren't looking for too much from the other person. If we don't just go out and say: Well, come on in here and make me happy."

Another wife put it this way: "Too many people expect marriage to give them something, to do something for them, and it doesn't work that way. Marriage is something that the two people *do for.*"

At the same time, I expect that married women will continue to have more opportunities than their mothers did. Women are not going to go back to the kitchen and close the door. They will continue to work and to enjoy the sense of self-worth that comes from having a life apart from the family. As women are able to let go of the inappropriate standards taken from an earlier, less-dimensional version of what a wife should be, the pressure on them should ease.

3. *Husbands are beginning to share in the work of keeping house and especially in the work of raising children.* As things have changed so much for married women in the past two decades, they have also changed for married men. If you assume that most women were doing all or almost all of the housekeeping

and child raising twenty years ago, then the *Wifestyles* study shows that husbands are doing more at home. Measured on the 5-point scale (where 1 = she does all or almost all, 2 = she does most, 3 = they split it fifty-fifty, 4 = he does most, and 5 = he does all or almost all), housework has moved from 1.0 to 2.2 and child care has moved from 1.0 to 2.6. All qualifications aside for the moment, that *is* progress. It's not enough. But it's a start.

It is also clear that some husbands would do more with the children and around the house if their wives would let them. Many women have a perfectly understandable feeling of possessiveness about the tasks that were traditionally theirs. They enjoy doing woman's work and don't want to give it up. And, of course, most women are more skillful in these tasks than most men. For all of these reasons, some wives are finding that the chief obstacle to a more equal sharing of household and child-care tasks is their own inability to surrender the traditional role. To paraphrase Pogo, she has met the enemy, and it is herself.

The question of who washes the dishes has become symbolic of the whole struggle to get wives out from under the domestic yoke of their traditional role, but very few of the women I talked to are going to the barricades over this issue. No matter who's washing the dishes in a particular household, the woman's marital satisfaction is not affected by her housework score. Sharing housework and child-care responsibility is terribly important to me and a few of the *Wifestyles* women, but it is not central to the majority.

Nevertheless, I expect the movement toward more equal sharing of housework and child care to continue. The results of the *Wifestyles* study hint at which women are more likely to get help from their husbands at home. We have seen that a woman who has a job does not necessarily have a higher housework score (indicating more help from her husband) than a woman who is unemployed. There is no significant difference in the *Wifestyles* study between working and non-working wives in housework scores.* There *is* a significant relationship, however, between a woman's housework score and her answer to the question "Who earns the money [in your family]?" Almost half (44 percent) of the wives who see themselves as earning on an equal basis with their husbands have high housework scores (2.5 or better). Among wives who say that their husbands earn all or almost all of the money, exactly half have low housework scores (less than 1.76).† So the women who say their work makes a significant contribution to the support of their family are also the women whose husbands help out the most at home, while those who are not employed or who see their earnings as insignificant when compared with their husbands' earnings are also the women who are still doing most of the housework.

The relationship suggests a connection between a working woman's self-esteem and a husband who washes the dishes. In families in which the wife feels proud of her own earning power and the couple is not threatened by her working, conditions are good for the sharing of housework. On the other hand, if a wife diminishes the importance of her own earning —because she is uncomfortable in the working woman's role,

---

*See Table 2 in the Technical Appendix.
†See Table 16 in the Technical Appendix.

out of deference to her husband's feelings, or because she earns so little in comparison to him—then she is less likely to get help from her husband with the work at home. As more wives become comfortable in their roles as working women, it seems reasonable to hope that both wives and husbands will find ways to share the work at home more equally.

I believe that this movement toward a greater domestic role for men is the necessary and inevitable counterbalance of the return of married women to the world of work. And I think that together these two changes have the potential to transform the relationship between wives and husbands in a truly revolutionary way. As women *leave* home and men *come* home they can begin to understand and appreciate each other in ways that have not been possible since the industrial revolution.

Approaching a more equal balance in their domestic and working roles, both wives and husbands can become fuller, richer, more dimensional people. Women who are comfortable in the world of work have the opportunity to develop more independence, assertiveness, and self-esteem. Men who have a genuine role at home have a chance to become more loving, patient, tender, and nurturing. As the differences between the sexes diminish, women and men will be able to share their lives more completely and to feel a sympathy for each other that is often impossible under the traditional arrangement.

4. *In the midst of an era of great social change among married women, some very important things have stayed the same.* (This is the sort of conclusion that drives my friend who makes the

rum punch crazy. "Oh, come on," he says. "Have things changed or haven't they?") Life has certainly changed in the last twenty years, especially for women. But the things that were most important to married women a generation ago—home, husband, children, family—are still the most important.

Some of the *Wifestyles* women were self-conscious about their love of the simple, everyday pleasures. I wish I had counted the number of times the women who talked to me said their lives were boring. In New York City Doris Sullivan described the quiet, ordinary life she shares with her husband. "We read a lot. We go to the library. We walk. We shop. We play Scrabble almost every day. . . . It doesn't sound very exciting, and it probably isn't."

Thousands of miles away in Dallas, Texas, another woman described her everyday life. "We lead the kind of life that they don't play up in the movies or anything anymore because they think nobody lives that way. But we sure do. You know, we go to bed at ten-thirty and we get up at six and everybody goes to work. And we all sit around and have breakfast. A very square type of life that probably most people think doesn't exist anymore. I have always made his breakfast. I would never give him hot dogs during the week. We have meat and potato and vegetable dinner every night."

And in Iowa, I asked a farm woman what she would change about her marriage if she could change one thing. She said, "I can't think of a single thing, isn't that boring?"

"No," I replied. "That's satisfied."

Even Deborah Rosen, who has what she and I both consider to be an unusually happy marriage, described the relationship at one point as if it were nothing special. "We are committed to our marriage in, I think, a positive way. And we've had no crises in that sense. We have our disagreements about things, but that's not a matter of whether the marriage will continue or not. So we're kind of mundane. We're not really dramatic, in a soap opera sense."

One of the things that moved me most in the year that I spent interviewing was a growing sense of the beauty and importance of a married woman's day-to-day life. The rhythm and texture of her ordinary days seem more and more extraordinary to me because so much of what a woman does is tied to the very essence of life. Whether she is feeding her family or nurturing her children, the work that a woman does in her role as wife and mother is among the most essential work there is.

A deep continuity pervades the ordinary things that women do—I do what my mother did and her mother before her. No matter how much women change, this somehow stays the same and links us together.

Some of the women who talked with me had a clear sense of the beauty and wonder in their lives. One told me that she celebrates every day as it comes. Another said, "It's taken me a long time but I've come to the conclusion: Appreciate what you have and be happy right now because happiness is right in front of you."

A woman who had been successfully treated for cancer expressed her pleasure in her family and their everyday life more clearly than anyone else in the study.

Once you know that you could die, everything changes. And you just appreciate things a lot better and a lot more. And you just don't let a lot of crappy things get in the way. The important things suddenly become right in front of you. And I guess that's always been a background of everything in our family. We focus in on the kids and our relationships and things we do together. So you don't have to live for a lot of other things or a lot of other people. . . . I don't think I'm going to die of cancer anymore. I think a lot of other things are going to get me first, but it does help you to kind of just realize that you're not here all the time and you only live once and you . . . if you're going to live, you got to enjoy things now and do what you're going to do. I know that I appreciate what I have.

The fact that people stay married day after ordinary day seems extraordinary to me too. In the face of all the odds, couples go right on dreaming the impossible dream and making it work, putting one foot in front of the other. When I started this book I was looking for another conclusion. I wanted to find the wide world full of angry women struggling to loosen the bonds of traditional marriage. I did not find them. Oh, I found anger and pain, to be sure, but not mostly. Mostly I found women who were working it out, women who were satisfied with their marriage. Some of them do some variation of the traditional thing; others are trying new patterns of accommodation. But the *Wifestyles* women are neither burning for change nor chafing under their marital constraints. I went looking for the new rules that make marriage work today, and what I found is that the rules are the same.

And now I do have to tell a couple more stories. . . . I was driving to meet Ruth Miller, up over the Idaho mountains in my brother's little blue Gremlin, when the state trooper pulled me over. He had one of those new radar guns; I was doing almost seventy in a fifty-five-mile-an-hour zone, just dreaming along that wide-open road with nobody on it but me. I had never been stopped for speeding before. I could feel my face get hot as I handed over my out-of-state driver's license and mumbled through the requisite excuses: unfamiliar road, late for my appointment, just wasn't paying very much attention, sir. He was businesslike and let me go with a warning.

My face was still hot when I pulled into Ruth's driveway ten minutes later. (She was amused. "That old Brian, he just sits up there behind the filling station, waiting for his daily victim to go by.") She is a small, almost fragile-looking woman in her early fifties, very ladylike and utterly calm. She looked as if she had just come from a good beauty parlor, although there isn't a beauty parlor for fifty miles. Ruth seemed quite uneasy when we first sat down. The trooper had made me late, and she had had too much time to wonder what I would ask her. But even when she was most nervous, I had the sense of a deep peace in this woman. She told me some of it: the loneliness of a bitter childhood, the death of their own first child at birth, the pain of a debilitating illness misdiagnosed for several years and then difficult to treat. But, she said, these things are in the past. Adversity overcome is what I saw on her face.

She and her husband both grew up in this valley. They got married the summer after she finished high school. He has always farmed, except when he was in the service, first as a hired man on another man's place and then on their own farm. When I asked her occupation, she smiled. "Oh, I'm a housewife." Her husband earns all the money, she said. "It's the way it should be. I guess it's just the way—the time I was raised, the women just didn't work. And it's, ah, a protected feeling to me, that he wants to do it and that I am sort of the pampered one who doesn't have to do this." She has always stayed at home.

"At home" is on the farm, of course: the house, the big sheds full of machinery behind the house, and the land all around, fourteen hundred acres in wheat and hay. Her husband stays at home too, since home is where he works. And, it turns out, Ruth works with him. She didn't put it this way, but she's a farmer too.

When they were first married, she used to stay in the house, but she didn't like it, even then. "It always hurt to be separated from him, even just for the hours that he worked, because we were so close." After they got their own place, she worked out in the field with him whenever she could. And when the children were big enough to help, they both had regular chores.

Now that it's just the two of them again, they work together all the time. "I work in the field with him when it's necessary. Not so much of the heavy work as I did a few years back, but. . . . We share everything. We're together all the time. In the mornings he'll go check the stacks and the hay haulers and the ground or something, and I go with him, whether anything else gets done or not. I go. And whenever he has to go for parts or something, I go. We very seldom go anyplace alone."

Ruth and I talked a little about the times when she and her husband disagree. They don't actually fight, she said. "We sort of argue. Not really that we get mad. We've never done that. But if I don't agree or something, I push it until we get it worked out to see which is right or wrong. And he does the same way. But we never fight never, really, where it gets so bad there has to be make up. It's just a discussion. There's just never been anything to fight about. We've always talked." I asked about yelling, and she said they never raise their voices at each other. Later she said they always listen to each other, and neither of them has bad moods. I asked her to name one disadvantage of being married. Ruth couldn't think of anything.

On the 1–10 satisfaction scale, she gave her marriage a 10. She said the best thing about the marriage is "the companionship and the closeness we have. I just can't believe it. I just marvel at it. When I see so many people—one goes one way and one goes the other. This is my money and this is yours. It's just almost overwhelming." I asked Ruth if she had any idea why her marriage worked so well. "I had a rough childhood, and I just wanted a home. I never really had one. He's a very affectionate man, from the very beginning. And it was something I wanted so bad. I think we both just wanted it so bad."

We saw Ruth's husband working in one of the sheds when she walked with me out the back door to the car. "Did you want to meet him?" she asked.

"Oh. Sure." I was almost always uncomfortable when I was introduced to the husband of a woman I had interviewed. Generally the man would seem suspicious: What had passed between his wife and me about him? And I would feel guilty, as if I were harboring secrets. But Ruth's husband just smiled and nodded. He has the same steady sense of calm that she does. Adversity overcome.

Driving back over the mountain, staying carefully at fifty-five, I had time to think about Ruth's story. "Well, I just don't believe it," I said to myself at first. "It's too good to be true. . . . Together *all* the time and *no* fighting? Come on—she's got to be hiding something." But it was a long way to town, and my disbelief didn't hold up. By the time I got there I had recognized the feeling underneath. It was pure and simple, and once I saw it, perfectly clear. I felt jealous of Ruth Miller.

Marjorie Barnes has spent most of her thirty-odd married years in one sort of combat or another. As soon as her last toddler was finally out of diapers she began fighting for herself: to go to school, to stay in school, to finish school, to get a job, to get some help at home. And the children went on needing—new shoes, summer camp, prom dresses, college. When all of that was finally over, when the kids were grown and she got tenure and it seemed that life would finally settle down, Marjorie's husband suddenly turned into a monster. It started around his fortieth birthday. He became moody, easily upset, angry at everybody all the time. Marjorie was beside herself. "I felt either I'm going crazy or he is. The kids were finally grown and I wondered if I was just finally seeing him as he was. If this was the man he had become, then I think I would have ended it. And I finally got a book that helped me a great deal to get a perspective and really hang on long enough to see if he was going through a crisis. So I hung on, learned to keep my mouth shut. . . . All I could think of was the elephant bulls in rutting season that just go mad for no reason. And nobody could do anything with them. So I just got out of the way and let it happen."

The crisis continued for several years and then it gradually abated. Looking back on it now, Marjorie is glad she stuck it out.

If you can ride it out the marriage will be much better, and he will appreciate you so much more for having gone through it with him. Now, it's never been said —but I definitely feel that way. Now he'll do things like come out and offer to help with the dishes. I'm sure his mother almost fainted Easter Sunday when he did that. . . . He's become much more aware of what I'm doing and much more helpful. Even after supper some nights he'll say, "Gee, I'll do the dishes tonight. You go in and sit down." And *that* is just unheard of.

Even our daughter said when she came up, "Boy, Dad. This is a new one. I never saw you in the dishpan."

He said, "Well, don't talk about it."

Now we're building a relationship, and we're really having fun together again. We look forward to the weekends. He never used to go to the grocery store. He hated grocery shopping or any kind of shopping. And now all of a sudden here we are on Saturdays shopping together—and not fighting about what we're going to buy. So it's just all kind of going back to the way it was before we had the children. Just really enjoying each other again.

When I asked Marjorie to rate her marriage for satisfaction, she said, "I don't see, knowing people as they are, how it could be much better than it is. I'd say 9 or 10."

Both Ruth Miller and Marjorie Barnes are in their fifties. Each woman has invested over thirty years in her marriage— that's all of her adult life, more than ten thousand mornings sitting across from the same man at the breakfast table. They have buried her parents and his parents. Their children have grown up and left home. And still her toothbrush sits next to his on the bathroom shelf.

Among the *Wifestyles* women, it is the older ones who are most satisfied with their marriages.[2] Just over half (51 percent) of the over-forty group gave their marriages a 9 or a 10 for satisfaction. Among the younger group, those twenty to forty years old, only a third (34 percent) gave a rating of 9 or 10. The difference is even more striking at the other end of the scale among the least-satisfied women, those who gave their marriages a rating of 1 to 7. Thirty-five percent of the younger women are in this least-satisfied group, while only 15 percent of the older women are.*

*See Table 17 in the Technical Appendix.

It is not surprising, then, that the older women are committed to the way things are. Asked what they would change in their marriages if they could change one thing, 30 percent of the women over forty said "Nothing." Only 7 percent of the younger women said that. Asked to name a disadvantage of marriage, 48 percent of the older women said they couldn't think of one. Among the younger wives, only 15 percent suffered from this singular failure of imagination. The pattern is repeated in the responses to the question about leaving ("Have you ever thought of leaving your husband?"). Only 29 percent of the over-forty group said that they had thought of leaving him, but 64 percent of the forty-and-under group admit to such thoughts.

The satisfaction question, the question about change, the disadvantage question, and the question about leaving were all designed to get at the woman's basic evaluation of her marriage. In each case there are significant differences between the responses of the older and younger women. I suppose the simplest and most obvious explanation is that women who aren't satisfied with their marriage these days don't stay married. As a wife continues her commitment to her marriage year after year, she becomes part of a group who have chosen to stay with the marital relationship. Among women over forty are many who have been divorced and some who have been widowed. Those who are still married after twenty or thirty or forty years are the survivors.

The older women have been married longer, of course.[3] They have had more time to make it work, more time to shape their marriage into something that satisfies them. And they've come to accept their marriage, to take it for what it is. One woman, married over twenty years, has just come to peace with herself in the recent past.

It finally leveled out a few years ago. I don't get upset with him any more. I used to really get upset with him, and it just isn't worth it. He is a good father. He's a good husband. I know he doesn't chase. He is a good guy. Oh, sure, there are a lot of things I wish he would do—he's overweight now; I wish he were not overweight. I wish he had more stamina, more get up and go. Everything has to be organized for him. I'm more venturesome. I wish we had more sex. . . . It took me a long time to say "This is a good guy you've got here. You're not going to make him into a model." I've adjusted. I counted my blessings, I guess.

People have asked me if I've ever considered divorce, and I say, "Murder, yes. Divorce, never!" I had to train him. I had to bring him up my way. I've got too much time invested now, and it takes too long to train one.

Her satisfaction rating? She gave the marriage a good solid 9.

The longer a woman stays with something, the more of herself she has invested in it. After all those years of whatever compromises the marriage has required, it surely becomes harder to think of giving it up. We are creatures of habit, after all, and the way we are living often seems best because it is most familiar. Some of the older women's satisfaction may come just from their years of investment in the marriage.

Then, too, the older *Wifestyles* woman was raised in an era in which there were few options to marriage. She may be more likely than the younger woman to value being a wife and to see other ways of living as less desirable than marriage. The forty-and-under wives are children of the sixties and seventies, people who grew up and got married in a time of incredible social change. They have had lots of new choices and few role models to follow. The over-forty women grew up and got married in the 1950s and 40s and 30s, eras when cultural values and women's lives were more uniform and stable.

There are a lot of different ways to second-guess the women who say they're satisfied with their marriages, but I am finally inclined to take them at their word. More of the older women say they're satisfied. I believe them. And I believe the younger women who say they're satisfied too. As we have seen, a large percentage of both age groups rate their marriages high on a 1 to 10 satisfaction scale; 65 percent of the younger women and 85 percent of the older women gave a score of 8, 9, or 10. More of the older women are more highly satisfied, but most of both groups chose the high end of the scale. So most of these women agree that being married is a satisfying way to live. If they had it to do over again, almost all of them (88 percent) say they would get married again, and even more (92 percent) say that they would marry their present husband again.

And that's how women stay married. By being satisfied with what they've got. By doing what has to be done. It's a terrible and wonderful thing. A woman in her early thirties who has been struggling for more than ten years with a difficult marriage explained to me why she's still trying.

I always feel that at some point some flash of light is going to hit me and I'm going to understand why anybody gets married. I think it's because there aren't too many other alternatives, as far as emotional satisfaction. There is no other structure in the society that has the constancy and the possibility of emotional support that marriage has. A group of people living together or two women living together—those other living arrangements just don't have the same possibilities for intimate, supporting relationships. At least with marriage there's that expectation that it might happen. There's that hope that it will.

Another woman in her late forties who has been married for more than twenty years told me why her marriage has survived.

We married with the idea that we're committed to marriage as an institution and to each other. And the obligation is to maintain it. And there's enough going, there's enough reason. Although one after another of our colleagues and our peers and our friends are finding that marriage is no damn good, that has just not been a question for us. Marriage is worthwhile, and we like it.

We want the marriage to work. We're not looking for it not to work. We could go out, I guess, and find ways to muck it up. I suppose we could. If you don't work at keeping things going, then you're going to muck it up. But we care that we do things to make the other person comfortable or happy or meet their needs in some way. And at the same time maintain our own lives. So we can live. We can be ourselves but together. And I think that's probably where it's at. If we didn't give a damn about the marriage, I guess it could go to hell. But we're committed to the marriage.

In the end it's deceptively simple. In spite of all the changes, the thing that makes marriage work is the same old thing. Call it commitment. Call it accommodation. Call it being satisfied with what you've got. At the end of the study I did a computer analysis of the responses of the most-satisfied women to several key questions. Of those questions, the highest correlation was with question 173—think of leaving. The *Wifestyles* women who are most satisfied with their marriages are the ones least likely to think of leaving their husbands.[4] I suspect that that's not so much a circle as it is a self-fulfilling prophecy. They *expect to stay married.* And they're willing to do what it takes. They know that marriage is more than an impossible dream; it's also a precious possibility.

Acknowledgments

I am grateful for my family—Dorothy and Abram, Dwight, Dean, Don, Elet, Paul, and Christopher—because they always stick by me no matter what, which is exactly what they're supposed to do.

This book would never have been started without the help of Stanley Lieberfreund and Janet Ginandes.

It would never have been finished without the help of more people than I can hope to name, though I must try. Harriet Arnone has been godmother to *Wifestyles* since the day it was conceived. She has influenced my work in more ways than I know—it was Hattie, for example, who first taught me the difference between the data and the stories. Officially she has been research consultant and interviewer, but those roles are just a small part of her contribution. She is always there when I need her—an extraordinary thing—and I will never be able to thank her enough.

Elaine Markson believed in this book even after we had the party and nobody came; she kept right on looking for the editor who would do the book justice until she found her. All else follows this.

Cynthia Vartan has been patient and kind; her criticism is laser sharp, penetrating but painless, and always, always on target.

Judith Thomas did a very special group of interviews that

are striking for their consistency, insight, and respect for the women she talked to; I am proud to be associated with the work that she did.

David Lucido helped me in the early stages of the computer analysis when I was still learning the language.

Pearl Beck has brought sensitivity, creativity, and the warmth of her friendship to the later stages of the analysis; she just wouldn't quit!

Sara Rubloff spent hour after patient hour listening to the interviews and coding them. And Helen Tretera, who can work from a manuscript in any condition and make it come out right, typed and typed and typed.

The women who took care of my son so that I could write have been crucial every working day. Thanks to Doris Krebser, Karen and Jill Krebser, Susan and Carol Keane, and Lisa Beckman.

Many friends read portions of the manuscript and gave me encouragement and support. I especially appreciate the faithfulness and perception of Lady Borton and Merrily Miller, each of whom has had a major impact on the final shape of the work.

And, of course, I never could have written *Wifestyles* without the gatekeepers who introduced me to the women who talked or without the interest and frankness of the women themselves.

Dawn Sangrey
September 1982

Notes

INTRODUCTION

1 D. Yankelovich, *New Rules* (New York: Random House, 1981), p. *xiv*.

2 How do the women in the *Wifestyles* study compare, in terms of satisfaction, with married women in other studies? It is not easy to make a comparison because the "satisfaction" measure used here is not the same as that used in many of the other studies. Satisfaction with marriage varies with the external situation and also with the stage of the marriage. For example, wives with young children are usually less satisfied with their marriage than wives either before the birth of their first child or after their children have grown older. Wives in families of high socioeconomic status are more satisfied than wives in families with lower socioeconomic status. On the whole, however, it looks as if the wives in this book are more satisfied with their marriages than American wives as a group, or at least they want to look that way.

For a detailed discussion of the relationship of marital satisfaction to a host of other variables, see: N. Bradburn, *The Structure of Psychological Well-Being,* (Chicago: Aldine, 1969); H. T. Christensen, "Children in the Family: Relationship of Number and Spacing to Marital Success," *Journal of Marriage and the Family,* vol. 25 (1968); B. C. Collins and H. Feldman, "Marital Satisfaction over the Family Life Cycle," *Journal of Marriage and the Family,* vol. 32 (1970); E. B. Luckey and J. K. Bain, "Children: A Factor in Marital Satisfaction," *Journal of Marriage and the Family,* vol. 32 (1970); A. Rossi, "Transition to Parenthood," *Journal of Marriage and the Family,* vol. 30

(1968); and H. Waldron and D. Routh, "The Effect of the First Child on the Marital Relationship," *Journal of Marriage and the Family*, vol. 43 (1981).

CHAPTER 1: GETTING MARRIED

1 In their recent book, *The Nation's Families: 1960–1990*, (Cambridge, Mass.: Joint Center for Urban Studies, 1980), G. Masnick and M. J. Bane explain that even with all the changes that have occurred in the last few decades, most people marry at one time or another in their lives (p. 7). It is not hard to understand this tendency to marry when you look at the things that seem to make people happy in our society. The Institute for Social Research at the University of Michigan has conducted numerous studies of people's perceptions of the quality of their lives and the things they believe influence it. Two reports published in 1974 show that Americans see marriage and family life as the most satisfying parts of their lives. The studies also found that being married has a big impact on whether or not people feel satisfied with life in general. See A. J. Norton and P. C. Glick, "Marital Instability in America: Past, Present, and Future," in G. Levinger and O. C. Moles, eds., *Divorce and Separation* (New York: Basic Books, 1979), p. 18.

2 The U.S. Bureau of the Census estimates that four out of every five divorced persons remarry eventually (*Statistical Abstract of the U.S.* [Washington, D.C.: U.S. Government Printing Office, 1980]). A discussion of what our high divorce rate and our high remarriage rate may mean can be found in "Marital Instability in America" by Norton and Glick.

CHAPTER 2: KEEPING HOUSE

1 "Click! The Housewife's Moment of Truth" has been reprinted in F. Klagsbrun, ed., *The First Ms. Reader* (New York: Warner Paperback Library, 1973) and in J. O'Reilly, *The Girl I Left Behind* (New York: Macmillan, 1980).

[2] It depends, of course, on the specific jobs one uses to define housework, but the evidence from sociological studies of the division of labor in families is clear, regardless of when in the last few decades the study was done or what methods were used. Wives keep house. Their responsibilities include, at a minimum, those recurrent household tasks—such as meal preparation, doing dishes, laundry, and bed making—that get "undone" almost as soon as they are done. Husbands are in charge of the car and other repairs, yardwork, and (about half the time) taking out the garbage. Like the world of paid employment, housework is sex segregated: Men and women do different tasks.

Good sources of information about housework include: C.W. Berheide, S. Berk, and R. Berk, "Household Work in the Suburbs: The Job and Its Participants," *Pacific Sociological Review,* vol. 19 (1976); A. Oakley, *The Sociology of Housework* (New York: Pantheon, 1974); A. Oakley, *Woman's Work: The Housewife Past and Present* (New York: Pantheon, 1974).

As you can see from the chart on page 294, which compares *Wifestyles* results with those of Berheide, Berk, and Berk and of L. Lein, *The Working Family Project* (Cambridge, Mass.: Center for the Study of Public Policy, 1974), there is pretty fair agreement on division of labor in the household, and *Wifestyles* women are not very different from most.

[3] Studies that keep track of how families allocate their time have looked at whether the fact that a wife works outside the home influences the extent to which the husband contributes to household work. The findings are consistent: A wife's employment makes very little difference. The only exception is that husbands who are the fathers of young children spend somewhat more time taking care of children when their wives work outside the home. See: M. Meissner et al., "No Exit for Wives: Sexual Division of Labor and the Cumulation of Household Demands," *Canadian Review of Sociology and Anthropology,* vol. 12 (1975); J. Pleck and M. Rustad, *Husbands' and Wives' Time in Family Work and Paid Work in the 1975–76 Study of Time Use* (Wellesley, Mass.: Center for Research on Women, 1980); J. Robinson,

Wife's Percentage of the Responsibility for Housework

	WIFESTYLES %*	BERHEIDE, BERK, AND BERK %†	LEIN %‡
Cooking	87	88	67
Home Repairs	17	—	0
Washing Dishes	63	86	54
Yardwork and Gardening	26	—	17
Food Shopping	74	74	57
Laundry	82	92	64
Picking up the House	70	89	—
Cleaning the House	79	—	62

*All of the wives who answered 1 or 2, where 1 = I do all or almost all of the task and 2 = I do most of the task, were included in these figures.

†This study included 309 suburban households. Forty-three percent of the wives were employed (20 percent part time); 60 percent had at least one child at home. The mean age was forty-three years, ranging from twenty-one to eighty-four.

‡This was a small intensive study of fourteen middle-class urban families. All wives were employed outside the home; all had at least one preschool child.

How Americans Use Time: A Social-Psychological Analysis (New York: Praeger, 1977); and K. Walker and M. Woods, *Time Use: A Measure of Household Production of Family Goods and Services* (Washington, D.C.: American Home Economics Association, 1976).

4   The women in the *Wifestyles* study did not differ much from women in other research in how they evaluated their household arrangements. In general, wives express much concern about housework, think a lot about it, talk about it, but they tell researchers that they don't fight much with their husbands about housework and aren't necessarily unhappy with their current household division of labor. For example, in *American's Use of Time*, J. Robinson, T. Juster, and F. Stafford report that in a national sample of married women surveyed during 1965–1966, only 19 percent answered yes to the question "Do you wish your husband would give you more help with the household chores?" (Ann Arbor, Mich.: Institute for Social Research, 1976). Repeating the question in another survey eight years later, they found the percentage of agreement rose only 4 points, to 23 percent.

Careful analysis of differences in the lives of women who are more or less satisfied shows some unsurprising patterns. Women who work outside the home are more ready to admit that they want "help" from their husbands with household tasks. Women with small children are also more able to say they want help. The greatest change over time has come from young wives, educated wives, and black wives.

According to Lein in *The Working Family Project*, satisfaction and dissatisfaction seem to have more to do with the values and relationships in families than they do with any specific distribution of tasks. There is an emotional/psychological connection between wives and housework; Berheide, Berk, and Berk describe it this way in "Household Work in the Suburbs": ". . . most of our respondents felt strong emotional ties to the household members for whom they labored. While it is extremely hard to gauge, altruism was clearly a factor that should not be neglected. A labor of love may at times not seem like labor at all. Again, the benefits which accrued from the roles of wife and mother may have outweighed the specifics of household work" (p. 511).

Additional sources of information include: W. Goode, "Why Men Resist," in *Rethinking the Family,* ed. B. Thorne (New York: Longman, 1982); and J. H. Pleck, "Work-Family Role Systems," *Social Problems,* vol. 24 (1977).

5 In *The Mermaid and the Minotaur: Sexual Arrangements and the Human Malaise* (New York: Harper & Row, 1976), D. Dinnerstein says that "women and men will regard each other, respectively, as silly, overgrown children" (p. 36) so long as we are all raised primarily by women in our most formative first years of life. Dinnerstein's book argues that female-dominated child care is at the root of misogyny because women alone are the object of the infant's dependence and rage.

CHAPTER 3: RAISING CHILDREN

1 Recent studies show that most younger women who are married or plan to marry also plan to have children. For example, Jessie Bernard reports the results of a study showing that 89 percent of young people expect to have children in *Women, Wives, Mothers* (Chicago: Aldine, 1975). In "Female Freshmen View Their Role as Women" (*Journal of Marriage and the Family,* vol. 34 (1972), C. Epstein and A. Bronzaft indicate similar percentages among college women: 77 percent in 1965 and 76 percent in 1970 said that they planned to have children.

2 Recently more popular and scientific attention has been paid to women who do not want to bear and raise children. In "Voluntary Childlessness: A Review of Issues and Evidence," *Marriage and Family Review,* vol. 2 (1979), J. E. Veevers estimates the group to be about 5 percent of all ever-married women. Research shows that this (possibly increasing) trend is, in part, a postponement of childbearing. Women in the past decade had

their first children at a later age than did women of past generations. Postponement seems related to women's participation in
the labor force. But there is also a growing number of women
and men—usually professionals or business executives—who are
deciding not to have children at all.

Research shows that Americans in general are strongly in
favor of married couples having children and most childless
couples experience some social disapproval. See H. Kearney,
"Feminist Challenges to the Social Structure of Sex Roles,"
Psychology of Women Quarterly, vol 4 (1979) and E. Macklin,
"Nontraditional Family Forms: A Decade of Research," *Journal
of Marriage and the Family,* vol. 42 (1980).

3   In *Themes of Work and Love in Adulthood* (Cambridge, Mass.:
Harvard University Press, 1980), Neil J. Smelser makes the same
observation about motherhood and marriage in a discussion of
adult development in which he describes the kinds of events that
give an individual life its characteristic shape: "Contours vary
according to the degree to which events and sequences are reversible or revocable. Becoming a Ph.D. is not normally a reversible
act; neither is becoming a mother. Marrying, however, can be
revoked by divorce, and taking a job can be revoked by quitting
or being discharged." (My pencil note in the margin: "Why
doesn't he say *becoming a parent?*)

4   Other studies that asked approximately the same question got
widely divergent answers. The most famous survey—albeit an
unscientific one—was done by Ann Landers, the newspaper
columnist. In November 1975 she received a letter from a young
couple who were trying to decide whether or not to have
children. The question Ann Landers put to her readers in turn
was this: "If you had it to do over again, would you do it?" The
response was overwhelming; people of all ages, races, religions
—male and female—wrote in, and most of them said no. Overall, 70 percent said they wouldn't have children again. (The tally
was reported in a column published January 23, 1976.) On the
other hand, D. Yankelovich reports that of people asked in the
late 1970s if they would have children if they "had it to do over

again," 90 percent said yes (*New Rules,* New York: Random House, 1981, p. 89).

5 Attitudes in this country about the best way to organize parent roles in a family are changing. There was a time when just about everyone believed that mother should stay at home with the children while father went off and earned money. Nowadays some people, certainly not all, would agree with Dr. Benjamin Spock, who has changed his mind. Spock said in an August 1971 *Newsweek* interview, "Women should have as much choice as men as to where their place will be. . . . If a mother wants an uninterrupted career, it is up to the two parents to decide, without prejudice, how to divide the child care or get part-time assistance from a grandmother or suitable sitter. I admit my sexism in having previously assumed that the mother would be the one who would limit her outside work at least to part-time until her children are three."

According to a 1975 National Child Care Consumer Study, a child's third birthday does mark a time of change. Only a maximum of 13 percent of children zero to two years old spend thirty hours or more a week in the care of someone other than their parents. As the children grow older, the amount of time increases (NCCS data cited by M. J. Bare et al., *Child Care in the United States* [Wellesley, Mass.: Wellesley College Center for Research on Women, December 1978]).

Of course, there are still differences of opinion. Much of the controversy over the Equal Rights Amendment, abortion, and the women's movement in general is based in part on fundamental disagreements about what a change in the role of wife (especially as it pertains to the care of children) will do to society. See L. Gordon, "Why Nineteenth-Century Feminists Did Not Support Birth Control and Twentieth-Century Feminists Do: Feminism, Reproduction, and the Family," in B. Thorne, ed., *Rethinking the Family* (New York: Longman, 1982).

6 Several studies indicate that men are beginning to take more responsibility for the care of their children. See W. Goode, "Why Men Resist," in B. Thorne, ed., *Rethinking the Family,*

and J. Pleck and M. Rustad, *Husbands' and Wives' Time in Family Work and Paid Work* (Wellesley, Mass.: Wellesley College Center for Research on Women, 1980).

7 In their analysis of time-use data from 1975–76, Pleck and Rustad found, for example, that unemployed wives spent 289 minutes a week in basic child care tasks while their husbands spent only 43 minutes in basic child care. Among couples in which the wife was employed, she spent 152 minutes a week in basic child care while her husband spent only 39 minutes (*Husbands' and Wives' Time,* p. 12).

8 And that person would be *a male.* Both N. Chodorow, in *The Reproduction of Mothering: Psycho-analysis and the Sociology of Gender* (Berkeley: University of California Press, 1978), and D. Dinnerstein, in *The Mermaid and the Minotaur,* argue convincingly that our culture's basic attitudes about women and men arise from the fact that most people are tended almost exclusively by female caregivers in infancy and early childhood.

9 In a well-respected study of family violence, *Behind Closed Doors: Violence in the American Family,* by M. A. Straus, R. J. Gelles, and S. K. Steinmetz (Garden City, N.Y.: Anchor Press, 1980), conflict over the children was found to be the most-common cause of physical violence between husband and wife.

CHAPTER 4: "WORKING"

1 "The problem is always being the children's mommy, or the minister's wife, and never being myself. . . .

"There's no problem you can even put a name to. But I'm desperate. I begin to feel I have no personality. I'm a server of food and putter-on of pants and a bedmaker, somebody who can be called on when you want something. But who am I?" (B. Friedan, *The Feminine Mystique* [New York: Dell, 1963], pp. 17, 23).

2 The sociology of work takes as a basic tenet the fact that most people have to provide for themselves one way or another. It also explores the ways in which society organizes work so that

it satisfies other human requirements, such as companionship and achievement. Basically most people understand that work has its good and its bad points. A classic research finding is that most people say they would continue working even if they could afford not to (N. C. Morse and R. S. Weiss, "The Function and Meaning of Work and the Job," *American Sociological Review*, vol. 20 [1955]). Another classic finding (P. Warr and T. Wall, *Work and Well-Being* [London: Penguin, 1975]) is that people find purpose and meaning in their work.

Historically, however, women's (paid) work has been a separate research issue. For researchers, the interesting question when women went out to work was always the effect on other things: the family, the children, the social fabric, the workplace. Women's work was seen as something of a social problem.

The research focus is changing somewhat as researchers (like wives and husbands) are beginning to understand how complex is the fact that most married women also have paying jobs. For one thing (L. Hoffman, "Effects of Maternal Employment on the Child," *Child Development*, vol. 32, [1961]) it is now understood that all jobs are not the same for women any more than they are for men; when women take high-status jobs the effect on them and their families tends to be more positive than when they take low-status jobs.

People are also beginning to understand that a marriage involves at least two people and the effects of something like the wife working depend on what those two people want and need. In *Work and Family in the United States* (New York: Russell Sage, 1977), R. M. Kantor puts it this way: ". . . to study *only* the husband or, more likely, *only* the wife, is to miss a set of interactions that may be critical for shaping the quality of interactions in the family" (p. 64).

Many studies tell what happens in particular spheres of family life when the wife goes out to work. In summary, it has been found that there is some impact on the relationship between the husband and wife. She may or may not get him to do more housework (J. Aldous, "Occupational Characteristics and Males'

Role Performance in the Family," *Journal of Marriage and the Family,* vol. 31 [1969]). She may become more dominant, especially over economic issues (R. O. Blood and D. M. Wolfe, *Husbands and Wives* [New York: Free Press, 1960]). If she is working out of choice and not economic necessity, a happier marriage for both husband and wife results (S. R. Orden and N. M. Bradburn, "Working Wives and Marriage Happiness," *American Journal of Sociology,* vol. 74 [1969]).

It has also been found that the wife generally feels better. She is healthier, accepts herself more, feels more satisfied with life, and has fewer emotional disturbances or physical symptoms (S. Feld, "Feelings of Adjustment," in F. I. Nye and L. W. Hoffman, eds., *The Employed Mother in America* [Chicago: Rand McNally, 1963]). According to E. B. Palmore and V. Stone in "Predictors of Longevity: A Follow-up of the Aged in Chapel Hill" (*The Gerontologist,* vol. 13 [1973]), she is likely to live longer; and in *The Depressed Woman: A Study of Social Relationships* (Chicago: University of Chicago Press, 1974), M. M. Weissman and E. Paykel cite evidence that she is able to function better, even if depressed.

See also L. Bailyn, "Career and Family Orientation of Husbands and Wives in Relation to Marital Happiness," *Human Relations,* vol. 23 (1970); L. Hoffman and I. F. Nye, *Working Mothers* (San Francisco: Jossey-Bass, 1974); C. Hornung and B. McCullough, "Status Relationships in Dual-Employment Marriages: Consequences for Psychological Well-Being," *Journal of Marriage and the Family,* vol. 43 (1981); S. Houseknecht and A. Mache, "Combining Marriage and Career: the Marital Adjustment of Professional Women," *Journal of Marriage and the Family,* vol. 43 (1981); and G. Spitze and L. Waite, "Wives' Employment: the Role of Husbands' Perceived Attitudes," *Journal of Marriage and the Family,* vol. 43 (1981).

[3] According to *Women in the Labor Force* (Washington, D.C.: U.S. Department of Labor, 1979), most women work because of economic need. That is, in fact, the reason why most *people* work. The sociological finding that people would be likely to

keep working even if they didn't need the money (see note 2 above) points to the second major reason why people work: (here's that same word, again) "fulfillment." We know now that people usually have more than one reason for working and that what they get most from working (money or satisfaction or something to do, etc.) depends to a great extent on what kind of work they do. In sociological terms, there is an "occupationally stratified" response. See M. Ferree, "Working Class Jobs: Housework and Paid Work as Sources of Satisfaction," *Social Problems,* vol. 23 (1976); N. C. Morse and R. S. Weiss, "The Function and Meaning of Work and the Job," *American Sociological Review,* vol. 20 (1955); and C. Rosenfeld and V. Perrella, "Why Women Start and Stop Working: A Study in Mobility," *Monthly Labor Review,* September 1965.

4 Avery Corman, *Kramer vs. Kramer* (New York: The New American Library, 1978), p. 54.

5 Recent studies indicate that young single women are incredibly optimistic about their ability to avoid some of the problems inherent in trying to combine marriage (and, in some cases, motherhood) with a full-time demanding career. See, for example, S. Bolotin, "Voices from the Post-Feminist Generation," *The New York Times Magazine,* October 17, 1982; J. Farley, "Graduate Women: Career Aspirations and Desired Family Size," *American Psychologist,* vol. 25 (1970); and C. Tavris, "The Love-Work Questionnaire—Who Will You Be Tomorrow?" *Mademoiselle,* vol. 88 (March 1982). In *Dilemmas of Masculinity* (New York: Norton, 1976), M. Kamarovsky indicates that the men they marry share their optimism. She says, "The young [college] men appeared unrealistic in describing the future . . . they did not foresee that the zestful, competent, independent women they hoped to marry might not easily fit into the semitraditional roles they preferred for their future wives."

6 The middle-class bias of the sample is obviously working here. (See the Technical Appendix.) Most of these families are reasonably comfortable, and they know it. Asked "Do you have enough money?" 67 percent of the women in the study said "yes."

[7] Working women generally earn much less money than working men do. In the *Wifestyles* sample, for example, 61 percent of the women who have jobs earn less than $10,000 a year, while only 11 percent of their husbands earn less than $10,000 a year. National averages show similar discrepancies: among full-time workers in 1978, the median income for women was $7,464 and for men, $13,588 (U.S. Bureau of the Census, 1978).

CHAPTER 5: LOVING AND HATING

[1] The standard wisdom among counselors of most persuasions goes like this: A sexual relationship reflects the relationship as a whole; if it's good out of bed, it will, for the most part, be good in bed too. And the reverse: If something is wrong in the relationship, it will show up in sex sooner or later. There does not, however, seem to be much empirical research which asks "How satisfied are you with your marriage? Your sex life?" and then runs correlations. We know that about half of all married couples experience some sexual problems (W. Masters and V. Johnson, *Human Sexual Response* [Boston: Little, Brown, 1966]). We also know that everyday pressures (work, children, etc.) can interfere with sexual enjoyment and that, especially in long-term marriages, routine or boredom become common complaints (J. Laws and P. Schwartz, *Sexual Scripts* [Hinsdale, Ill.: Dryden, 1977]).

The relationship between satisfaction with marriage and satisfaction with sex is surely a complex one. A hint of this complexity may be seen in a study conducted at an Ohio university in which people were asked about sex and marital satisfaction. Both people who said their marriages were "satisfactory" and those who said their marriages were "unsatisfactory" said that their frequency of intercourse was twice a week. The husbands in the unhappy marriages, however, said that this frequency was more sex than their wives wanted but all right with them, while their wives said the frequency of their intercourse was right for them but less than their husbands wanted. In the "satisfactory" marriages, both husbands and wives reported that their frequency of intercourse was satisfying to both partners.

2 "As business, politics, and diplomacy grow more savage and warlike, men seek a haven in private life, in personal relations, above all in the family—the last refuge of love and decency. Domestic life, however, seems increasingly incapable of providing these comforts. Hence the undercurrent of anxiety that runs through the vast and growing commentary on the state of the family" (Christopher Lasch, *Haven in a Heartless World: The Family Beseiged* [New York: Basic Books, 1977], p. xiii). Lasch makes no mention, I notice, of the needs of the women who are expected to provide these comforts.

3 *Concepts of Modern Psychiatry* (New York: W. W. Norton, 1953), pp. 42–43.

4 The *Wifestyles* questions ("Have you been faithful to your husband? And he to you?") were coded for husband and wife and for past and present separately. The results were:

Infidelity Ever?	Percent
No, neither	76
Him only, past only	8
Her only, past only	6
Both, past only	6
Him only, now	3
Her only, now	1

It is hard to be sure just how much actual infidelity is going on these days. Some studies ask questions about behavior ("Have you ever had sexual intercourse with someone other than a spouse while you were married?"). Others ask about attitudes ("What do you think of extramarital sex?"). Taking other studies of behavior for comparison, since that's what the *Wifestyles* questions ask about, it would appear that the women in the study had marriages of greater than average fidelity. For instance, in *Playing Around: Women and Extramarital Sex* (New York: Morrow, 1975), L. Wolfe reports that 25 percent of married women have extramarital sex at some time, compared with only 13 percent of *Wifestyles* women.

Why do the *Wifestyles* women seem so different in this regard? It is possible that, by chance, this is an unusually faithful group of wives. However, the attitude research about extramarital sex suggests another interpretation: The *Wifestyles* women may have been reporting not their behavior but their conviction (which most Americans hold, even after the sexual revolution) that sexual fidelity is a very important ingredient in a good marriage. Compare these two sets of statistics:

Wifestyles (Anyone unfaithful ever?)		National Opinion Research Center question (1977) ("Extramarital sex is . . .")	
No infidelity	76%	73%	always wrong
Him, her, both past	20%	14%	almost always wrong
Him, her, now	4%	3%	not wrong

It's always the case that what people tell you about their behavior is a mixture of what they actually do and what they expect/want/need you to hear from them. My guess is that the 13 percent is underreporting.

See also A. C. Kinsey, et al., *Sexual Behavior in the Human Female* (Philadelphia: Saunders, 1953); R. J. Levin, "The Redbook Report on Premarital and Extramarital Sex: The End of the Double Standard, *Redbook,* vol. 145 (October 1975); and E. Morrison and V. Borosage, eds., *Human Sexuality: Contemporary Perspectives* (Palo Alto, Calif.: National Press Books, 1973).

CHAPTER 6: MAKING THE BEST OF IT

1 D. Yankelovich (*New Rules,* New York: Random House, 1981, p. 252) has found a strong and continuing belief among Americans in the couple, with or without children, as the best unit for

living. In 1970, 96 percent of the population agreed that living in pairs was the best arrangement. In 1980, in spite of everything, the percentage who agreed was still 96 percent.

2   This may be another case of the *Wifestyles* women reporting what they believe to be the ideal rather than their actual condition (see note 4, Chapter 5). Other studies show more unhappiness in long-term marriages. In *Husbands and Wives* (New York: The Free Press, 1960), for example, R. O. Blood and D. M. Wolfe speak of "the corrosive influence of time . . . wearing away at the strengths of marriage" (p. 263). According to their data (based on interviews with 731 city families and 178 farm families), the average wife's marital satisfaction decreases consistently over the duration of the marriage.

3   There is a very high correlation between age and length of marriage among the *Wifestyles* women. Only 6 percent of the over-forty women have been married zero to seven years; most of them (80 percent) have been married more than twenty years. Among the twenty- to forty-year-old group, thirty (40 percent) have been married zero to seven years, forty-two (57 percent) have been married eight to twenty years, and two (3 percent) have been married more than twenty years.

4   The relationship between "Think of leaving him?" and satisfaction was compared with the relationship between satisfaction and several other questions: "If you could change one thing about your marriage, what would you change?" "How satisfied are you with your sex life?" and "If you could change one thing about the way you and your husband divide the household work, what would you change?" To find out whether "leave him" was related to marital satisfaction above and beyond these other variables, a statistical procedure called a partial correlation was conducted. This correlation took into consideration the effect of the other variables. The results indicated that "leave him" had a strong independent relationship with satisfaction, even when the effects of these other questions were statistically controlled for.

Partial Correlations Between Variables That Predict Marital
Satisfaction and Responses to "How Satisfied Are You, Overall,
with Your Marriage Today?"

	Partial Correlation	Significance
1. Think of leaving him: No	.34	.001*
2. Change in the marriage: Nothing	.23	.02*
3. Satisfied with sex: Yes	.21	.04*
4. Change in housework: Nothing	.18	.07

*Partial correlation is significant. For a discussion of statistical significance, see pp.
322–323.

Technical Appendix

> What we . . . refer to confidently as memory—meaning a moment, a scene, a fact that has been subjected to a fixative and thereby rescued from oblivion—is really a form of storytelling that goes on continually in the mind and often changes with the telling. Too many conflicting emotional interests are involved for life ever to be wholly acceptable, and possibly it is the work of the storyteller to rearrange things so that they conform to this end. In any case, in talking about the past we lie with every breath we draw.
>
> —William Maxwell, So Long, See You Tomorrow

I asked my good friend Morton Bard, who is the Director of the Center for Social Research and a professor of psychology at the Graduate Center, the City University of New York, to read the first draft of *Wifestyles*. He said he liked the work a lot, but as a social scientist he couldn't help noticing that I was trying to have my cake and eat it too. I want to have a base in objective data for the things I say; at the same time I want to insist that there are other ways of learning about human experience that are at least as valid. And since I have been trained as a writer and a reader but not as a scientist, I will always like the stories better.

The book is a maverick, then—at best, original; at worst, heretical. I hope that the parts of it that do not conform to scientific convention are all intentionally deviant and that the reasons for the deviance are clear. I hope for the work to be taken seriously in the scientific community and for others to pursue paths that have been broken here. This appendix is designed to further those ends.

But the appendix too is a maverick since I also want to use it to introduce the interested lay reader to the data. So what follows is written in everyday language rather than in the idiom of journal articles and doctoral dissertations. And it is undoubtedly colored by the point of view of the storyteller.

Finding the *Wifestyles* Women

I was determined to include as many different parts of the country as I could, so I started with a map of the United States divided into the nine census divisions designated by the U.S. Bureau of the Census. I decided to visit several different sites in each of the nine divisions, including rural, suburban, and urban locations.*

It seemed unlikely that a woman would be willing to talk to a total stranger about something as intimate as her married life unless the stranger was introduced to her by someone she already knew. So I needed a connection, a person who would help me locate the women to interview and also vouch for my trustworthiness. These connecting people are called gatekeepers.

The individual sites within each census division were chosen because gatekeepers, people already known to me or to one of the other interviewers, lived there. The gatekeepers were asked to invite married women they knew to participate in the study. I said, in my instruction letter to gatekeepers, that I wanted to interview as many different kinds of wives as possible—"rich, middle-class, and poor; white and nonwhite; brides and veterans of fifty married years; mothers and women without children; those who work outside the home and those who do not; women who are happy in their marriages and those who are not so happy." The gatekeepers prepared a list of the names and phone numbers of women who

---

*Rural was defined as outside of what the U.S. Office of Federal Statistical Policy and Standards calls a standard metropolitan statistical area (SMSA); suburban was defined as within an SMSA but outside the central city; urban was defined as within a central city. See Appendix II, Metropolitan Area Concepts and Components, *Statistical Abstract of the United States: 1979,* p. 935.

expressed interest. The interviewer then called the women, explained the interview, and made appointments with those who were willing to participate.

The system worked well. Of seventeen people asked to be gatekeepers, only one hesitated and finally refused to help. Almost all of the women approached by the gatekeepers were willing to talk about participating. Only five of the 130 who were approached by phone to set up interview appointments were unable or unwilling to be interviewed. And of all the interviews for which appointments were made, only one woman failed to keep her appointment.

Among social scientists this method of choosing women to interview might be called "purposive sampling" or "snowball sampling" or "network sampling." It is a practical approach when the research requires wide variety among the people interviewed and a random sample cannot be drawn. The principal limitation of network sampling is that you cannot base generalizations about the population as a whole on the statistics from the study. The research gives you ideas rather than projections.

Comparing the *Wifestyles* Women with the National Population

The women who participated in the study were a richly varied group, but they were not strictly representative of the population as a whole. This means that we do not know how their experience and opinions compare with the national population. But if you compare the *Wifestyles* women with the national population, you can get some idea of how the two differ.

Geographically the women in the study were distributed in roughly the same way that married couples are distributed in the population as a whole. The following chart geographically compares *Wifestyles* women with all married couples in the United States in 1978.*

---

*Figures for the population as a whole are all taken from *Statistical Abstract of the United States: 1980* (Washington, D.C.: U.S. Bureau of the Census, 1980).

Wifestyles

	Wifestyles (%)	All Married Couples (%)
North East	18	22
North Central	25	27
West	22	18
South	35	33

The two groups are also similar in their distribution in rural, suburban, and urban areas, as this chart shows.

	Wifestyles (%)	Total U.S. Population (1977) (%)
Urban	31	28
Suburban	38	45
Rural	31	27

Since the *Wifestyles* group had only 124 women in it, I decided to try to get a good spread of ages and of marital length rather than to make any attempt to mirror the national population for these variables. The age distribution was as follows: 24 percent were thirty and under; 36 percent were thirty-one to forty; 25 percent were forty-one to fifty; and 15 percent were over fifty. For length of marriage, 27 percent were married zero to seven years; 39 percent were married eight to twenty years, and 34 percent were married more than twenty years. Eighty-five percent of the women were in their first marriage; 15 percent had been divorced and remarried.

The racial distribution of *Wifestyles* women compares favorably with the population as a whole: Eighty-nine percent of the study group were white; 7 percent were black; 4 percent were of other racial minorities. In the U.S. population in 1979, 86 percent were white; 12 percent were black; 2 percent were of other racial minorities. In a sample of this size, of course, the actual number of nonwhite participants is so small that it is safe to say that the *Wifestyles* group is much more representative of white women than it is of nonwhite women.

The *Wifestyles* women are also better educated and have higher family incomes than the married women in the country as a whole.

Technical Appendix

A larger percentage of *Wifestyles* women are employed outside the home, as well. This chart compares the educational level of the women in the study with those of all women in the United States in 1979.

Last Grade Completed	*Wifestyles* (%)	All U.S. Women (%)
1–8	3	18
Partial high school	4	15
High-school graduate	18	40
Partial college	24	14
College graduate	51	13

The mean family income for all U.S. families in 1978 was $19,340. For all families in which both husband and wife were employed, the mean family income in 1978 was $22,280. Among the *Wifestyles* women, the mean family income was $33,232.

Fifty-two percent of the women in the study were employed full time and 27 percent were employed part time. In the population as a whole in 1979, 49 percent of married women with husband present were in the labor force, both employed and unemployed and looking for work. You will recall from the chapter on work that I am inclined to include all sorts of unorthodox occupations as "work" and it may be that some of the women whom I counted as being employed would not be considered to be in the labor force by the U.S. Department of Labor. Even so, I think many more of the *Wifestyles* women were employed than are wives in the population as a whole.

Education and occupation are often used to determine a family's social class. I did an analysis of the *Wifestyles* women to determine their family social status, using a weighted formula that includes four factors: sex, marital status, occupation, and education.* According to that formula, 3 percent of the women were in the

*August B. Hollingshead, "Four Factor Index of Social Status," Working Paper, Yale University Dept. of Sociology, June 1975.

lower group; 7 percent were in the lower-middle group; 12 percent were in the middle-middle group; 35 percent were in the upper-middle group; and 43 percent were in the upper group.* It would certainly be safe to say that the *Wifestyles* women have, as a group, a higher social status than a representative group of married women.

More women in the study have children than the national average, as can be seen from the chart that follows. (Note that only children under eighteen years of age are included.)

Number of Children Under Eighteen	*Wifestyles* (%)	All U.S. Married Couples—1979 (%)
None	42	49
One Child	20	19
Two Children	27	19
Three or More	11	13

In terms of age distribution, 26 percent of *Wifestyles* women have at least one preschooler compared with 23 percent of all U.S. couples; 58 percent of the *Wifestyles* women have at least one child under the age of eighteen, while 51 percent of married couples in the U.S. have at least one child under that age.

The Interview Questions

Since I wanted to compare each woman's answers with those of the others in the study, I had to ask everyone the same questions. But I also wanted to gather as many stories as possible and to encourage each woman to talk about whatever was important to her. So I didn't want to just hand out the same printed list of questions

*Hollingshead does not use the lower, lower-middle, middle-middle, upper-middle, upper labels. He does give a range of scores in five categories that allow one to assign a status to an individual or family; the categories are named according to occupational levels—the highest category is called "major business and professional," for example.

for everyone to fill in. Instead the interview was conceived as a conversation, and the questions were grouped around broad themes so that each woman would have the room to talk about her own life in relation to these themes. Many of the questions were phrased to elicit a long, anecdotal response ("Tell me the story of the day you decided to get married."). Others, especially in the second half of the interview, were short-answer questions that needed only a brief response.

Some of the questions elicited wonderful, provocative answers —they encouraged lots of good stories and/or the kind of sharp distinctions that allowed the answers to be easily categorized for computer analysis.* In answering the question about the women's movement ("Some people say that the women's movement has had a good effect on marriage and some people say it has had a bad effect. What do you think?"), for example, the wives I talked to had one of five responses: They had strong opinions (pro or con); they straddled the fence; they said they didn't know; or they said the women's movement had no effect on marriage. The answers were easy to code (good, bad, good and bad, don't know, or no effect), and the stories were wonderful.

Other questions produced nothing worth talking about. All the answers were the same or they were all boring or they were so diffuse that it was difficult to categorize them. At the end of the section on marital disagreements in the interview, for example, I asked this question: "Some people say that in the perfect family there are no fights. What do you think?" Almost every single woman I talked to said she thought that statement was silly because there have to be some disagreements in any family. Finally I stopped asking the question. The questions that produced nothing of interest have not been discussed in the book, but they are

---

*Information for the computer analysis was taken from the interview tapes by two people. (The process is call "coding.") Ten percent of the tapes were coded twice, once by each coder, so that their answers could be compared. On 80 percent of the items, the coders' responses agreed.

included here so that the reader has a sense of the continuity of the entire interview.

The first thing that happened in the interview was that I went over the ground rules that had been covered in our telephone conversation again to be sure that the woman understood the purpose of the study, the fact that the interview was confidential, the reason for my using a tape recorder, and the importance of stories to the study. Then I asked a series of demographic questions (age, length of marriage, marital history, children, wife's education, husband's education, wife's occupation, husband's occupation, wife's employment history, wife's income, husband's income, religion, race). Then we got to the good part, the questions designed to elicit stories.

The first group of story questions are about the history of the marriage.

Tell me about the day you met.

Tell me about the day you decided to get married.

Tell me about the day you got married.

And then, what was the first year like?

Now, take me from the end of the first year up to the present in highlights, turning points, major events that changed the marriage in some way.

When you were a teenager and you imagined your adult life, did you imagine this life?

Think about your marriage now in comparison with your mother's marriage. How is it the same? How is it different? Is it more different or more the same?

Now let's do some summary questions: How satisfied are you, overall, with your marriage today? Do it on a scale from 1 to 10, where 10 is high. If you had it to do over again and you could get married or stay single, would you get married again? Would you marry this man again?

Technical Appendix

The second group of questions are about your days.

> I'd like to get an idea of how you spend your time.
> Let's take a typical day, yesterday or the day before, and
> just run me through it. You get up in the morning
> and . . .
> What's a weekend like around here? How do you spend
> your weekend time?

The next group of questions was asked only of women who had
children or stepchildren.

> What do you like best about being a parent?
> What do you like least about being a parent?
> Your husband is a parent too. How does his parenting differ
> from yours?
> What do you think the effect of having the children has
> been on the marriage?
> If you had it to do over again, would you have the chil-
> dren?

The next group of questions are about your work:

> I want to get an idea of how you and your husband divide
> up the responsibilities of your household, and I've made a
> little card so that everyone will answer this question the
> same way.

WHO DOES IT?
1. I do all or almost all of it.
2. I do most of it.
3. We split it 50–50.
4. He does most of it.
5. He does all or almost all of it.

> Cooking
> Home maintenance and repairs
> Washing dishes
> Yardwork, gardening
> Food shopping
> Car maintenance and repairs
> Laundry
> Child care
> Picking up the house
> Disciplining the children
> Earning the money
> Cleaning the house
> Major decisions about the children

At the top is a scale from 1 to 5: 1 means you do all or almost all of the task; 5 means your husband does all or almost all of it; 3 means you two split it fifty-fifty, and there are some grades in between. Underneath the line is a list of tasks. Read through the list of tasks and give each one a number that shows who does it at your house.

How do you feel about the way you and your husband have divided up your household work? If you could change one thing about the way you divide it up, what would you change?

Do you have enough time for yourself? If you had more time for yourself, what would you do with it?

The next questions were asked only of women who had some kind of paid work outside of the home.

We've already talked a little about your job. [I took an employment history at the beginning of the interview.] Now I'd like to know a few more things.

First, why are you working now? Do you consider your work to be a job or a career? What do you think the impact of your working has been on your marriage?

Technical Appendix

Now we're going to talk about three areas of your relationship that reveal how you and your husband interact with each other: money, loving, and disagreements. We'll start with money.

You get a paycheck and he gets a paycheck [or, if she is not employed: your husband gets a paycheck]. What happens to the money? Where is it kept? Whose job is it to pay the monthly bills, like the electric bill? Where would you get money if you needed to buy groceries? If you needed to buy some new clothes? If you needed to buy a present for your husband? Where would he get the money to buy a present for you? How about a major purchase like a new clothes dryer, where would the money come from for that? Whose name is the title of the house [lease] in? Do you spend money without talking to him about it? Does he spend money without talking to you?
Do you ever fight about money?
What do you think the effect of his earning all [most] [more] of the money is on your marriage?
Do you have enough money?

Loving. Do you like your husband? Do you love him? When you and he were courting and you wanted to let him know that you cared for him, what did you do? What did he do to show that he cared for you when you were courting? How do you show him that you love him now? How does he show you? Do you love him more, less, or about the same as you did when you married him?

How easy is it for you two to express intimate feelings? For example, if you're making love and you want him to touch you in a certain way, can you ask for what you want? How about your husband?
How important is the sexual side of your relationship to you? How important is it to your husband?
Are you satisfied with your sex life? Are you having any problem with sex now?

Have you and your husband agreed to be faithful to each other? And have you been faithful to him? And he to you?

Disagreements. What do you two do when you disagree about something? If never, why? What do you usually fight about? Do you ever yell at him? Does he ever yell at you? Has either of you ever hit the other in anger? How long does a fight usually go on? And how do you know when it's over? Have you ever had a fight that was so memorable that it sticks in your mind? Some people say that in the perfect family there are no fights. What do you think?

Are you ever afraid that your husband will leave you? Have you ever thought of leaving him?

These questions are quickies. I want you to answer them as briefly as you can.

Suppose that you want to get your husband to do something that he doesn't want to do. What do you do?

How does he get you to do something that you don't want to do?

What do you do when he's in a bad mood (nothing to do with you, just a bad mood)? What does he do when you're in a bad mood?

Suppose that he's talking to you about something that you're not interested in. What do you do? What does he do when you talk to him about something he's not interested in?

Who do you think gives more to the marriage, you or he? Whose job is it to make the marriage work?

Can you tell me one advantage of being married? One disadvantage?

There are people who say the women's movement has had a good effect on marriage and people who say it's had a bad effect on marriage. What do you think?

Pretend that you're back in school, and give yourself a

grade for being a wife: A, B, C, D, or F. Give yourself a grade for being a mother.

If you could change one thing about your marriage, what would you change?

What's the best thing about your marriage?

And what have I left out? Is there anything that we haven't covered that you thought we would or anything that you want to say that you haven't had a chance to?

The Tables

The tables that follow are mathematical expressions of ways in which various subgroups of the *Wifestyles* women differ (or do not differ) from one another. Table 1, for example, summarizes the responses of the younger and older women to the first-year question ("Tell me about the first year of your marriage."). The women's responses were coded for how much happiness or unhappiness they included. The coder listened to the interview tape of the story that each woman told about her first year: If she mentioned mostly happy events, her answer was rated "mostly happy"; mostly unhappy stories got that rating, and very mixed first-year stories got the "mixed" rating.

Table 1 (bottom line) shows that the responses of a total of ninety-three women were coded for this question. Of these, 16 percent (fifteen women) told mostly unhappy stories, 30 percent (twenty-eight women) told mixed stories, and 54 percent (fifty) told mostly happy stories about their first year. The table also shows how each subgroup (unhappy, mixed, happy) breaks down by the age of the women responding. Those twenty to forty (a total of fifty-three women) are separated from those over forty (a total of forty women). There is a lot of difference between the two age groups. The older women tell mostly happy first-year stories a lot more often than the younger women do; only 38 percent of the twenty-to-forty group told mostly happy stories, but 75 percent of the older group did.

Finding and explaining the differences between groups of people is a basic task of social science research. In Chapter 1, I speculate about some of the reasons why so many more of the older *Wifestyles* women report a happy first year of marriage. But before I began to think about what the reasons might be, I needed to be sure that the difference between the older and younger women wasn't just an accident.

At the very bottom of Table 1 is an expression (p < .01) which reads "the probability is less than .01 (or 1 out of 100, or 1%)." This number is my reassurance that the differences I see in the table are not just a matter of chance. It is called the significance level of the results shown in the table. Tests of statistical significance are conducted to determine whether the differences that have been found among two or more groups are large enough that we can say they did not occur by chance. A significance level reports the probability of a particular finding occurring by chance.

In the social sciences a .05 probability level is considered sufficient for statistical significance. This means that there is only a 5 percent probability that this finding could have occurred by chance. In Table 1, a significance test was performed to find out whether the differences between the first-year stories of the younger and older women could have occurred by chance. The significance level was found to be less than .01. This means that the size differences shown in the table could only have occurred by chance once out of one hundred times. All significant differences in the tables are starred.

Sometimes it is important to note that a difference is *not* significant. If the significance level is greater than .10, the probability is said to be "not significant" (n.s.). In Table 2, for example, there is no significant difference among the housework scores of *Wifestyles* women who have full-time jobs, those who have part-time jobs, and those who are not working outside the home. Note that there are some differences among the three groups, but the differences are not great enough to pass the test of statistical significance.

The finding is surprising. I had expected that women who had jobs would be more likely to get help with the housework. The fact that an expected relationship does not exist stimulates the search for

Technical Appendix

other differences that are significant; in this case a statistically significant difference was found in the housework scores of women who
see themselves as contributing to the earning in their families compared with women who see their husbands as the main person who
earns money in the family (Table 16). (Note that the percentage
breakdowns in the tables occasionally add up to more or less than
100; this is due to rounding the figures.)

Table 1 Age Group $\times$ Happiness Level of First Year of Marriage

Age	Mostly Unhappy	Mixed	Mostly Happy	Totals
20–40	21%	41%	38%	57% (53)
41+	10%	15%	75%	43% (40)
	16% (15)	30% (28)	54% (50)	100% (93)

$p < .01$*

Table 2 Employment Status $\times$ Housework Score

	Housework = 1.0 to 1.75	Housework = 1.76 to 2.49	Housework = 2.5+	Totals
Employed full time	27%	31%	42%	49% (48)
Employed part time	35%	46%	19%	27% (26)
Not employed	39%	39%	22%	25% (23)
	32% (31)	37% (36)	31% (30)	100% (97)

n.s.

Table 3 Age Group × Housework Score

Age	Housework = 1.0 to 1.75	Housework = 1.76 to 2.49	Housework = 2.5+	Totals
20–40	36%	34%	30%	61% (59)
41+	26%	42%	32%	39% (38)
	32% (31)	37% (36)	31% (30)	100% (97)

n.s.

Table 4 Housework Score × What Do You Want to Change in Household Division of Labor?

	Nothing	Split It 50–50	Husband to Help More	Totals
Housework = 1.0 to 1.75	30%	13%	57%	33% (23)
Housework = 1.76 to 2.49	52%	7%	41%	41% (29)
Housework = 2.5+	66%	6%	28%	26% (18)
	49% (34)	8% (6)	43% (30)	100% (70)

n.s.

Table 5 Housework Score × Satisfaction Rating

	Low (1–7)	Middle (8)	High (9–10)	Totals
Housework = 1.0 to 1.75	41%	24%	35%	31% (29)
Housework = 1.76 to 2.49	29%	29%	43%	38% (35)
Housework = 2.5+	21%	48%	31%	31% (29)
	30% (28)	33% (31)	37% (34)	100% (93)

n.s.

Table 6 Kidswork Score × Satisfaction Rating

	Low (1–7)	Middle (8)	High (9–10)	Totals
Kidswork = 1.0 to 2.3	43%	29%	29%	22% (14)
Kidswork = 2.4 to 2.9	29%	33%	38%	33% (21)
Kidswork = 3.0+	21%	36%	43%	45% (28)
	29% (18)	33% (21)	38% (24)	100% (63)

n.s.

Table 7 Employment Status $\times$ Satisfaction Rating

	Low (1–7)	Middle (8)	High (9–10)	Totals
Employed full-time	28%	34%	38%	52% (61)
Employed part-time	32%	36%	32%	26% (31)
Not employed	19%	23%	58%	22% (26)
	27% (32)	32% (38)	41% (48)	100% (118)

n.s.

Table 8 Maternal and Employment Status $\times$ Enough Time for Yourself?

	No	Yes	Totals
Employed mother	77%	23%	52% (47)
Employed not-mother	28%	72%	27% (25)
Not employed mother	62%	38%	14% (13)
Not employed not-mother	none	100%	7% (6)
	56% (51)	44% (40)	100% (91)

$p < .001*$

Table 9 Employment Status × Who Earns the Money?

	I Do Most	We Split 50–50	He Does Most	He Does All	Totals
Employed full time	6%	53%	35%	6%	53% (51)
Employed part time	none	13%	57%	30%	24% (23)
Not employed	none	9%	17%	74%	24% (23)
	3% (3)	33% (32)	36% (35)	28% (27)	100% (97)

p < .001*

Table 10 Husband/Wife Income Difference × Who Earns the Money?

	I Do Most	We Split 50–50	He Does Most	He Does All	Totals
Income Difference					
Large	none	13%	34%	53%	41% (32)
Small	2%	39%	44%	15%	59% (46)
	1% (1)	28% (22)	40% (31)	31% (24)	100% (78)

p < .01*

Wifestyles

Table 11 Age Group × How Important Is Sex?

		Not to Either	Him More	Her More	Both Equally	Totals
Age	20–40	6%	42%	16%	36%	62% (64)
	40+	18%	43%	3%	38%	39% (40)
		11% (11)	43% (44)	11% (11)	37% (38)	100% (104)

p < .10

Table 12 Satisfied with Sex Life? × Satisfaction Rating

	Low (1–7)	Middle (8)	High (9–10)	Totals
Satisfied? No	48%	30%	22%	27% (27)
Yes	22%	33%	45%	73% (73)
	29% (29)	32% (32)	39% (39)	100% (100)

p < .05*

Table 13 Any Problem with Sex Now? × Satisfaction Rating

	Low (1–7)	Middle (8)	High (9–10)	Totals
Problems? No	14%	33%	52%	44% (42)
Yes	38%	32%	30%	56% (53)
	27% (26)	33% (31)	40% (38)	100% (95)

p. < .05*

Table 14 Effect of Women's Movement on Marriage ×
Satisfaction Rating

	Low (1–7)	Middle (8)	High (9–10)	Totals
Effect? Bad	13%	21%	67%	29% (24)
Good	23%	31%	46%	42% (35)
Good and Bad	57%	22%	22%	28% (23)
	29% (24)	26% (21)	45% (37)	100% (82)

p < .01*

Table 15 Age Group × Effect of Women's Movement
on Marriage

		Bad	Good	Good and Bad	Totals
Age	20–40	8%	59%	33%	59% (51)
	41 +	60%	20%	20%	41% (35)
		29% (25)	43% (37)	28% (24)	100% (86)

p < .001*

Table 16 Housework Score × Who Earns the Money?

	We Split 50–50	He Does Most	He Does All	Totals
Housework = 1.0 to 1.75	21%	29%	50%	31% (24)
Housework = 1.76 to 2.49	24%	38%	38%	37% (29)
Housework = 2.5+	44%	56%	none	32% (25)
	30% (23)	41% (32)	30% (23)	100% (78)

p < .01*

Table 17 Age Group × Satisfaction Rating

		Low (1–7)	Middle (8)	High (9–10)	Totals
Age	20–40	35%	31%	34%	60% (71)
	41+	15%	34%	51%	40% (47)
		27% (32)	32% (38)	41% (48)	100% (118)

p < .05*

Index

Y